Ghosts in the Neighborhood

WEISER CENTER FOR EMERGING DEMOCRACIES

Series Editor
Dan Slater is Professor of Political Science,
Ronald and Eileen Weiser Professor of Emerging Democracies,
and Director of the Weiser Center for Emerging Democracies (WCED)
at the University of Michigan. dnsltr@umich.edu

The series highlights the leading role of the University of Michigan Press, Weiser Center for Emerging Democracies, and International Institute as premier sites for the research and production of knowledge on the conditions that make democracies emerge and dictatorships endure.

Ghosts in the Neighborhood: Why Japan Is Haunted by Its Past and Germany Is Not
Walter F. Hatch

Struggles for Political Change in the Arab World: Regimes, Oppositions, and External Actors after the Spring
Edited by Lisa Blaydes, Amr Hamzawy, and Hesham Sallam

The Dictator's Dilemma at the Ballot Box: Electoral Manipulation, Economic Maneuvering, and Political Order in Autocracies
Masaaki Higashijima

Opposing Power: Building Opposition Alliances in Electoral Autocracies
Elvin Ong

The Development of Political Institutions: Power, Legitimacy, Democracy
Federico Ferrara

Aid Imperium: United States Foreign Policy and Human Rights in Post–Cold War Southeast Asia
Salvador Santino F. Regilme Jr.

Opposing Democracy in the Digital Age: The Yellow Shirts in Thailand
Aim Sinpeng

Normalizing Corruption: Failures of Accountability in Ukraine
Erik S. Herron

Economic Shocks and Authoritarian Stability: Duration, Financial Control, and Institutions
Victor C. Shih, Editor

Electoral Reform and the Fate of New Democracies: Lessons from the Indonesian Case
Sarah Shair-Rosenfield

Campaigns and Voters in Developing Democracies: Argentina in Comparative Perspective
Noam Lupu, Virginia Oliveros, and Luis Schiumerini, Editors

GHOSTS IN THE NEIGHBORHOOD

Why Japan Is Haunted by
Its Past and Germany Is Not

Walter F. Hatch

University of Michigan Press
Ann Arbor

Published in the United States of America by the
University of Michigan Press
Manufactured in the United States of America
Printed on acid-free paper
First published January 2023

A CIP catalog record for this book is available from the British Library.

Library of Congress Control Number: 2022946854
LC record available at https://lccn.loc.gov/2022946854

ISBN 978-0-472-07576-8 (hardcover : alk. paper)
ISBN 978-0-472-05576-0 (paper : alk. paper)
ISBN 978-0-472-90310-8 (open access ebook)

https://doi.org/10.3998/mpub.11683923

Walter F. Hatch and the University of Michigan Press gratefully acknowledge funding from
Colby College to support open access publication of this work.

The University of Michigan Press's open access publishing program is made possible
thanks to additional funding from the University of Michigan Office of the Provost and the
generous support of contributing libraries.

Cover image: *Takiyasha the Witch and the Skeleton Spectre* (c. 1844), by Utagawa Kuniyoshi.
Courtesy of Wikimedia Commons.

For my soulmate and muse, Laurie B. Mann

Contents

List of Illustrations   ix

Preface   xi

ONE Introduction: Ghosts, Regionalism, and Reconciliation   1

TWO Bloody History in Two Regions   17

THREE Germany and France: Creating Union   29

FOUR Japan and South Korea: Enmity between Allies   47

FIVE Germany and Poland: Enlarging the Tent   70

SIX Japan and China: Can't Buy Me Love   89

SEVEN Janus-Faced Superpower:
    The U.S. Role in Different Regionalisms   115

EIGHT The Healing Power of Institutions   135

Notes   141

References   157

Index   171

Digital materials related to this title can be found on the Fulcrum platform via the following citable URL: https://doi.org/10.3998/mpub.11683923

Illustrations

3.1 French Views of West Germany   40

3.2 Germany's Share of French Trade   42

3.3 French Trust in FRG vs. Trade Intensity   43

3.4 French Views of FRG vs. Trade Intensity   44

4.1 Korean Views of Japan (1984–2015)   61

4.2 Where Do Korean Exports Go?   65

4.3 From Where Do Korean Imports Come?   66

4.4 Korean Views of Japan (2014–21)   67

5.1 Polish Views of Germany (1993–2022)   80

5.2 Polish Views of Germany (%) vs. Trade Intensity   82

6.1 Chinese Views of Japan (2002–10)   103

6.2 Chinese Views of Japan (2005–21)   104

6.3 Chinese Views of Japan vs. Trade Intensity   108

6.4 China's Dependence on Trade with Japan (% by year)   109

Preface

I began contemplating this book many years ago, when Germany appeared to be consolidating friendships in Europe while Japan seemed mired in hostility from Asian countries. Both had faced ghosts in their neighborhood—lingering memories of their own bad, sometimes brutal behavior in the past; but only one remained haunted. This struck me as an intriguing puzzle.

But it also proved to be a challenging one to solve. My research ultimately covered two continents, six countries, centuries of history, and a lot of trade and investment data. I am an Asianist specializing in Japanese politics—so I had to also learn about Europe, especially Germany (but also France and Poland). And I have mostly been a political economist—so I had to learn about "squishier" but equally important issues such as state-to-state apologies and international reconciliation.

The process was very long, and I accumulated numerous debts along the way. Please allow me to acknowledge those creditors, without relinquishing any responsibility for the final product.

Colby College was a generous employer, providing several grants for travel to many places in Europe and Asia. As a small liberal arts college, it also pushed me to acquire new areas of expertise beyond my training in graduate school. I ended up teaching courses on Chinese and Korean politics, as well as Japanese politics. And I taught a course on regionalism, comparing the mix of thin or relatively weak institutions in Asia with the thicker, stronger set of institutions in North America and Europe. This expanded curriculum made me a more competent researcher.

The college also helped me hire a small army of brilliant students as research assistants: Angie Sohn, Ryu Matsuura, Josh Brause, Anna Simeonova, Tammi Choi, Clara Devers, Haolu Wang, Xinyi Chen, Mingwei ("Julian") Zhu, Josh Connell, Vicky Yuan, Jill Greenstein, Valerie Coit, Anran Zhang, Eleanor ("Ella") Jackson, Vicky Ni, Hannah Kim, Jayadev Vadakkanmarveettil, Jacob Marx, and Pawel Brodalka. Thanks to all of you.

I relied heavily on guidance from wonderful mentors Jim Caporaso, Peter Katzenstein, and T. J. Pempel—thank you, gentlemen. Kaz Poznanski, Günter Heiduk, and Agnieszka McCaleb opened doors for me in Poland; Jon Weiss and John Keeler were helpful with French sources; Sabine Seidler and Paul Talcott connected me with German diplomats; Choi Pyung Arm introduced me to Korean ones. Nicolas Jabko helped me secure a brief affiliation with Sciences Po in Paris; Verena Blechinger-Talcott helped me secure a similar affiliation with Free University Berlin. Dziękuję. Merci. Danke. Gam-sa-ham-ni-da—to each of you.

Thanks also to four anonymous reviewers, as well as the strong team at University of Michigan Press, especially editorial director Elizabeth Demers and editorial associate Haley Winkle. In addition, I am grateful to Dan Slater, head of the Weiser Center for Emerging Democracies, for including this book in the center's series.

My greatest debt, though, is to my wife, Laurie B. Mann, who stood lovingly by me throughout this long process. I dedicate this work to her.

ONE

Introduction

Ghosts, Regionalism, and Reconciliation

The past often creeps into contemporary international relations, especially when abused states conjure up memories of horrible crimes committed by abusers. But some nations that have engaged in brutal aggression or colonialism are able, over time, to escape the ghosts, the angry reminders and recriminations from neighbors, while others simply remain haunted. Consider these two images from fall 2018:

- In the forest where combatants signed an armistice ending World War I, German chancellor Angela Merkel and French president Emmanuel Macron embrace warmly, grab one another's hands, and commit to deepening the already-close relationship between their countries.
- Japanese prime minister Abe Shinzo travels to Beijing for the first bilateral meeting with a Chinese leader in more than seven years. In front of giant flags, he and President Xi Jinping stand far apart and awkwardly shake hands, staring glumly at the camera—never at one another.

Yes, these are just snapshots. Mere anecdotes. But they illustrate very different realities about the ghostly influence of history in Europe and Asia today. While Germany has been liberated, more or less, from its bloody past in places like France and Poland, Japan is still tightly tethered to its earlier record of violent domination in places like China and Korea.[1] Why has Germany been relatively successful in making amends with neighbors that it conquered and mistreated in an earlier period, while Japan has, for the most part, failed to turn old enemies and victims into new friends? Most observers (see, for example, Berger 2012) focus on official discourse, and argue that Germany has been appropriately "penitent," while Japan has failed to apologize for its previous "sins." I disagree, arguing instead that:

1. Japan has repeatedly expressed regret for its past behavior in China and Korea, but to no avail.
2. Germany did not become fully contrite until the 1970s, long after it had managed to reconcile with its most important neighbor (France).
3. What actually distinguishes Germany from Japan has been its use of political institutions such as the EU and NATO to demonstrate a credible commitment to cooperation. Germany has proven that it can be a reliable partner, while Japan has not.
4. The United States, which promoted multilateralism in Europe but a U.S.-dominated bilateralism in Asia after World War II, is largely responsible for these competing outcomes. It viewed each region quite differently.

Put simply, I show that, when it comes to interstate reconciliation, actions speak louder than words. Institutions fostering cooperation do more than official apologies to heal old wounds. And the U.S., guided by both racial and power politics, encouraged such institution-building in Europe but not in Asia.

The analysis presented here is timely. Collective memory, ironically, appears to matter more than ever in global affairs—unless, as Trouillot (1995) notes, you have the awesome capability to suppress it. Russia's invasion of Ukraine in February 2022 was at least partly a function of Vladimir Putin's revanchist nostalgia for the Soviet empire, while Ukraine's fierce resistance was undoubtedly a function of lingering resentment over the 1932–33 Holodomor, to say nothing of Moscow's relatively recent annexation of Crimea and incursion into the Donbas.

Generally, states today face tremendous outside pressure to acknowledge and repent for what Dixon (2018) calls "dark pasts," including genocide, crimes against humanity, and so on. Barkan (2000: xi) believes history plays a bigger role today in shaping international relations because of a global consciousness hastened by the end of the Cold War: "This desire to redress the past is a growing trend, which touches our life at multiple levels, and it is central to our moral self-understanding as individuals and members of groups the world over."

While many scholars have written about the influence of the past on the present in international relations, only a few have tried to explain why some states have managed to overcome it and others have not. That is my ambition here, using the regional experience of Germany and Japan to understand how the former achieved reconciliation with neighbors in Europe while the latter has not been able to do so in Asia.

Before spelling out alternative answers, as well as my own, I face two analytical challenges. First, I need to clarify what I mean by the otherwise murky concept of "reconciliation." Second, I must briefly demonstrate the veracity, or at least the plausibility, of the critical assumption embedded in the overall puzzle that propels this study. In other words, has Germany *truly* fared better than Japan in achieving reconciliation with brutalized neighbors? Let me tackle these challenges in order.

Defining a Key Term: "Reconciliation"

Every adult understands this concept intuitively, but in personal and thus vastly different ways. We can agree that reconciliation generally has to do with the restoration of harmony and goodwill following a rupture in relations between those, such as family, friends, or neighbors, who previously had been close. To make this broad definition analytically useful, however, we need to specify its four core elements. Reconciliation consists of:

1. History. Some painful, perhaps even traumatic or humiliating event occurred in the past, locking two parties into a long-standing pattern of enmity.[2]
2. Propinquity. The two parties are emotionally connected or are geographically proximate.
3. Transcendence. The two parties manage to make the leap from enmity to amity. But how? Some, especially those who may be influenced by Judeo-Christian scripture, believe reconciliation requires a public and heartfelt act of "contrition" or "penitence" on the part of the perpetrator, and forgiveness on the part of the victim.[3] Others, including me, believe the process is more

prosaic (or less biblical), requiring only a simple recognition of
wrongdoing on the part of the perpetrator and a desire on the
part of the victim to move forward.

4. Mutuality. Reconciliation cannot be achieved unilaterally; it
comes about when two parties "agree" to prioritize a rosier
future over a bloody past.

In political science, we have analyzed the concept of reconciliation most
carefully in the context of domestic conflict, especially ethnic strife and
civil war. Scholars such as Priscilla Hayner (2010) have written extensively
about schemes to build national harmony through "truth and reconciliation commissions." Although they have been established all over the world,
from Chile to Peru, from East Timor to the Solomon Islands, from Liberia
to Sierra Leone, and from South Korea to Canada, the best-known truth
and reconciliation commission was created in 1995 by President Nelson
Mandela and Archbishop Desmond Tutu of South Africa. It heard testimony about otherwise unspeakable violence committed during the dark
days of apartheid. Remarkably, it not only offered solace to many victims
of misdeeds, it promised amnesty to perpetrators, who voluntarily came
forward and openly acknowledged their violent actions.[4] Political scientists explained this "soft" approach to justice, an alternative to the so-called
"Nuremberg method," as an imperfect means to an important end: national
healing.

International relations scholars have tended to shy away from using the
concept of reconciliation, preferring instead to talk about "stable peace"
between two countries. This is not merely the condition of "no war," and
can be distinguished from a "precarious peace" or even a "conditional
peace," both of which are maintained by military deterrence.[5] Boulding
(1978: 13) defines stable peace as "a situation in which the probability of
war is so small that it does not really enter into the calculations of any of
the people involved." This is a helpful concept, but it does not necessarily
encompass the fundamental elements of reconciliation I outlined earlier.
Most importantly, two countries could experience a stable peace without
ever having to transcend an historic breakdown in their relationship. For
example, Canada and the United States enjoy a stable peace that did not
require grappling with a traumatic past.

Those IR scholars willing to use the concept seem to treat interstate
reconciliation as a social and not merely a political process. This may happen, as Carroll (2008) suggests, at the global level, when a guilty nation
is forgiven not only by an aggrieved party but by "international society"

(which includes third parties).[6] Or it may happen, as others suggest, at the level of civil society. Yinan He (2009: 14) believes that reconciliation requires "an amicable people-to-people relationship." Likewise, Ann Phillips (2000: 53) notes that goodwill between previously hostile countries cannot be "legislated or imposed" by political leaders; it requires a widespread transformation (for the better) in perceptions held by the citizens of one country about another country.

I do not challenge these sociological characterizations of interstate reconciliation, but contend that states can trigger such a broad change in public opinion through government action that, over time, cultivates more positive attitudes and interests among citizens. It should also be noted that states often engage in such behavior for strategic reasons, as well as perhaps moral and ethical ones.

Defending a Critical Assumption: Germany's Relative "Success"

I argue that since 1945, when World War II came to an end, Germany has been able to largely regain the trust of its brutalized neighbors while Japan largely has not. This conclusion is shared, more or less, by nearly all scholars who have engaged in comparative analysis, from He (2009) to Lind (2008), from Berger (2012) to Timmerman (2014), from Feldman (2012) to Heo (2012), from Sato and Frei (2011) to Conrad (2003), and from Shoji (2011a) to Buruma (2002).

More persuasive than good company, of course, is supporting data, and I think I have these on my side, too. They include the results of public opinion surveys. For example, in Poland, where anti-German feeling has traditionally been strong but declining, only 27 percent of respondents in surveys between 2020 and 2022 said they had an unfavorable view of Germany—down significantly from 45 percent in 1993–95, the first years that the Polish polling firm asked this question.[7] By contrast, in China, where anti-Japanese feeling has been consistently strong, 57 percent of respondents in surveys from 2019 to 2021 said they had an unfavorable view of Japan—up from 52 percent between 2005 and 2007, the first years Chinese pollsters asked this question.[8]

It is undeniable that the Eurozone crisis (2010–17) undermined Germany's standing in some parts of Europe. By insisting on austerity, especially massive cuts in government spending, in exchange for bailouts from the European Central Bank, Angela Merkel became persona non grata in southern Europe, especially Greece. On a long ferry ride in the Aegean

Sea (June 2015), I sat next to an amateur Greek historian who expressed profound, nearly endless contempt for the German chancellor and her domestic supporters. By contrast, Greek prime minister Tsipras sounded almost banal when he claimed that Europe's paymaster had a "moral obligation" to make amends for the Nazi occupation (and associated atrocities) in Greece.[9] But this anger has subsided as financial conditions have improved. Greece adopted a balanced budget in 2016 and quit relying on external relief in 2018.

Another way to evaluate my claim is to engage in a thought exercise. When West Germany absorbed East Germany in 1990, dramatically expanding the size and prospective power of a unified state, many citizens elsewhere in the region expressed concern. But very few openly opposed German unification. Now imagine how Chinese and South Koreans might react if Japan were to undergo a similar expansion in size and power. They already protest loudly whenever it tries to assert authority over small but disputed islands. The regional response to an actual and significant expansion of territory and power by Japan would be explosive, probably even violent.

Considering Alternative Explanations

Unlike other academic questions I have pondered, this one about Germany, Japan, and interstate reconciliation immediately elicits answers, often quite confident ones, across the human spectrum. As a result, I have thoroughly enjoyed discussing my research not only with academic colleagues but also with intelligent laypeople. Some tell me that Japan has been less successful than Germany because its war crimes were less "forgivable," far less forgettable. But this seems dubious, even if we exclude the Holocaust (which I do here, since I am examining reconciliation between nearby states rather than between ethnic groups).[10] For many years, Germany and Prussia (which led the German confederation before unification in 1871), earned a reputation among Europeans for callous militarism. German troops pioneered "modern warfare" by murdering French civilians in the Franco-Prussian War (Stoneman 2008), gassing their enemies in World War I, and mowing down millions of Poles "mercilessly and without compassion," as Hitler advised his Wehrmacht (Lochner 1942), in World War II. Like their Japanese counterparts, German military doctors also carried out horrible experiments on live patients during that conflict, hoping to advance their knowledge about biological warfare.

Others have declared that the difference must have to do with geography. Japan is an "island nation," isolated from its neighbors, while Germany is a continental power with land borders, and thus had to learn to get along with neighbors able to mobilize tanks. "To some respect, Japan's geographic isolation makes it difficult for them to be in sync with others. They tend to think differently," argued Kim Chang-gi, former managing editor of *Chosun Ilbo*, one of South Korea's leading daily newspapers.[11] This explanation, however, fails the test of time. Germany has always been a continental power, and its geographical setting probably fostered war as much as it did peace. Before World War II, imperial Germany—or its precursor, Prussia— waged more wars of aggression than imperial Japan ever did.

But the response I have heard perhaps most often from nonspecialists has to do with something they call "culture." The Japanese and German people, they repeatedly tell me, are completely different—so naturally they have related to their own histories differently, and those different recollections and reconstructions have triggered different reactions from people in neighboring countries. It often boils down to this: Germans know how to apologize; the Japanese do not. A crude version of the cultural answer recycles the work of Ruth Benedict (1946), the Columbia University anthropologist who was commissioned by the U.S. Office of War Information to "explain" Japanese society to Americans at the end of World War II, even though she had never traveled there. She calls Japan a "shame culture" in which individuals are guided not by their own conscience or their internal evaluation of absolute principles ("right versus wrong"), as in the "guilt culture" of the West, but by a fear of ostracism for not conforming to external or social expectations.

Many friends tell me that Japan is unable to display real contrition because of its social "wiring." I even heard something like this from a prominent German historian who lived through Polish-German territorial conflict and played a lead role in strengthening the European community. Rudolf von Thadden, who died a few years after I spoke with him, lost his family estate in Pomerania at the end of World War II, when that region was absorbed into a new Poland. In his youth, he attended a lycée in Geneva and became fluent in French—a skill that helped him become an expert on Franco-German ties, serving for a time as Chancellor Gerhard Schröder's adviser on the bilateral relationship. In an interview, he said Japan could not escape its own bloody history with China and Korea as easily as Germany did with both Poland and France because East Asia is not Christian, and thus lacks not only the political prerequisites but also the necessary moral foundation. "Reconciliation requires a belief in forgiveness."[12]

Ian Buruma (2002: 116), the Dutch journalist, flatly rejects the argument that Japan, unlike Germany, struggles to achieve reconciliation with its neighbors because it is non-Christian, or because it is a "shame culture." He accurately labels this a "mechanistic view of human behavior" that is belied by the fact that many Germans have no desire to "confess" and many Japanese have struggled to expose the "sins" of their country. In the end, though, Buruma seems to rely on a different kind of cultural argument to explain Japan's failure to achieve reconciliation with its neighbors. The Japanese, he writes, have been infantilized by U.S. security protection, transformed into

> people longing to be twelve-year-olds, or even younger, to be at that golden age when everything was secure and responsibility and conformity were not yet required. There they sit, the Japanese, in their pachinko halls, in long straight rows, glass-eyed in front of pinball machines, oblivious to both past and present, watching the cascade of little silver balls, while listening to the din of the "Battleship March" beating away in the background. (295)

I recognize the salience of culture. In fact, I use this concept to help explain the different attitudes about Europe and Asia adopted by U.S. elites in the post–World War II environment, and thereby answer a part of our puzzle here. But many observers of Japan and Germany use culture in a rather ham-handed way, treating it as a fixed or apolitical construct. This is unfortunate. Cultural norms change over time in response to political contests in society. For this reason, contemporary Japanese are as different from the Japanese of 1937 as they are from today's Germans. If we want to understand why Japan has failed to achieve reconciliation, while Germany has largely succeeded, we must dig deeper.

Among students of international relations, the question posed here spawns a variety of answers that can be linked to different schools of thought. Realists such as Friedberg (1993/94) point to a relatively stable balance of power in Europe and a relatively unstable balance of power in Asia. It is true that Germany's neighbors tend to accept, if not always embrace, German power, while Japan's neighbors, especially China and Korea, are exceedingly anxious about Japanese power. The Chinese, in particular, bristle over Japan's claim to what they call "Diaoyu" (and the Japanese call "Senkaku"), a set of islands in the East China Sea, while the Koreans grumble over Japan's claim to what they call "Dokdo" (and the Japanese call "Takeshima"), located in the East Sea (or Sea of Japan). But this difference in the behavior of other states doesn't answer our original question; rather, it begs a second one: Why do states in Europe trust Germany while states in Asia distrust Japan? A neo- (or structural) realist might encourage us to go further in our analysis, to examine the configuration of power. In fact, however, the power structures in the two regions are not so dissimilar. Germany has the largest economy in Europe, but not an overwhelmingly strong one (especially compared to France), while Japan is the second-largest (behind China) in Asia; but Japan's runner-up status is relatively new (since 2010), while its "history problem" goes back to at least the late 1970s.

Liberals answer the question posed here in a couple different ways. Classical liberals consider the domestic politics of the various countries in each region. They argue that European states, being democratic, are naturally disinclined to wage war with one another. In Asia, by contrast, China remains authoritarian. As a result, they conclude, one should not be surprised at all to find latent conflict between China and its democratic neighbor, Japan. The problem with this argument is that South Korea, a democratic regime, also is distrustful of and sometimes even hostile to Japan—far more than Germany's neighbors are toward that country. Commercial (and neo-) liberals consider the level of economic interdependence in each region.[13] Europe is deeply integrated, with intraregional trade accounting for nearly 64 percent of the region's total trade in 2019. But East Asia is increasingly integrated as well (more than North America); intraregional trade accounted for almost 59 percent of its total trade in 2019 (ADB 2022: 20). China is now Japan's leading trade partner, supplying by far the largest volume of Japanese imports and absorbing about the same amount of Japanese exports as the U.S.; China and Japan are South Korea's first- and second-most-important trading partners. But interdependence has failed to help Japan improve its diplomatic standing with neighbors in Asia.

Constructivists focus on nonmaterial or intangible forces: ideas, discourse, myth, values, or norms, the different ways in which Germans and Japanese conceptualize, discuss, or identify with the past. This is a more sophisticated use of "culture" as a concept. For example, Yinan He (2009) argues that Japan and China have been unable to reconcile because their political and intellectual elites have constructed conflicting narratives about the past that are reinforced in textbooks, museums, and public statements. By contrast, she claims that Germany and Poland have managed to reconcile because their narratives mesh far more neatly. This is a fascinating analysis, but ultimately not persuasive. Reconciliation can happen without overlapping narratives. Consider the United States and Vietnam. The two states have relatively good relations, even though they have completely different narratives about the protracted and bloody war they fought in the 1960s and early 1970s. Many Americans tend to think of that conflict as a noble but unsuccessful effort to help a democratic ally (South Vietnam), while Vietnamese view it as nothing more than U.S. imperialism.

Carroll (2008) suggests that Germany has achieved reconciliation with its neighbors, while Japan has not, because the former felt compelled to secure readmission into "international society." Although he does not state this explicitly, he seems to suggest that Japan apparently could stand to continue living as a "pariah nation." This just begs the question: Why is Japan different?

Some academics have adopted a hybrid approach to explain Germany's success and Japan's relative failure in achieving reconciliation. Jennifer Lind (2008) uses "balance of threat" realism to suggest that states not only mobilize against other states with large militaries but also those that display hostile intent by, for example, failing to acknowledge their own militarist histories. In the end, she also invokes constructivism by focusing on the discourse of "sorry states." Although she accepts the conventional wisdom that Japan has not been as consistently contrite toward South Korea as Germany has toward France, Lind also notes that its official statements of apology have triggered a domestic backlash, undermining their effectiveness. At the same time, she notes that Germany managed to regain the confidence of France without twisting itself into a pretzel of contrition. As a tool of diplomacy, then, she concludes that apologies are necessary, but also potentially dangerous at home.

Thomas Berger (2012) uses an approach he calls "historical realism," which is not IR realism at all. Indeed, this is an idiographic or case-by-case understanding of the politics of reconciliation. Berger, too, ultimately endorses the popular understanding that Japan has been less successful than Germany in achieving reconciliation because it has been less contrite. But he also suggests that this outcome, in turn, can be attributed to a variety of factors, including international politics (Japan, as an island nation, was not forced by Cold War exigencies to accommodate its neighbors, while Germany was), domestic politics (conservative elements in Japanese society became ascendant, and their narrative about World War II cast the nation in the role of victim, not victimizer), and culture (the dominant narrative about World War II became embedded in Japan's collective identity). This is a wide-ranging, messy claim.

About State Apologies

As I have noted, the conventional wisdom here is that Germany has shown contrition, especially through the discourse and gestures of apology, while Japan has not. I reject this approach, for a few reasons.

First, it tends to anthropomorphize states. A human may need to hear an apology from another person who has wronged them before they can fully reconcile with the other. But a state is a political entity designed to represent an entire nation, a broad community with often competing interests and preferences. Second, this approach is ahistorical; it fails to recognize that states don't typically apologize openly to other states. The Turkish state, for example, has never apologized for the genocide of Armenians; it even prohibits its own citizens from acknowledging this history.[14] For many decades, France not only failed to apologize for enslaving Haitians; in 1825, it used its military power to demand repayment from Haiti for the loss of its slave colony. The U.S. has never apologized for invading various countries, or dropping nuclear bombs on Japan. Third, this approach ignores the domestic consequences of apologizing. When they do express contrition, state leaders often stir up resentment at home. Nationalists, who tend to view their own country as blameless, dislike leaders who display "weakness" by "prostrating themselves" before others. In June 2009, addressing a crowd in Cairo, Egypt, then–U.S. president Barack Obama acknowledged that the United States had not always behaved well in the Middle East. It was a vague, mostly tepid statement, but it was enough to upset right-wing pundits on Fox News and other domestic media outlets, who accused the president of betraying the nation on an "apology tour" of that region.[15]

Lind (2009) understands this phenomenon of domestic backlash, and thus discourages state leaders from engaging in "deep" apologies. Interestingly, though, even she believes apologies are necessary for reconciliation, as long as they remain "shallow."

Advancing a New Approach:
Institutions, Credible Commitments, and Power

Talk is often very cheap. I believe we should focus on words only as far as they reflect ideas that actually help shape our behavior. To really understand international relations, we need to examine ideas and structures that matter. My own explanation for Germany's relative success and Japan's relative failure to achieve reconciliation first highlights the capability of institutions (especially multilateral ones) to help each country demonstrate to neighboring states a genuine or credible commitment to cooperate. I argue that Germany has used the project of economic and defense cooperation in Europe to regain the trust of its neighbors, while Japan has been unable to assemble anything remotely like this thick web of ties in East Asia. Moreover, the difference in these two examples of regionalism is, I contend, largely a function of U.S. policy discretion, which in turn is a function of cultural norms and influence. In building a new international order after World War II, the United States used its unparalleled power to foster multilateralism in Europe, centered on Franco-German rapprochement. In East Asia, by contrast, the U.S. chose to build a hub-and-spokes pattern of bilateral ties, with itself at the center. Even in the contemporary moment, the United States has insisted on serving as the broker of last resort in that region. Finally, I argue that the U.S. has made these different choices because its political elites have identified with Europeans, viewing them as nearly equal partners, while they have looked down on Asians as "immature" junior partners who are unprepared for a robust regionalism that excludes the world's superpower.

Readers have good reason to wonder, then, about my own theoretical mooring. In highlighting the productive work of regional institutions, I suppose I sound like a neoliberal institutionalist. In fact, however, I explicitly reject that school's unsubstantiated faith in the healing powers of economic exchange or "complex interdependence." So am I then an orthodox realist? No, this label has only a limited application. Although I do recognize state power (especially United States hegemony) as the political force shaping different forms of regionalism, I also recognize collective identity as the source of U.S.-centered "hub-and-spokes" bilateralism in Asia and U.S.-sponsored multilateralism in Europe. Does this then make me a constructivist? Not really.

The approach used here is eclectic and inspired by Sil and Katzenstein (2010); it is driven more by questions than by theoretical assumptions. But it does aspire to use the hard logic of game theory to understand what until now has been considered a "soft" problem in social science—the problem of historical memory and interstate reconciliation. Game theory is not really a theory at all; rather, it is a mathematical tool that can help us think more clearly about strategic decision-making and the collective action problems that tend to preoccupy social scientists. In general, game theory examines how we as individuals (or groups, or states) try to secure the optimal outcome for ourselves in a social and therefore uncertain environment, with other individuals (or groups, or states) striving to do the same for themselves.

The most common scenario modeled in game theory is the "prisoner's dilemma," which shows why two individuals (or groups, or states) might not cooperate even when it is in their best interest to do so. Imagine two suspects in a crime. They have been detained, but the police do not yet have enough evidence to convict either one of them. By cooperating with one another (that is, by holding out; by refusing to confess to authorities or place the other at the scene of the crime), the two prisoners can achieve the optimal outcome—going free. But the authorities have an advantage. They can separate the two prisoners, and create a set of incentives that will cause each to confess and implicate the other. (This is obvious in the matrix of payoffs; each prisoner is induced to defect, to "sing" rather than cooperate by staying quiet, because the recalcitrant one would be punished more harshly.) The outcome—prison for both—is a stable equilibrium, but not optimal.

International relations scholars, especially realists, have long argued that states in the dog-eat-dog international system routinely face a prisoner's dilemma. They are naturally inclined to defect (not act cooperatively), because other states will take advantage of any unilateral decision to drop one's guard by, for example, reducing military capabilities or removing protections against imports. But other IR scholars, particularly neoliberals, believe cooperation is possible, even in a world of anarchy, when games become "iterated" or repeated. They cite Axelrod and Hamilton (1981), who demonstrate that, when a game is played repeatedly, players learn to cooperate over time by using a "nice" strategy (cooperation) on the first play and then tit-for-tat (or reciprocity) after that. By lengthening the "shadow of the future," Lipson (1984), Keohane (1984), and others argue that iteration creates stable expectations, which in turn foster durable rules and patterns of behavior (institutions) that facilitate information-sharing. Cooperation is possible without a central authority.

The idea of an "iterated game" is useful, but the contention that it will lead to cooperation is, for our study, problematic because it ignores the effect of traumatic history. States subjected to extreme or protracted violence or humiliation in the past cannot be expected to take a chance by playing "nice" on the first move with the state that has victimized them. Wholly lacking in trust, they will always defect.

But there is still some hope for a positive-sum outcome. If the stronger (or once-dominant state) makes the first move and backs that up with a credible commitment to cooperation, then the weaker (or previously dominated) state can be expected to follow in the end. What the weaker state requires is some kind of reassurance; that is, it needs a clear demonstration, a credible commitment, that the stronger state will not renege on its initial pledge to "play nice." Such a commitment is one that is difficult, or even very costly, to reverse; it entails a significant level of nondiscretion or inflexibility. For example, when the United States set up the United Nations at the end of World War II, it made a credible commitment to its wartime allies—the United Kingdom, France, the Soviet Union, and the Republic of China—that it would not abuse its overwhelming power. The U.S. could not, according to the UN Charter, impose its will on the others; each of the five permanent members of the Security Council had veto power over the binding resolutions of the new intergovernmental organization.

Surprisingly, it took a study of corporate management to really make sense of this. Gary J. Miller (1992) treats the organizational behavior of a firm as an iterated prisoner's dilemma, one in which employees have a built-in incentive to shirk, because they will be paid a fixed wage even if they don't exert maximal effort, and the employer has a built-incentive to restrict rewards. The boss might try to overcome this dilemma by implementing a system of "Taylorism" or scientific management, paying piece rates for each individual worker's output. But when the boss comes around with his stopwatch, the worker is unlikely to cooperate. Given the way the firm has operated in the past, she has good reason to suspect that the employer will use that precious information to reduce piece rates or even to lay her off. So both players lose in the end: Employees receive suboptimal wages, while the employer earns a suboptimal profit. Is there a solution? Yes, but only one, according to Miller: By demonstrating a credible commitment to cooperate, management can ultimately achieve a Pareto-optimal outcome. As the dominant player in this game, it has to stick its neck out and show workers that it will not violate their trust. It can do this by, for example, allowing employees a voice in restructuring the workplace to improve productivity (and then allowing them to pocket a significant share of the increased revenue), or by refusing to cut employment in an economic downturn.

Miller tells the story of Lincoln Electric, a successful manufacturer of arc-welding tools in Euclid, Ohio. The firm fared well in the long run, but only after it took a risk by making a credible commitment to cooperate with its increasingly productive workers. Those employees now "are convinced that their employer will neither lower piece rates nor fire excess workers if they work their hardest, earn high wages, and increase productivity" (117).

We can use this insight to understand how West Germany (between

1949 and 1990) and then unified Germany managed to achieve reconciliation with its former victims in Europe, including France and Poland. By embedding themselves in European and trans-Atlantic projects, first with the Treaty of Paris in 1951 and NATO in 1955, when they linked arms with France, and later with the Treaties of Maastricht (1992) and Nice (2001), when Poland was a key target, the Germans demonstrated a credible commitment to cooperate with nearby states. These projects of integration and alliance-building represented, according to Chancellor Helmut Kohl, "the most effective insurance against a reemergence of nationalism, chauvinism, and racism."[16] He and other German leaders gambled, tied their hands in a knot of regional ties, and eventually won over their neighbors. The Japanese, by contrast, have done no such thing. They have a security alliance with the United States, and economic partnership agreements with a number of Southeast Asian states, but have not forged significant pacts with neighbors in Northeast Asia. As I will argue, this is not entirely Japan's fault.

It is true, of course, that institutions in Europe have experienced some erosion in recent years, while new institutions in Asia have taken root. Specifically, the U.K.'s 2016 referendum to leave the European Union ("Brexit") has undermined the solidarity of the European Union, and former U.S. President Donald Trump's harsh critique of low defense spending by members of NATO weakened that alliance—at least until 2021. At the same time, Japan and China, as well as Japan and South Korea, found new reasons to cooperate in the face of U.S. unilateralism by Trump in Asia, especially on trade policy.

I realize that my argument is unconventional. According to some of Europe and Asia's leading intellectuals, it might even be alarming or perplexing. For example, several years ago, I received an email from Alfred Grosser, a French political scientist whose father, a Jewish socialist, emigrated from Nazi Germany in 1933. Grosser is France's leading authority on Franco-German relations, and he was responding to a prospectus I had sent him about this book: "I must confess to being quite appalled [*épouvanté*] by what you have written."[17] He reaffirmed the point he has made so eloquently in his own works—that the Franco-German rapprochement is built on top of a "human architecture" that includes thousands of youths, artists, businessmen, and lovers who have crossed the border over the years, and not due primarily to intergovernmental agreements. Likewise, I reconnected in Tokyo with a longtime acquaintance, Keiichi Tsunekawa, professor emeritus of Tokyo University, and a former president of the Japan International Cooperation Agency's Research Institute. "Might you have the causation backwards?" he asked politely but firmly. "You say that regionalism will resolve the history problem, and I agree that it could help. But the conflict over history in our region is so stubborn that it seems to block real progress toward anything like an EU in East Asia."[18]

Both Grosser and Tsunekawa raise important points. I acknowledge that individuals and groups in society play a critical role in transnational relations, but contend that states still create the conditions (including the rules) under which social forces operate. And I acknowledge that global conflict often becomes self-reinforcing, but contend that bold action by political leaders can break the cycle of mistrust.

This book proceeds as follows: In the next chapter, I offer some background about the two regions studied here, and discuss the case study methodology used to carry out this analysis. Chapter 3 examines the process of Franco-German reconciliation; chapter 4 investigates Japan-South Korean relations; chapter 5 analyzes the process of German-Polish reconciliation; chapter 6 considers Sino-Japanese relations; chapter 7 discusses the U.S. role in both regions. I conclude in chapter 8 by highlighting the role of institutions. I show how states must take the critical step of forging regional bonds, not just uttering words of contrition, before they can regain the trust of nearby states they brutally dominated in the past. Germany has fared better than Japan in this regard; as the stronger (or once-dominant) state, it had to break a cycle of mistrust and demonstrate a credible commitment to cooperate. It did this through the European project of integration and the transatlantic process of alliance-building; Japan has yet to take this step.

TWO

Bloody History in Two Regions

History is replete with stories of terrible war crimes committed by one group against another. But if we want to study interstate reconciliation between long-standing rivals, we cannot focus on tragedies that occurred inside one nation's (or perhaps even one empire's) borders, such as the Great Crime against Armenians in the early 20th century, the Nazi Holocaust of the 1930s and 1940s, the 1994 genocide in Rwanda, or the ethnic cleansing of Bosniaks following the breakup of Yugoslavia. And we cannot focus on short-lived conflicts, such as Iraq's conquest of Kuwait in 1990, or recent conflicts, such as the U.S. invasion of Iraq in 2003.

The Vietnam War had its share of atrocities, but that conflict between the United States and North Vietnam and the Viet Cong was a one-time affair, which scholars tend to treat as either an American extension of France's imperialism over that land or a proxy war between the U.S. and the Soviet Union. Interstate conflicts in South America and Africa, including the border wars between Peru and Ecuador in 1941 and 1995 and those between Eritrea and Ethiopia in 1998–2000, as well as briefly in 2010 and 2016, were not exceptionally bloody or long.

India and Pakistan have fought a few times since 1947, when Britain partitioned its empire in South Asia. At first blush, this conflict appears to meet our criteria: it has been protracted and bloody, and it has been carried out by two independent states. But it has been waged, for the most part, in the confined territory of Kashmir. (An exception was 1971, when India invaded East Pakistan under the pretext of helping Bengalis caught up in the national liberation struggle that led to the creation of Bangladesh.) Neither state's army ever seized the other's capital.

Well, what about the one and only deployment of nuclear weapons against a civilian population, the U.S. bombing of Hiroshima and Nagasaki in August 1945?[1] We cannot use this case for a couple reasons. First, some historians—especially Americans—claim the U.S. had almost no other recourse; although the Japanese were losing badly after Iwo Jima and Okinawa, they refused to surrender. Second, and most importantly, the U.S. was the ultimate victor in that war. Winners get to write the history, or at least they typically get to avoid the harshest judgment.

This leaves us with four obvious cases: (1) Germany's violent invasions of France (in the Franco-Prussian War, 1870–71, World War I, and World War II); (2) Germany's domination of Poland, including the evisceration of that country by Prussia, Russia, and others in a series of partitions in the latter half of the 18th century, and the Nazi invasion and occupation from 1939–45; (3) Japan's wars of aggression against China (1894–95 and 1931–45); and (4) Japan's domination of Korea in the early 20th century (1910–45), as well as its samurai invasion near the end of the 16th century. In the next two sections, I offer background on all of these cases, focusing less on what actually happened in the past and more on how history is remembered in different countries. Then I outline the methodology used in this comparative study.

Iron Cross over Europe

In the mid-19th century, Europe's balance of power shifted slowly but steadily: as England declined, Prussia rose. Guided by the wily statesman Chancellor Otto von Bismarck, the leading kingdom in the German confederation forged a variety of useful alliances and waged a series of successful battles—against Denmark (1848–51, and 1864), against Austria (1866) and then against France (1870–71)—culminating in the unification of a new empire.

Imperial Germany's military might was based on manufacturing, which in turn was based on the rapid adoption of technology. The state encouraged investment in emerging industries, from railroads to chemicals to steel. By 1913, Germany accounted for 15 percent of the world's industrial output; by contrast, England's share had fallen to 10 percent. But by then, Bismarck was gone. And so was the flexible, multipolar system of alliances he had helped to construct, with Germany at the center.

Germany's Aggression against France

Many contemporary citizens of France cannot remember a time when Germany was their enemy. This is true even for some French intellectuals. On a pleasant summer day in 2009, I met Bruno Rémond at a small café in Paris. A popular professor of public administration and the son of one of France's best-known political historians, he arrived for our rendezvous with a marked-up copy of the prospectus for this book, which I had mailed to him, and an ominous frown on his face. "Your study is wrong," Rémond declared soon after taking a seat.[2] One might be able to compare Germany's testy relationship with Poland to Japan's troubled ties with its Asian neighbors, but the Franco-German relationship, he insisted, was completely different. "France and Germany have deep and long-standing cultural ties," he argued. "The relationship has always been very close—nothing like Japan and the other countries in Asia, which are completely alien to one another, where there is terrible hatred based on misunderstanding." I pushed back, pointing out that Japan also shares long-standing cultural bonds with both Korea and China. Then I asked about the three bloody invasions of France by German troops over a span of just 70 years. "Those were territorial wars, not ideological wars. They were no big deal, really—more like the fighting between brothers."[3]

One normally should not argue about history or politics with a Rémond, but here I must. Indeed, I believe his view is testament to the remarkable level of goodwill, based on rebooted collective memory, that now exists between Germany and France. But it wasn't always so. Before, during, and after World War I, for example, French educators taught their students to despise Germans as bloodthirsty militarists. This was not a random lesson here or there; it was official French education policy.[4] In autumn 1915, for example, the Ministry of Public Instruction hosted pedagogical conferences across the country that revolved around Germany's treachery. A record of one such conference, convened in Dordogne, a department (or district) in southwestern France, includes this resolution from the teachers in attendance:

> The capital duty of educators will be to see to it that *France does not forget.* . . . If we forget, we are destined to perish, and the schools can help keep the hatred of the Teutons alive in the hearts of all French people. Teachers must make Germany known to children. They will

point out its extreme, unbounded *arrogance*, which remains a menace for all civilizations. They will show that the Germans remain
veritable barbarians. . . . The German race is despicable, detestable,
and dangerous. Our children must learn this so that they may come
to consider Germany as an enemy that will never disarm. . . . *France
must remember!*[5]

Six years later, with the fighting behind him, Lavisse (1921: 266) issued
an equally urgent message to French pupils in his history textbook: "Germany, arrogant and rapacious, sought to dominate the World in order to
exploit it." Even later, in yet another history text, Gauthier and Deschamps
(1923: 233) blamed the war on "Germany's determined will to dominate
the world."

In those days, French citizens routinely and excitedly shared stories
about German atrocities in both the Franco-Prussian War (1870–71) and
in World War I (1914–18).[6] In the case of the former, they complained that
invading German soldiers encountering "guerrilla" resistance had murdered French civilians, burned down homes, and taken hostages. They also
grumbled about the loss of national land (Alsace-Lorraine) to the Prus-
sians. In the case of the latter, they stewed over the unprecedented use of
chlorine gas against French (as well as British and Canadian) soldiers in the
battle for Ypres, Belgium, in May 1915. And they accused German troops
of various war crimes, from slaughtering noncombatants to raping women.
In sum, the French viewed Germany as a vicious military machine, "brutal
as a steamroller."[7]

Although French hostility toward Germany peaked in the early 20th
century, and French distrust of its military prompted construction of the
Maginot Line in the 1930s, both were still quite evident in the early years
after World War II. Massacres such as the one at Oradour-sur-Glane reinforced the already-solid view of France's neighbor as a serial war criminal.
On June 10, 1944, German soldiers machine-gunned or burned 642 residents of that village (including 247 women and 205 children) in retaliation
for the alleged kidnapping of an SS officer. After the war, General Charles
de Gaulle decided to leave Oradour-sur-Glane in its ravaged condition—a
visible, very public reminder of Nazi occupation.

As head of the provisional government of France in 1946, de Gaulle
vowed to block the re-establishment of a centralized Reich that had been
"the instrument of Bismarck, William II and Hitler."[8] And when his successor capitulated to U.S. pressure for an Allied effort to rebuild Germany,
French critics howled in protest. In one especially fiery session of Parlia-

ment (June 12, 1948), Pierre Cot, who had been a leader of the Popular Front, warned of a "renaissance of the German peril," and proclaimed that "the victims of Nazi barbarism" must not be forgotten.[9]

Within a decade or so, public sentiment in France had shifted dramatically. This is a fascinating riddle I intend to solve in chapter 3.

Germany's Domination of Poland

Once upon a time (in fact, three centuries before the establishment of a unified Germany), Prussia was nothing more than a fief, a Teutonic and mostly Protestant duchy inside a predominantly Catholic Poland. But under Frederick I, his son Frederick William I, and his grandson Frederick II ("Frederick the Great"), it became one of Europe's rising powers with a modern bureaucracy and a strong military. How did Prussia evolve into the powerful leader of the German confederation? One significant piece of the answer has to do with a land grab. In three greedy strokes between 1772 and 1795, Prussia conspired with two other powers, imperial Austria and imperial Russia, to carve up Poland. Over time, Poles came to view the partitions in religious terms, with the victim-nation representing a Christ-like martyr "nailed to the cross," and its perpetrator-neighbors representing "satanic charlatans" (Prokop 1993: 53). By the end of the 18th century, Prussia had expanded to encompass most of what had been western Poland, including important commercial centers such as Danzig (now Gdansk) and Breslau (Wrocław), as well as a swath of central Poland, including Warsaw.[10]

Prussia quickly went about "Germanizing" its new lands, bringing in thousands of colonists and pushing out much of the Polish gentry. The policy was informed by chauvinistic feelings of ethnic superiority. For example, Frederick the Great referred to long-standing residents of this area as "slovenly Polish trash," and likened them to Native Americans facing "civilization" or extinction at the hands of white settlers.[11] German intellectuals such as Johann Georg Forster, a travel writer and naturalist who had been born in Poland, disparaged Poles as "backwards" and compared them to the "barbarians" of Southeast Asia.[12]

In the early 19th century, following the setback of the Napoleonic Wars, Prussian leaders renewed and accelerated the policy of Germanization by, for example, establishing German as the official language in public schools, requiring German priests to lead Catholic services, and installing German officials in administrative and judicial positions. These efforts triggered Polish resistance, which was routinely crushed by the Prussian military.

Bismarck, who became chancellor of the unified Germany in 1871, established a Prussian Settlement Commission to strengthen the colonization campaign. The goal was to isolate and eventually undermine Polish communities, which represented pockets of potential opposition to a rapidly growing empire. Bismarck himself viewed Poles as dangerous animals (wolves) who must be exterminated whenever possible.[13]

Unsurprisingly, Poles came to hate Germans just as much. Stripped of their homeland, many joined the fight against imperial Germany in the waning days of World War I. The Treaty of Versailles (1919) partially reconstituted Poland, though it transformed Danzig into a stateless city under the jurisdiction of the newly established League of Nations. Germany's eastern border was pushed back to the west.

But then Hitler, an unalloyed revanchist, rose to power. Guided by a perverse chauvinism, he absolutely despised Jews, homosexuals, Roma, and communists; but he also looked down on Poles, who after all had helped roll back the German empire. On August 23, 1939, the Führer took a diplomatic bite out of Poland, negotiating a secret protocol with Stalin to divide that cursed country into German and Soviet "spheres of influence."[14] Within a few days, Nazi troops moved into western Poland; within a few weeks, the Red Army gobbled up the rest, finalizing what Poles later came to call the "Fourth Partition."

Germany's conquest, motivated by a renewed desire to finally obliterate Polish national identity, was particularly nasty.[15] This became obvious in the very first month, when invading troops massacred the residents of more than 30 Polish towns and villages. The Luftwaffe, Hitler's air force, played an active role, bombing those population centers and then strafing refugees as they fled. In the end, Nazi Germany killed one out of every five Polish citizens living under its occupation. Half of these six million people were Jews, who died in ghettoes, concentration camps, and gas chambers. But ethnic Poles also faced Nazi terror, including mass executions, slave labor, and brutal medical experiments.

In addition to the loss of human life, Poland also suffered massive property destruction—38 percent of the nation's wealth. Warsaw, the capital city, where the Polish Home Army staged a heroic but unsuccessful uprising in 1944, was all but razed; only a quarter of its buildings survived Hitler's fury. Other major cities also experienced heavy if less extensive damage.

Although Catholic clerics in both countries launched an unofficial campaign for reconciliation in the 1960s, Polish-German relations would not rebound until the 1990s. We explore how this happened in chapter 5.

Rising Sun Over Asia

The Meiji oligarchs who led Japan in the late 19th century gradually came to emulate the "West." First they adopted its economic institutions, from a banking system to insurance; then they embraced its political institutions, from political parties to a constitution; finally, they endorsed its ideas, from social Darwinism to imperialism. After reading Herbert Spencer, the British liberal philosopher who argued that "civilization" marched forward in a straight line from the most "primitive" to the most "advanced" societies, Meiji thinkers understood their nation's place in this presumed pecking order: Japan ranked behind Europe, but well ahead of the rest of the Asia, especially "uncivilized" China. And they quickly took steps to demonstrate Japan's new place in the world.

In 1894, Japan went to war against China over control of the Korean Peninsula. By winning a quick and decisive victory, it gained Taiwan, the Pescadores, and, for a short while, the Liaodong Peninsula.[16] Then, in 1904, it went to war against Russia to defend its strategic interests in Korea and Manchuria. The imperial navy ultimately prevailed in a pivotal battle that U.S. President Theodore Roosevelt called "the greatest phenomenon the world has ever seen."[17] In the Portsmouth Treaty brokered by Roosevelt, Japan won substantial concessions, including half of Sakhalin and railway rights in Manchuria. Most importantly, though, it cemented its global reputation as an *ittōkoku* (or first-class nation), the most powerful country in East Asia.

Japan eventually (1942) conquered the entire region, from Indonesia to China, calling it a "Greater East Asia Co-Prosperity Sphere." It first posed as a liberator, training nationalist forces and professing to lift the yoke of Western colonialism. But it quickly revealed itself to be just another occupier, subjugating local residents and brutalizing dissidents.

Even today, the Japanese struggle to name this war in which they or their ancestors fought. Is it simply "World War II?" Or is it the "Pacific War?" Or is it the "Greater East Asia War?" Or is it something else? The domestic debate, according to Shoji (2011b), suggests the legacies of this conflict still reverberate inside Japan.[18]

Japan's Domination of Korea

Seoul, the capital of South Korea, has been reconfigured as a monument to Japanese cruelty. You hear about it at the majestically rebuilt Gyeongbokgung, the National Palace that was, according to a sign for tourists, "completely destroyed by fire during the Japanese invasion of 1592" and then "cruelly destroyed by Japan's wicked policy of aggression" during the occupation of the early 20th century.[19] And you witness it at the Seodaemun Prison, now a museum dedicated to educating Koreans about the movement against Japanese colonialism. A plaque there tells visitors, "Japan cruelly oppressed the resistance, arrested and imprisoned patriotic fighters in prisons they had built, and conducted ruthless tortures."

South Korea has spent centuries fighting for survival in the shadow of more powerful neighbors. Today, however, its nationalism is mostly fueled by anti-Japanese feelings.

The seething anger and deep resentment go way back, all the way to the last decade of the 16th century, when Hideyoshi Toyotomi, one of Japan's feudal "unifiers," invaded Korea in two different campaigns. Although he wreaked plenty of havoc, he failed to conquer the peninsula—a fact that is celebrated in Seoul by its most prominent statue, a towering replica of Admiral Yi Sun-sin, whose agile "turtle ships" bedeviled the bigger Japanese warships.

But Japan's occupation of Korea generated the greatest political blowback. In the very late 19th century, as Japan emerged from its victory in the first Sino-Japanese War, it began to exercise tighter and tighter control over the peninsula. Some prominent Koreans resisted Japan's growing influence, calling for closer ties with Russia to counter the trend. So Japan's resident minister sent assassins into the imperial palace to murder Korea's leading opponent of Japanese rule, Empress Min. When the Russo-Japanese War concluded in 1905, Japan further strengthened its grip by establishing a protectorate and implementing 25 "reforms" that included gutting Korea's national army. Five years later, it fully annexed the peninsula.

The colonial period (1910–45) was bitter. Japan's military overlords ruled directly and brutally, replacing Korean officials, censoring the media, and violently suppressing dissent. Thousands of Korean nationalists were jailed, and many were tortured during detention; others were summarily executed. Japan came to view the peninsula as an important part of its empire, and pushed to "Japanize" the economy and the culture. Japanese merchants moved into Korean cities, establishing shops and factories, while Japanese farmers took over agricultural land. By 1940, McNamara (1990: 53) notes, Japanese investors controlled 95 percent of the capital in larger firms on the peninsula. In schools, teachers used the Japanese language, not Korean, and taught the history of Japan, not Korea. Individuals were pressed if not always required to adopt Japanese names.

With the outbreak of the Pacific War, matters quickly went from bad to worse. Colonial authorities deported as many as two million Koreans, forcing them to work in Japan-based factories.[20] (Indeed, among the victims of the atomic bombings of Hiroshima and Nagasaki were an estimated 70,000 Koreans.) At the same time, the Japanese military conscripted thousands of Korean men, requiring them to serve on the front lines, while luring, deceiving, and even coercing as many as 100,000 Korean women into sexual slavery at so-called "comfort stations" (or military brothels).[21]

One can argue, of course, that Japan's colonization of Korea created real benefits: infrastructure, enhanced agricultural productivity, a solid education system, and a strong, bureaucratic state. But the fact that Japan and South Korea spent 14 painful years (from 1951 to 1965) negotiating a normalization treaty may demonstrate that Koreans did not then feel so positive about the past. What is remarkable is that they still harbor deep resentment, even though the two countries were politically aligned during the Cold War and even though they remain economically integrated partners. We investigate all this in chapter 4.

Japan's Aggression against China

Although Japan was never as deeply enmeshed as, say, Korea in the China-centered East Asian Order that reached its peak during the Ming Dynasty, it did borrow heavily—religion, architecture, an alphabet, political institutions, and more—from the Middle Kingdom. So it was ironic when, in the late 19th century, a rapidly industrializing and "Westernizing" Japan began to look down on its once-powerful neighbor. On the eve of the first Sino-Japanese war, religious leader Uchimura Kanzo referred to Japan, his homeland, as "the champion of progress in the East" and to China as "the incorrigible hater of progress."[22]

Defeated by a former vassal state, Chinese elites felt deeply humiliated. And that was just the beginning. In 1915, Japan issued its infamous "21 Demands," pushing China to recognize its expanded sphere of influence in Manchuria and the Shandong Peninsula, grant new rights for Japanese investors, and guarantee additional legal protections for Japanese residents. Then, in 1931, Japan used a phony incident to justify establishing the puppet state of Manchukuo in northeast China. Six years later, vowing to bring law and order to its new sphere of influence, the military regime in Tokyo launched an all-out war on China.

The war was exceptionally ugly, and—for the Chinese—came to be symbolized by the Nanjing Massacre. In December 1937, after capturing the southern capital, Chinese, Western, and some Japanese sources say the occupying army went berserk, wantonly slaughtering Chinese civilians, pillaging and burning homes, and raping women. Historians outside China continue to debate the number of casualties, but the Chinese Communist Party has no doubt: In history textbooks and at an impressively renovated museum in Nanjing, it repeatedly asserts that 300,000, precisely, were murdered.[23]

While the Nanjing Massacre became a symbol of the Japanese military's brutality, it was not a completely isolated event. Other coastal cities in China suffered heavy casualties, and rural villages faced harsh "pacification" campaigns as the war spread. The military became notorious for its slogan: "Kill all, burn all, destroy all." Chinese men were forced to do hard labor on Japanese projects, including the Burma railroad, while Chinese women were forced to serve as prostitutes for the Japanese military. Back in Manchuria, Unit 731 of the Japanese Army carried out medical experiments on live Chinese patients (*maruta*, or "logs," as the military called them), hoping to develop chemical and biological weapons and better understand the human threshold for pain. Military doctors committed horrible atrocities by, for example, injecting deadly germs into their patients. They even cut off limbs and reattached them in different places. This history lives on, grimly and grotesquely, at the Unit 731 Museum outside Harbin.[24]

The government of China estimates that as many as 10 million Chinese died in the second Sino-Japanese War. Many more were injured and traumatized by Japan's violent occupation and nightly air raids. And the country's already weak economy was devastated, with roads and bridges utterly destroyed. In October 1949, about four years after Japan's surrender, Mao Zedong and the Chinese Communist Party won a civil war against Chiang Kai-shek and the Nationalists, who fled to Taiwan.

For the first three decades of "New China" (the People's Republic of China), Mao suppressed historical evidence of Japanese war crimes, including the Nanjing Massacre. Anxious to consolidate support at home, his regime chose to highlight the heroic resistance of the Communist Party and the Chinese people rather than dwell any further on the country's humiliation. Eager to break free of U.S.-led containment and secure a new (and, it was hoped, socialist) ally in East Asia, China also pursued a charm offensive, placing the blame for its neighbor's wartime behavior solely on the Japanese military—not the Japanese people.

But then Mao died. In the 1980s, as the Communist Party began to embrace market liberalization (capitalism), the new regime in Beijing— eager to retain legitimacy—revised its historiography. It suddenly began to focus attention on Japan's earlier misdeeds and its alleged failure, in the present, to acknowledge the past. Although trade and investment ties have drawn the two nations ever closer economically, they remain far apart politically. I document this process in chapter 6.

Methodology

Some scholars, such as Lieberson (1991), claim that qualitative analysis is a hopelessly blunt tool for solving a puzzle like the one posed in this book. But I disagree.[25] Designed and executed properly, a comparative case study can be just as useful as a quantitative (or large-N statistical) analysis. The trick is to follow Mill's method of difference: investigate cases that differ significantly in their outcomes, and then isolate the causal factor or explanatory variable by controlling for others. That is exactly what I do here.

Germany has achieved reconciliation with France and Poland, while Japan has not achieved reconciliation with South Korea and China. What explains this difference? By examining four distinct cases, we can highlight the strongest factor among the following possible causes:

- Geopolitics, especially the effect of the Cold War on bilateral relations
- Regime type, or the nature of the two political systems in a bilateral relationship
- Development level, or the per-capita GDP of different members of a dyad
- Economic interdependence, or the intensity of bilateral trade
- Discourse, or the nature of apologies (including compensation) for a perpetrator's behavior in past relations with a victim
- Institutions, or the depth of political cooperation within a region.

We can easily anticipate some of the results. For example, it is possible to preemptively dismiss "geopolitics" as our explanatory variable, since West Germany and France were capitalist, pro-U.S. allies during the Cold War—just like Japan and South Korea. Likewise, West Germany and Poland were rivals during the Cold War—just like Japan and China. If a factor does not vary between our European and Asian cases, it cannot explain the different results.

We also can rule out "regime type." Of the six states studied here, only one—China—has been consistently authoritarian over the past half century. If the Republic of Korea, once a military dictatorship, also had been authoritarian during this entire period, then this variable might have explanatory power. But it democratized in the late 1980s, and yet its hostility toward Japan actually deepened.

Finally, we can rule out "development level." Germans were, in 2021, a little richer than the French, on average, but almost three times wealthier than their counterparts in Poland. The data for Asia are equally instructive. Japan's per-capita GDP in 2021 was a tad larger than South Korea's, but nearly four times larger than China's.[26] Levels of development differ more between the cases with similar outcomes than they do between the cases with different outcomes.

In the case studies that follow, I make at least some mention of these variables, but focus my attention on those (economic interdependence, discourse, and institutions) that are still in the running as explanatory factors. The stories themselves are fascinating and, I hope, revealing.

THREE

Germany and France

Creating Union

In the 1950s and first half of the 1960s, West Germany's conservative political elite shied away from public statements of contrition. Konrad Adenauer, the first elected chancellor, famously said that Nazi war crimes were committed "in Germany's name," as though the nation itself could not blamed.[1] His government did apologize to the new state of Israel, but failed to express similar remorse to its European neighbors. If anything, Bonn was in those days eager to forget its own wartime history. But this stubborn refusal to acknowledge past misdeeds did not block the path to a relatively quick Franco-German reconciliation. Alfred Grosser (1967: 6) writes that, at the end of World War II, the French looked out at the world and saw "no enemy but Germany"; just a decade and half later, he writes, they saw "no friend but Germany." Likewise, Deutsch, Edinger, Macridis, and Merritt note that positive impressions of Germany among French poll respondents "rose spectacularly" during that same early postwar period, and conclude, "The anti-German attitude . . . immediately after World War II seems to have disappeared almost entirely" (1967: 247 and 67, respectively).

Obviously, something other than apologizing was going on, and that something was Franco-German cooperation on Europe's defense and, even more, its economic integration. Six years after the liberation of Paris, Robert Schuman, the foreign minister of France, began to put history in the past as he justified his proposal to create a European Coal and Steel Community (ECSC) based on the pooling of raw materials and manufacturing capacity: "The solidarity in production thus established will make it plain that any war between France and Germany becomes not merely unthinkable, but materially impossible."[2] The ECSC was successful, and its success led to the European Economic Community (EEC), which led to the European Communities (EC), which led to the European Union (EU), and so on—almost always with France and Germany in the driver's seat, together.

"It was a matter of building trust," explains Sylvie Goulard, a French bureaucrat who became a member of the European Parliament, then minister of the armed forces, and then deputy governor of the Bank of France.[3] "You don't create trust or mutual understanding through speeches. You get there through action, through joint projects. And that's what French and German leaders did in the 1950s. They dedicated themselves to a joint initiative to forge a new Europe, a peaceful and prosperous Europe."

This is a remarkable story of reconciliation that was achieved primarily through collaborative work on the evolving European project. I recount it in broad strokes before looking more closely at the competing explanatory variables.

Getting to "Oui"

Phase One (1945–1951): Becoming Partners

Joseph Rovan was a French philosopher who converted from Judaism to Catholicism, played an active role in the Resistance, and spent 10 months in the Dachau concentration camp after being arrested by the Gestapo. Among his compatriots, he was truly extraordinary. At the end of World War II, he returned to France and wrote a seminal essay arguing that the Allies, especially the French, had a moral responsibility to build a democratic Germany out of the wreckage of the Third Reich. "We must love man and men, his nation and all nations," Rovan declared (1945: 11). "This is why the French, who will participate in German re-education in the name of principles espoused by France, are obliged by these very principles to honor, respect and love the German spirit, which is now entrusted to them."[4]

Rovan was exceptional in that early post–World War II moment because the French then generally did not want to rehabilitate or reform Germany; they wanted to control or corral it—just as they had tried to do after World War I. In fact, they wanted to avoid a repeat of German resur-

gence. The initial impulse at the end of the war was overwhelmingly puni-
tive, not charitable. Charles de Gaulle, the head of the provisional government, opposed even the unification of the three (U.S., British, and French)
zones of occupation, predicting that a reconstituted Germany, even just a
West Germany, would once again attack France: "Realize that we are the
neighbors of Germany, that we have been invaded by Germany three times
in one lifetime, and conclude that never again do we want a Reich."[5] A few
years later, French president Vincent Auriol (1947–54) warned American
officials that the Germans were "revengeful, nationalistic and could not
be trusted."[6] He and other French leaders advocated a plan to divide the
German state into a weak, decentralized confederation, permanently pacify
its military, and shut down its strategic factories. French citizens strongly
supported this draconian approach. There was, according to Markovits and
Reich (1997: 125), a widespread consensus for "the harshest treatment for
Germany, any solution leaving her in a state of inferiority . . . any measure
seemed acceptable as long as it was radical and severe."

But that consensus could not hold. When the U.S. began to insist on
transforming the Federal Republic of Germany into a solid bulwark against
communism in Europe, French political elites had to adapt.[7] To secure
American aid under the Marshall Plan, they had to support the rearming
and redevelopment of their longtime rival next door.

So France adopted plan B, an elaborate, U.S.-approved scheme to
embed West Germany in multilateral institutions. The Schuman Plan was
a modified version of the Monnet Plan, named after the French socialist
and diplomat Jean Monnet, who declared: "The Franco-German problem
must become a European problem."[8] Adenauer (1966: 245), the chancellor
of West Germany, hailed the proposal to jointly exploit coal in the Ruhr
Valley and cooperate in the production and distribution of steel: "A union
between France and Germany would give new life and vigor to a Europe
that is seriously ill. . . . It would cause the rivalry between the two countries
to disappear."

The 1951 Treaty of Paris created the ECSC, but—more significantly—it
also established many of the key institutions of the contemporary European Union: a council to develop policy, a commission to set the rules,
and even a court to settle disputes. West Germany and France now were
partners, along with Italy, Belgium, the Netherlands, and Luxembourg, in
a European project of economic and—increasingly—social governance.
It would grow stronger over time, engendering greater and greater trust
between its members, and especially its coleaders.

Phase Two (1952–1963): Consolidating the Partnership

Thomas Mann, the famous novelist, issued a lonely statement during the interwar period that ultimately became the prevailing philosophy of the center-right government of the 1950s and early 1960s: "We do not want a German Europe, but a European Germany."[9] The ruling Christian Democratic Union eagerly sought to anchor the nation in a united region that was capitalist, democratic, and pro-U.S. For West Germany, Europe was more than a place; it was a political vehicle for overcoming history through two related goals: international integration (*verflechtungen*) and national self-restraint (*selbsteinbindung*).

It took France some time to appreciate the sincerity of this new German vision. In 1954, the National Assembly rejected a proposed European Defense Community, which would have incorporated West Germany into a continental security alliance. Critics feared that West Germany would eventually come to dominate the supposedly supranational institution, allowing it to subjugate France once again. The French did, however, support an alternative: They backed West Germany's entry into NATO in 1955, but only after Bonn promised not to produce any nuclear weapons, long-range missiles or large battleships, and only after it pledged to operate its armed forces under the Alliance's command structure. In the end, France reluctantly accepted West German rearmament under NATO, but only after the United States fully committed to station its own troops on the continent.

It is true that some French and German individuals and groups reached out to one another during this period. For example, business interests hoping to spur trade and investment created the Franco-German Chamber of Commerce. Municipalities began to "twin," promoting tourism, education, and other cross-border connections. (As of 2021, there were 2,317 such "sister city" or "sister region" organizations.[10]) Historians began to share notes, while peace activists (especially Action Reconciliation Service for Peace, a group founded by evangelical Lutherans in West Germany) began to collaborate. But these grassroots efforts were limited; to gain any momentum, they needed a push from Paris and Bonn.

In 1957, France and West Germany led the multilateral negotiations that culminated in the Treaties of Rome, transforming the ECSC into the European Economic Community, which was designed to promote intra-regional trade and support agriculture, and creating a European Atomic Energy Community (Euratom). The deepening of European integration helped further diminish French apprehensions about West Germany, leading to a series of bilateral summits (Chancellor Adenauer visited France in July 1962, overseeing a Franco-German military parade and attending mass at Reims Cathedral; President de Gaulle returned the favor in September) and finally to a treaty of reconciliation signed by the two leaders.

The Elysée Treaty of 1963 not only normalized ties between these long-standing enemies; it created a roadmap for future cooperation. It called for semiannual meetings between the heads of state, between ministers of foreign affairs and defense, and between officials in education and youth affairs. The treaty also established a framework for a network of civil society linkages. For example, it set up the Franco-German Youth Office, which now helps about 200,000 students travel across the border every year.[11] Roland Schäfer, who used to oversee relations with France in Germany's Foreign Ministry, joined the early wave of German youth who studied in France, and eventually married a French woman. His personal experience informed his professional work, as well as his strong belief in reconciliation through regional cooperation. "The bilateral relationship with France is only permanent and effective within the institutional framework of the European Union," he told me.[12]

Phase Three (1964–2010): The End of Franco-German "History?"

Like many others, Schäfer is blunt about the Elysée Treaty. "For quite some time, it didn't work very well." This had at least something to do with the personalities of political elites: de Gaulle famously sparred with Adenauer's successors; de Gaulle's replacement, Georges Pompidou, another center-right leader, got along better, but only slightly better, with Willy Brandt, the head of the Social Democratic Party, who became chancellor in 1969. But the treaty's ambitions also went unfulfilled because of the two states' different strategic orientations: France remained focused on national interests, jealously guarding its autonomy inside NATO and consistently resisting proposals to widen Europe; West Germany, on the other hand, was enthusiastically transatlantic as well as European, committed to both the U.S.-led military alliance and to the enlargement of integrated Europe.

This is not to suggest that Franco-German cooperation collapsed in the two decades following the birth of Elysée. Summit and ministerial meetings went on as scheduled. And leaders signed important agreements, including the 1969 plan to jointly manufacture airplanes (as Airbus) and the 1972 plan for more collaboration on monetary policy. But the relationship seemed to coast.

That changed in the early 1980s, when Chancellor Helmut Kohl and President Francois Mitterand came to power. The two leaders invested heavily in the relationship, creating Franco-German working groups on defense, economics and finance, culture, and the environment. They invited officials from the other country to serve in their own embassies and foreign ministries. They established a Franco-German television channel (Arte) dedicated to cultural programming. And they even organized a Franco-German military brigade (which became the foundation for Eurocorps)—a small but serious step toward security cooperation that once would have been unthinkable.

The decade did, of course, present bilateral challenges, and none was bigger than Kohl's plan, announced in November 1989, for West Germany to absorb East Germany. Mitterand, like almost everyone else in France, initially was quite nervous. Would a bigger and stronger Germany become unhinged, re-revanchist? Would it once again try to dominate the continent? To reassure himself and others about unification, the French president demanded that Bonn recommit itself to Europe: "German unity will be undertaken after European unity, or you will find against you a triple alliance (France, Britain, and Russia, the same alliance that fought Germany and Austria in World War I), and that will end in war. If German unity is enacted after European unity, we can help you."[13] Kohl responded by signaling support for monetary union—a dramatic move, officially enacted in the Maastricht Treaty of February 1992, which foreshadowed the death of the Deutschmark, the strongest and thus de facto currency of the European monetary system, and the birth of the Euro.

By the 1990s, the relationship between France and Germany was solid and stable. Although it did not completely disappear, the past no longer seemed to haunt the two countries.[14] Indeed, they focused their attention on joint efforts to strengthen Europe, pursuing enlargement, inviting Poland into an EU policy caucus known as the Weimar Triangle, crafting a common foreign policy, and enacting budget reforms. "Franco-German cooperation is the heart of every new development in the European project," writes Claudie Haigneré (2004: 69). French president Jacques Chirac put it even more emphatically: "So long as Germany and France get along, Europe advances; when they cease to get along, Europe stagnates."[15]

There were, to be sure, bumps along the way. For example, in the run-up to 2004, when the European Union was scheduled to take on 10 new members, most of them from central and eastern Europe, France resisted. Like Germany, it was very enthusiastic about "deepening" the EU with new responsibilities, but unlike Germany, it was quite unenthusiastic about "widening" it with new members that would compete for agricultural subsidies previously received, in large part, by French farmers.

Personality differences at the top also exacerbated underlying tensions in Franco-German relations. The flamboyant Nicolas Sarkozy, who became French president in 2007, was not a good match for the disciplined and cautious Angela Merkel, who became German chancellor in 2005. They famously clashed on a couple of occasions, including the negotiations over how to respond to the defeat of the Constitutional Treaty (Merkel wanted to rescue its most important provisions in a new Lisbon Treaty; Sarkozy was reluctant), and how to respond to the global financial crisis (Sarkozy pushed an aggressive package of proposals, including an EU-wide stimulus; Merkel preferred a more modest bailout plan).

But the two countries always seemed to iron out their differences. Even on issues outside the EU framework, France and Germany appeared to operate as a team. For example, President Chirac and Chancellor Schröder joined in firm opposition to the 2003 invasion of Iraq, despite enormous pressure from the U.S. and U.K. Then, in 2009, in the wake of a global recession, President Sarkozy and Chancellor Merkel collaborated with U.S. president Barack Obama and the other 17 members of the G20, on banking reforms. On issues of European integration, France and Germany pledged in January 2003, on the 40th anniversary of the Elysée Treaty, to work even more closely, advancing EU policies in tandem. And in 2010, the two powers led EU efforts to rescue a failing Irish economy.

"History," as progress through conflict, had come to end. Or at least it appeared to be over, even when the countries were officially remembering history. In November 2009, President Sarkozy welcomed Chancellor Merkel to Paris for a ceremony commemorating the Armistice that ended World War I. He called Franco-German cooperation a "treasure," and proclaimed that the time for "repentance" was now in the past.[16]

Phase Four (2011–): From Crisis to Renewal

By 2011, the global recession had led to a grave crisis for Europe's fiscally precarious states. One of them, Greece, revealed that its financial standing had become so shaky that it would default without a European or global bailout. France was eager to help without attaching strings; Germany was not. Chancellor Merkel pushed hard to attach conditions, especially a requirement for massive government spending cuts, to any Greek bailout package.

The disagreement led to painful negotiations over fiscal and monetary policy for Europe. In essence, Germany sought to strengthen the autonomy of the European Central Bank and require more fiscal accountability from members of the Eurozone. In opposition, France sought greater political influence over the European Central Bank and greater macroeconomic flexibility for member states. In 2012, the EU ended up adopting a Fiscal Stability Treaty barring states from running budget deficits and financial debts above specified levels. In other words, Germany won the showdown.

French voters soon elected a socialist, François Hollande, as their president. He insisted on a plan to boost spending by the European Commission to stimulate EU member economies. But the agreed-upon amount was small, the French economy continued to stagnate, and its national debt began to rise. Sounding like a German scold, the Commission (2013: 43–44) pointed out that France was becoming less resilient as it fell into the red, and advised it to put "its debt firmly onto a downward path."

The austerity policies of the European Union rankled workers, students, and socialists in France. They blamed Germany, and Merkel specifically, for subjecting them to a fiscal discipline that limited economic growth, wages, and government spending. It felt, to them, like a new occupation—this time, one commandeered by macroeconomics rather than the German military. Poulos (2015) described it this way:

> The country's public, and its political class, have chafed for a long while at Europe's reigning ideology of Merkelism, an approach to budgetary penny-pinching somewhat like Sarkozy's but considerably more drastic, and infinitely more German in its commitment to following common rules. Merkel's approach to keeping the eurozone intact was viewed by many Europeans as everything from bunk economics to moral bankruptcy, and its dead yet grasping hand was invasive enough to stir up memories of the deceptively distant Nazi occupation.

Stokes (2013) reported a widening rift between Germany and France over their respective views of the EU. While Germans continued to be positive about European integration, the French—upset about high unemployment—expressed a new Euro-skepticism. In a 2013 poll by the Pew Research Center, only 41 percent of French respondents expressed a favorable opinion of the EU; six years earlier, 62 percent had.

The Eurozone crisis finally abated, with Greece and other countries in the "South" returning to positive GDP growth and better fiscal health. But in 2017, many Europeans, especially Germans, became worried about the presidential election in France. Populists on the far Right and far Left were united in anger against a Merkel-led EU, and they seemed ascendant.

In the end, though, Emmanuel Macron, a socialist turned centrist, won the election and recommitted France to the European project.

Macron and Merkel quickly moved to revive the Franco-German axis. Indeed, the leaders collaborated on two major initiatives for Europe. First, they jointly called for a permanent EU military force within the framework of Europe's common security policy. This new army would complement NATO, and would supplant the five-nation Eurocorps created in the 1990s to allow EU members to respond more rapidly to crises.[17] The two leaders also jointly hammered out a plan to create a new budget to help member states in the Eurozone carry out reforms to maintain their financial standing and stabilize their economies.[18]

In early 2019, Merkel and Macron met in Aachen, a border town that had served as the medieval residence of King Charlemagne, and was the first German town to be captured by Allied forces near the end of World War II. They signed a new bilateral treaty pledging to defend one another militarily (without weakening NATO), promote people-to-people exchange, collaborate on clean-energy projects, and build new cross-border infrastructure. Above all, the new treaty called for closer cooperation to integrate Europe, a project that suddenly seemed in jeopardy with the Eurocrisis, Brexit, and a rise of nationalism. Discontent in Germany already had led Chancellor Merkel to resign from her post as head of the Christian Democratic Union. Massive protests in France threatened the Macron regime.

In Aachen, Merkel called for "a re-establishment of the responsibility of Germany and France within the European Union." Macron went even further: Europe, he declared, "is the protective shield for our people against the new storms in the world."[19]

A 2021 poll confirms that French citizens have come to trust their neighbor, with 84 percent indicating that Germany was a reliable partner for France. This level of trust was higher than for any other European or North American countries, including the United States (60 percent).[20]

Factors

Discourse/Gestures of Contrition

As Jennifer Lind (2008: 155) notes, this case shows that reconciliation is possible without contrition: "West Germany's remarkable *Vergangenheitsbewältigung* [mastering the past] followed, rather than preceded, Franco-German rapprochement." She argues, more broadly, that official apologies may help ease tension between states, but are not always necessary.[21] This is a controversial claim; in our personal lives, most of us refuse to embrace bullies as friends until they have bowed their heads in a public expression of guilt, or perhaps shame. Scholars tend to think states in the international system operate much like individuals on the playground. For example, Thomas Berger (2012: 247) concedes that German "penance" in the early post–World War II period was "incomplete," but nonetheless insists that "German apologies and compensation helped make the project of ever-deepening European integration possible and allowed it to forge a lasting partnership . . . with France."

The evidence here supports Lind, not Berger. In the two decades following World War II, West Germany never apologized to France for its militarist past. Yes, there were high-profile summits, such as the meeting between Adenauer and de Gaulle at the French president's home in September 1958—but no words or gestures of contrition. As I noted earlier, the West German leader did acknowledge the suffering of the Jewish people under the Nazi regime, though he pointedly declined to accept the nation's collective guilt.[22] He also persuaded a reluctant Bundestag to pay DM3.5 billion in compensation to the state of Israel as part of the 1952 Luxembourg Agreement.[23] And, finally, Bonn did sign agreements with 12 European states, promising to pay restitution to individuals persecuted by the Nazis for their religion, nationality, ideology, or race. But Adenauer and the other prominent leaders of the Christian Democratic Union that ruled West Germany until 1969 did not apologize to France.

In those days, most Germans wanted to forget the past, or—if they were willing to recall anything from the period of national socialism—to focus on their own victimization. One of the few official commemorations of that time was a memorial, erected in 1952 at Mehringdamm, Berlin, for Germans expelled from their homes in Europe at the end of the war. Otherwise, mum was the word: Concentration camps and other sites of German atrocities were, for the most part, razed or converted to peacetime purposes. May 8, the anniversary of Germany's surrender, passed each year without notice or spectacle.[24] Even textbooks on German history fell silent, focusing instead on the glories of Bach, Goethe, and a more distant, bucolic past. "Teachers simply opted out of the teaching of contemporary history," explains Wulf Kansteiner (2006: 111).

The Christian Democratic Union's silence reflected popular opinion. It opposed calls for further denazification and trials of presumed war criminals, fearing that such efforts would divide West Germany at a time of all-out, domestic reconstruction. Adenauer encouraged the nation to "put the past behind us."[25]

To be sure, not everyone fell under the spell of amnesia. Social Democrats in West Germany campaigned for greater historical consciousness, and nongovernmental organizations such as Action Reconciliation Service pushed the government to focus on non-German victims of Nazism and previous militarism. But Thomas Lutz, head of memorial museums at "Topography of Terror," a network of German facilities dedicated to remembering the past, says he and others like him constituted a "small minority" until the late 1960s and early 1970s. "The student movement started the change. That's when we began to see a new interest among the German people in the suffering of others, not just themselves."[26]

In 1969, the Social Democratic Party (SPD) gained power for the first time in Bonn, and it immediately changed the discourse about history. Willy Brandt, the new German chancellor, told the Bundestag that German suffering at the end of World War II was indeed terrible, but was caused by none other than German aggression. His successor, Helmut Schmidt, another SPD politician, delivered an impassioned speech on November 9, 1978, the 40th anniversary of Kristallnacht, accusing Germans of complacency in the face of Nazi atrocities and calling this "a cause of bitterness and shame."[27]

But well before the SPD gained power, long before West Germany revised its discourse on history, it already had achieved reconciliation with France. It did so without ever saying "I'm sorry." By 1964, 53 percent of French respondents in a poll indicated they had a good or very good opinion of West Germany—up from only 9 percent a decade earlier. A breakthrough in bilateral relations actually came as early as 1957, when positive views, for the first time, outweighed negative ones (21 percent to 18 percent; a year later, in 1958, it was 37 percent to 8 percent; see fig. 3.1).

Nothing could reverse this trend—not even a conservative resurgence in the 1980s that led to new efforts to "normalize" German memory or ease German guilt. France and West Germany were now equal partners in, or co-hegemons of, a united Europe, and this geopolitical relationship was symbolized by Mitterand and Kohl's visit to Verdun, the French town destroyed by the German army in one of the First World War's bloodiest battles. There, in September 1984, the two leaders held hands in front of the graves of both French and German soldiers. Rosoux (2001: 193) paints the picture:

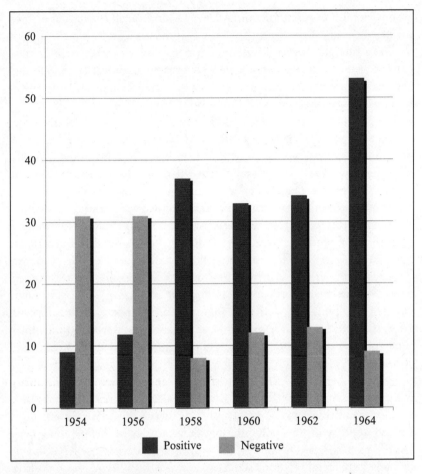

Fig. 3.1. French Views of West Germany
Source: Data from Merritt and Puchala (1968: 119).

Past wars fought between French and German were now presented as a common past of collective sufferings. The groups ceased to be described in the official memory as in opposition. They lost their heterogeneous character of groups living separately from one another and became brothers who mutually suffered a common tragedy.

French and German experts on the bilateral relationship acknowledge that words and gestures matter. But in the case of Franco-German rapprochement, most seem to know they didn't have as much impact as regional or trans-Atlantic agreements. "Of course there were apologies from Germany. Of course there were reparations," says Étienne François, a French scholar, now retired from the Free University of Berlin.[28] "But these were not the important factors; the most important factor was the development of common interests, the development of a common understanding, through the European project."

Economic Interdependence

France and Germany, the leading economies in continental Europe and next-door neighbors, are now close trading partners. But they did not become interdependent until well after they had achieved reconciliation.

In 1958, when French citizens began to express positive opinions about West Germany, the latter relied on France for only 5.5 percent of its total trade. That share rose to 13 percent by 1969, when Franco-German reconciliation already was firmly established. The French version of the story is similar. West Germany accounted for a modest amount (11 percent) of France's total trade in 1958. It was not until a decade later (1968), long after the two states had reconciled, that France came to rely on West Germany for 20 percent of its total trade (see fig. 3.2).

Another way to evaluate the effect of economic interdependence is by examining the intensity of trade between Germany and France, or the share of bilateral trade in the combined, overall trade of the two countries. That variable was relatively constant between 1980 and 1995, while French trust in Germany, measured in Eurobarometer polling, grew (see fig. 3.3). More evidence against the salience of this factor comes from an examination of bilateral trade intensity between 2002 and 2007; it fell modestly during that time, while French views of Germany, as measured by Pew, were consistently positive (see fig. 3.4). On the other hand, trade intensity fell modestly (again) from 2007 to 2017, while French views of Germany declined a bit. This is the only evidence, thus far, for the salience of economic interdependence as a factor in explaining Franco-German reconciliation.

France and Germany invest heavily in one another's economies; midway through 2021, more than 2,700 French firms were operating in Germany, and about 3,200 German firms were operating in France.[29] And the actual numbers may be far higher.[30] But high-volume, cross-border investment by French and German multinational corporations is relatively new; foreign direct investment did not flow heavily from one country to the other until the late 1990s, long after they had achieved reconciliation. And over the years, U.S. and British firms have invested far more in each country.[31]

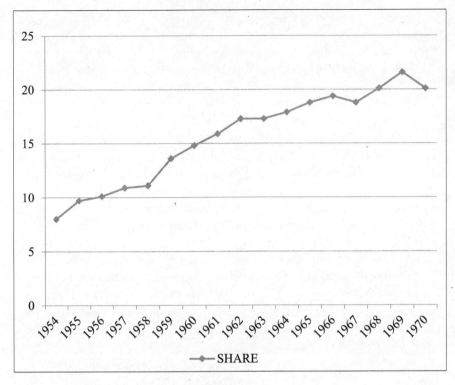

Fig. 3.2. Germany's Share of French Trade
Source: Data from World Bank, WITS.

So foreign direct investment is not a powerful indicator of economic interdependence between Germany and France. And neither is tourism. While Germany sends more short-term visitors to France than any other country, France is the sixth leading source of tourists visiting Germany, according to Destatis. If there is any interdependence in these flows, it is quite asymmetrical.

Formal Cooperation

The evidence here suggests that Germany achieved reconciliation with France by cooperating with its neighbor and the region. That is, it escaped the ghosts of the past by forging a series of bilateral and multilateral ties that embedded the nation in a European and trans-Atlantic community. By agreeing to participate in a thick web of economic and security institutions, the nation broke from its previous pattern of pursuing ultranationalism

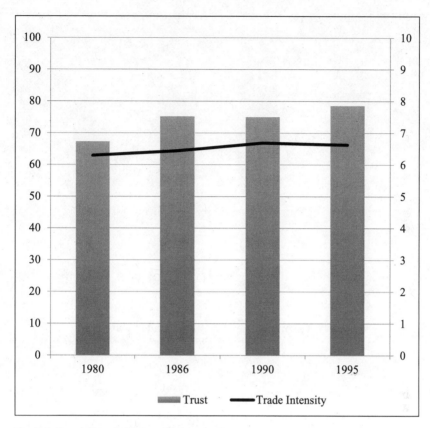

Fig. 3.3. French Trust in FRG vs. Trade Intensity
Source: Data from Eurobarometer and World Bank, WITS.

and engaging in brutal militarism. As West Germany (the FRG), it demonstrated a credible commitment to cooperate with, rather than dominate, its neighbors. The ECSC was the first step, but was followed by NATO, and then the Euratom and EEC—all of which represented, collectively, what French politician Maurice Faure called "a thousand small linkages" between France and the FRG, thereby curtailing future conflict between the two countries.[32]

West Germany's Europeanization was launched and accelerated during the 1950s, and its commitment to the process persuaded the French, by 1964, to relinquish ill will, to give up their feelings of suspicion and hostility, according to polling data. In other words, the two countries had achieved reconciliation by the mid-1960s, when the first phase of institutionalizing Europe was complete.

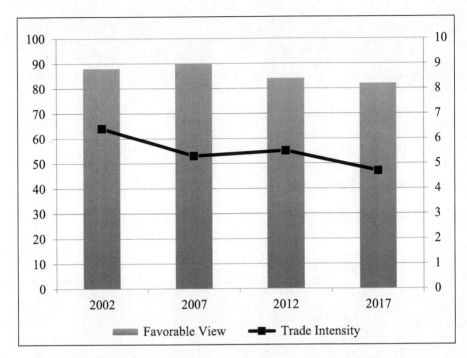

Fig. 3.4. French Views of FRG vs. Trade Intensity
Source: Data from Eurobarometer and World Bank, WITS.

"One can't just roll back history," explains Rudolf von Thadden, a German historian of France who served as Chancellor Schröder's advisor on Franco-German relations.[33] "We were required to make a new beginning after World War II, and we did it by dedicating ourselves to a cooperative effort to build a new Europe."

Of course, the European project continued to unfold beyond the mid-1960s, yielding additional institutions like European Monetary System, the EC, the EU, the European Monetary Union, and a host of new treaties. As the project advanced, memories of the bloody past retreated even further. Stephan Martens (2002–3: 14), a French political scientist, concludes: "The many problems that have plagued Franco-German relations over the years, especially the three wars that occurred in less than a century, could not have been solved outside of the multilateral framework of cooperation that is the European Union."

German leaders repeatedly have invoked the European project as their country's path out of a violent past and into a peaceful future. As noted in chapter 1, Chancellor Kohl in 1994 called it "the most effective insurance against a reemergence of nationalism, chauvinism and racism."[34] Wolfgang Schäuble, Kohl's heir-apparent as head of the Christian Democratic Union, told the German Council on Foreign Relations in June 1997: "The experiences of the first half of the twentieth century have taught us Germans to bet on integration [*verflechtungen*] . . . by tying ourselves [*selbsteinbindung*] to the West."[35]

French observers tend to agree. Regional institutions, especially the EU, served as the "glue" to cement Franco-German ties and facilitate rapprochement, according to Nicolas Jabko, a French political scientist affiliated with Johns Hopkins University and Sciences Po.[36] Sylvie Goulard, a French bureaucrat, and Étienne François, a French historian, both quoted previously, have come to the same conclusion.

Although political leaders in Bonn/Berlin and Paris launched the project, citizens in both countries eventually embraced Europeanization. This is evident in the activities of municipalities on each side of the border that have twinned, forging cooperative ties of their own. In 2009, I visited one such "sister region" organization in Dijon, France, which is twinned with Mainz, Germany. Till Meyer, a German national who, until recently, had directed Maison Rehanenie-Palatinat (in French) or Das Haus Rheinland-Pfalz (German), viewed his group as a part of the unfolding process of Europeanization. "It is a new way to create Europe—through local governments rather than central governments," he told me.[37] "Europe is now the practice of everyday life, not some abstract phenomenon."

Cooperation—through formal-legal agreements and now via daily practice—created Franco-German reconciliation. It began in the 1950s and continues today.

Summary

This case study shows that Germany and France achieved reconciliation by the mid-1960s, before the Social Democrats came to power in Bonn and began acknowledging past war crimes, and before the two economies became more or less interdependent. It came after the two nations, once bloody enemies, found common ground in bilateral, regional, and trans-Atlantic projects, from economic integration to a security alliance. Formal cooperation, which began in the 1950s, made the difference.

Representatives of France and Germany now anticipate the future; they no longer dwell on history. The ghosts of past hostility no longer seem to haunt this relationship.

"We are in a post-reconciliation time," says Claire Demesmay, a French scholar at the Deutsche Gesellschaft fur Auswartige Politik (DGAP), the German Council on Foreign Relations in Berlin.[38] France and Germany "are different countries with different political cultures, different economic structures. There is some tension, as there is in every bilateral relationship. But war between these powers is now unimaginable. And that's a big change from the past."

Wolfram Vogel, a German consultant who used to conduct research at the Institut Franco-Allemand in Paris, agrees. "We don't talk about reconciliation anymore. That word is no longer part of the public discourse. Reconciliation is over. It was completed a long time ago."[39]

FOUR

Japan and South Korea

Enmity between Allies

Since each has a democratic regime, an advanced capitalist economy, and a security alliance with the United States, Japan and South Korea appear to be natural partners in the international system and in their own neighborhood—much like Germany and France are today. And yet, in fact, Japan and South Korea (the Republic of Korea, or ROK) have not gotten along. They have consistently sparred over ownership of the Dokdo/ Takeshima islands, and they routinely clash over how to remember the past. In September 2021, nearly 40 percent of South Koreans indicated in a public opinion survey that they viewed Tokyo as a military threat.[1] Indeed, respondents to a different poll (in spring 2019) were far less favorable to Japan (3.32 out of 10) than to the United States (5.84) or China (3.64).[2] Most dramatically, 46 percent of South Koreans in a third survey (November 2019) indicated they would support North Korea if it ended up in a war with Japan; only 15 percent said they would support Japan. This preference for North Korea (over Japan) comes despite decades of belligerence against the south: a 1950 military invasion by the North; the kidnapping of numerous ROK citizens in the 1970s; the murder of many others in a bloody terrorist attack in 1987; the sinking of an ROK military ship and the shelling of a South Korean island in 2010; and the repeated threat in recent years to use Pyongyang's nuclear arsenal to turn Seoul into a "sea of fire."[3]

Between 2015 and 2018, anti-Japanese feeling in Korea diminished, leading to hope for improved relations. But a series of events at the end of that otherwise stable period reignited distrust and renewed pessimism.

This was familiar. Hope had also blossomed in the late 1990s, when diplomacy appeared to reduce tensions between Japan and South Korea. That moment, too, was short-lived; genuine reconciliation did not emerge.

Even Koreans who have spent significant time in Japan remain hostile. In 2009, I traveled to Brussels to visit Park Joon-woo, then South Korea's ambassador to the European Union. He had been a diplomat in Tokyo during the 1990s, and served for a time as director of the Japan division in Korea's Ministry of Foreign Affairs and Trade. "Japanese brutality toward Korea goes way back," Park told me.[4] "During the colonial period, they imprisoned and tortured our people, tried to steal our culture. They assassinated our empress before that. And they tried to completely destroy us in the 16th century."

Likewise, many otherwise mild-mannered Korean academics are still angry at Japan. For example, Shin Yong-ha, a sociologist and professor emeritus at Seoul National University, acknowledged that he becomes emotional over Japan's territorial claim to Dokdo. "It reflects a revival of Japanese imperialism that once again threatens Korean independence," he told me.[5] "This may be a small matter for Japan. But for us it is very important. Dokdo symbolizes our national sovereignty."

Why does the past, then, continue to haunt Japan's relations with South Korea? Japanese officials, including the emperor, have apologized to the Koreans, using the language of sincere contrition and identifying specific offenses. The government in Tokyo has offered limited compensation in the form of grants and loans, as well as an official fund to compensate those forced to serve as sex slaves or "comfort women" for the Japanese military during World War II. And the two economies are relatively interdependent with solid but informal investment and trade ties. What is really missing here, compared to the European cases, is regionalism—a set of formal trade or security agreements that otherwise would give Japan a chance to demonstrate a credible commitment to cooperation.

Before proceeding to an analysis of causal factors, we should explore how the ghostly past has not yielded to the present in Korea-Japan relations.

Enduring Hostility

Phase One (1948–1992):
From Patrimonialism to Dictatorship to Democracy

There is a remarkable continuity in South Korean attitudes toward Japan, and toward Japanese historiography about its relations with the peninsula.

Alexis Dudden (2008: 81) notes that, in the early years of independence, Korean opinion-makers condemned Japan in ways that "do not sound very different from now." In 1949, for example, a leading newspaper, *Chosun Ilbo*, assailed Japan for sponsoring "secret, illegal" fishing in Korean waters, while politicians in Seoul blasted their counterparts in Tokyo for harboring revanchist ambitions.[6] In 1951, President Syngman Rhee demanded that Japan show "concrete and constructive evidence of repentance for past misdeeds and of a new determination to deal fairly with us now and in the future" (Lee 1985: 37). Without such reassurance, he declared in a subsequent statement, Koreans have reason to believe that Japan simply wants to "redominate" the peninsula.[7]

Rhee was the corrupt if not completely incompetent leader installed by South Korea's patron, the United States. His legitimacy rested almost entirely on his anti-Japanese credentials—so he was loath to establish diplomatic ties with Korea's former colonial master. That job fell to Park Chung-hee, a former officer in the Imperial Japanese Army who seized power in a 1961 military coup. General Park, who spoke Japanese and held no obvious grudge toward his former employer, entered negotiations over a normalization treaty that would require Japan to pay $800 million in aid ($300 million in grants, $200 million in low-interest loans, and $300 million in commercial loans) in exchange for relief from reparations. The proposed pact was hugely controversial in South Korea, triggering massive street demonstrations over what critics called a "national sellout" (Lee 1990: 65).

Even though he was a ruthless dictator governing through martial law, Park nonetheless felt compelled in 1964 to demand that Japan publicly acknowledge its "past aggression" before he would sign off on a normalization treaty. This was tricky because many Japanese leaders then did not think their country had misbehaved in a terribly egregious way during Japan's colonization of Korea. But the U.S. ambassador to Japan, Edwin Reischauer, was eager to see the negotiations concluded; he urged Tokyo to deliver a statement, even a vague one. In February 1965, Foreign Minister Shiina Etsusaburo visited Seoul and expressed "true regret" and "deep remorse" for the "unfortunate period in the midst of our nations' long history." This must have been sufficient: The treaty was ratified a few months later.[8]

But relations between Japan and South Korea did not suddenly improve. Indeed, they seemed to worsen in 1973, when longtime opposition leader Kim Dae-jung was kidnapped by ROK intelligence officers in Tokyo; and again in 1974, when a Korean resident of Japan, entering Seoul on a Japanese passport and speaking Japanese, shot and killed South Korea's first lady in an assassination attempt on President Park.

Commerce drew the two economies together, but not always in a mutually satisfying way. South Korea traded heavily with Japan; from the late 1960s to the mid-1970s, its former colonizer sometimes accounted for as much as 40 percent of the country's total trade.[9] Indeed, Korean manufacturers became woefully dependent on Japanese technology, and their nation's trade deficit with Japan began to soar. In 1975, Chang Ki-young, a former deputy premier, complained bitterly about this asymmetry in a speech to the Japan-Korea Cooperation Society: "There is a saying in Korea that one not only eats the pheasant but also its eggs. Japan, however, not only eats the pheasant and eggs but also the chicks hatched from the eggs" (Lee 1985: 57). Japan conditions its loans to South Korea, he argued, on the purchase of Japanese goods, and it provides technology that requires the import of Japanese machinery and parts. In other words, Japanese business is able to dominate its smaller neighbor—just as it did in the past.

In the 1980s, the new Cold War drew the two states closer still. U.S. President Reagan wanted Tokyo and Seoul to form a united front, under America's nuclear umbrella, against Moscow and Pyongyang. South Korea's new military dictator, Chun Doo-hwan, was happy to receive funding from Japan—a low-interest loan of $4 billion over seven years. Prime Minister Nakasone Yasuhiro visited Seoul in 1983, sounding more penitent than earlier Japanese leaders. A year later, when Chun returned the favor by visiting the imperial palace in Tokyo, Emperor Hirohito himself stood up at a state dinner and apologized with a somewhat wispy reference to the colonial past.

However, the Japan-Korea relationship—characterized by one step forward and one if not two steps back—did not enjoy anything like a breakthrough. It was mired in controversies over language in Japanese textbooks authorized by the Ministry of Education in 1982, and over Nakasone's pilgrimage to the Yasukuni Shrine in 1985, the first official visit by a prime minister after Shinto priests decided to enshrine 14 Class-A war criminals there. Diplomacy suffered in the process.

Yet another military leader, Roh Tae-woo, paid a state visit to Tokyo in May 1990, where he met with Emperor Akihito, who had assumed the figurehead role following his father's death, and Prime Minister Kaifu Toshiki. Both of them granted President Roh's wish for additional statements of contrition. The new emperor used language that was clearer and more forceful than his father's, while the prime minister explicitly apologized.

It apparently wasn't enough. As the Cold War waned, creating an opening for democratization, civil society groups in South Korea began to raise new concerns about the past. For example, some complained about the forced mobilization of Koreans throughout Japan's "Co-Prosperity Sphere," where they had worked as slave laborers in factories and mines. Many ended up in Japan, where they were herded into industrial slums and treated as second-class citizens. Others were shipped off to far-flung places such as Sakhalin Island, off the coast of Siberia, which was reclaimed by the Soviet Union, and were then abandoned at the end of World War II. NGOs have represented these forced laborers in lawsuits filed in Japan and the United States.

In August 1991, an even bigger controversy erupted when Kim Hak-soon, an elderly Korean woman, stood before television cameras to tell her gripping story of being forced to work as a sex slave for Japanese troops during the Pacific War. Other women, encouraged to speak out by a grass-roots feminist organization (the Korean Council for the Women Drafted for Military Sexual Slavery by Japan; hereafter, "Women's Council"), soon followed suit. Media all over the world covered the tragic story of these "comfort women"—between 100,000 and 200,000 women, many of them Korean, who were coerced, coaxed, deceived, or sold into service at military brothels, and who now were approaching the end of often unhappy lives. The outrage was most fierce in South Korea.[10]

In January 1992, after historian Yoshimi Yoshiaki uncovered military records revealing the Japanese government's role in setting up and operating the "comfort stations," the cabinet of Prime Minister Miyazawa Ki'ichi expressed its "sincere apology . . . to those who endured suffering beyond description." But this statement, as we know, did not come close to ending the scandal—or just about any of the other controversies bedeviling the bilateral relationship.

Lee Jung-bok, a longtime friend who happens to be an expert on the bilateral relationship, delivered a passionate presentation at the Korea-Japan Intellectual Exchange Conference in Seoul in the summer of 1992. "Is the thick barrier between our two nations now broken down?" he asked (1992: 9). "Unfortunately, we cannot answer this question positively. It may be said that Korea has never been more frustrated with Japan than now in the postwar period."

Phase Two (1992–2001): Some Reason for Hope

In 1992, Kim Young-sam, a civilian, won what some regard as the first free and fair election for president of South Korea. The nation now was democratic. It also was youthful: More than 80 percent of the population had been born after Korea's liberation from Japanese occupation. Kim focused on the post–World War II and post–Cold War future in a speech to the Japanese Diet in March 1994: "We must put the past completely behind us. The Korean people are willing to look ahead and build a brighter future. To help forge a new Korea-Japan relationship crucial to ushering in a new Asia-Pacific age, the Japanese people should also muster the courage to squarely face the truths of history and live up to their lessons. We must not allow emotional residue or ethnic prejudices to remain unabated and obstruct the development of a mature bilateral partnership."

Japan, too, appeared to be moving forward in dramatic ways. In a stunning move, a coalition led by Hosokawa Morihiro of the Japan New Party had swept into power in 1993, unseating the conservative Liberal Democratic Party for the first time in 38 years. Hosokawa, an unusually youthful and telegenic leader, issued a series of statements that positioned Japan as newly cognizant of its past. He openly apologized for the nation's aggression in Asia, and its 35 years of physically brutal, culturally cruel colonialism in Korea.

A year later, in 1994, the Liberal Democratic Party regained power by teaming up with its old nemesis, the Japan Socialist Party, which required—as a precondition for partnership—that one of its own be installed as prime minister. Leftists in Japan have tended to share the Korean (and Chinese) perspective about Japanese imperialism, and Murayama Tomiichi, a pacifist as well as a socialist, was no exception. He used the occasion of the fiftieth anniversary of the end of World War II to set a new standard of contrition by offering a "heartfelt apology" and expressing "deep remorse" for Japan's militarist past. The Diet approved a watered-down statement of apology.

Even with one of the most vexing issues in the bilateral relationship, that of the "comfort women," Japan seemed eager to accommodate. The government investigated the allegations of sexual slavery and agreed in the landmark Kono statement that, in many cases, the military or its contractors, had coerced or pressured women to serve.[11] In 1995, Tokyo began soliciting private donations for an Asian Women's Fund, which promised compensation in the amount of two million yen—as well as a letter of apology from the prime minister in office—to any woman able to show she had been put to work as a sex slave.

The warming trend in bilateral relations reached a peak in 1998, when Korean president Kim Dae-jung, the hero of the Korean Left, met in Tokyo with his far less flashy counterpart, Japanese prime minister Obuchi Keizo. The two signed a joint communiqué, which included Japan's first written apology (modeled, like all subsequent apologies, on the Murayama statement) and Korea's acceptance. The two leaders called for a new "Japan-

Korea partnership for the 21st century," and agreed on economic terms of great significance for each side. Kim won a Japanese promise of $3 billion in aid to help his country overcome a financial crisis. And Obuchi secured a Korean commitment to gradually relax the long-standing ban on the import of Japanese cultural products, such as movies and music. In a subsequent meeting, the two sides even agreed to cohost the 2002 World Cup soccer tournament.

These otherwise halcyon days were not, however, entirely free of conflict. Korean voices, recently liberated from the yoke of government censorship, became even more shrill as they expressed *han*, or unabiding resentment, toward Japan. One example was *Ilbon-un ôpt'a* (The Japan That Does Not Exist), a 1993 memoir by the first Korean woman to work as a KBS TV correspondent in Tokyo. In profoundly emotional prose, Chŏn Yŏ-ok, the author, documents many unpleasant encounters with the Japanese, whom she describes as racist, sexist, and "infantile." The book quickly became a best seller. So did an explicitly anti-Japanese novel (*Mugunghwa kkochi pieot seumnida* [The Rose of Sharon Blooms Again]) published in the same year. "The Rose" depicts a Japanese attack on Dokdo/Takeshima that is repelled with the help of a nuclear weapon jointly produced by North and South Korea. The novel, by Kim Jin-myung, was quickly turned into a film. Moviegoers in Seoul apparently leaped to their feet and cheered when South Korea launched its deadly weapon against Japan.[12]

Even generally conciliatory politicians reverted to Japan-bashing to bolster their public standing. In 1995, Kim Young-sam celebrated the 50th anniversary of Japan's surrender by overseeing the demolition of Japan's colonial headquarters in Seoul, which had been transformed into the National Museum. A year later, he apparently became "indescribably outraged" when the Japanese foreign minister reasserted his nation's claim to Dokdo (Takeshima) and asked the Koreans to stop constructing a harbor on the island.[13] (Korean protesters shared the president's outrage, burning Japanese flags throughout the country and hurling salt at the Japanese embassy in Seoul.) In 1999, Kim Dae-jung, the leader who had vowed to bury history in the past, used the anniversary of *samilchol* (commemorating the March 1, 1919 protests against Japanese occupation) to blame Japan, along with other major powers, for the 1945 division of the Korean peninsula. On that same day, but two years later, he hectored the Japanese to adopt a "correct" view of history.[14]

In perhaps the most ironic commentary on Japan-Korea (or Korea-Japan) relations, the two sides squabbled repeatedly over plans for the 2002 World Cup soccer tournament, which they had agreed to cohost. At one point, Korean demonstrators demanded that FIFA, the international organization governing the competition, strip Japan of any role unless it complied with an apparent understanding that the event be described as the "FIFA World Cup Korea/Japan" rather than "Japan/Korea," as Japanese organizers were describing it. Even with a global sporting event, then, the pain of the past penetrated the present. Alastair McLauchlan (2001: 497) writes that South Korea's ambassador in Tokyo "issued an unequivocal warning that the 2002 World Cup would be placed in serious jeopardy should Japan's education system, textbooks, and official announcements 'distort the truth' about comfort women or other historical issues."

Phase Three (2001–2015): The Persistence of a Ghostly Past

The cohosted World Cup was, in the end, relatively successful, lifting spirits on both sides of the East Sea (as it is called in South Korea) or the Sea of Japan. Even though the Japanese team failed to advance beyond the opening round, "the fact that many ordinary Japanese, and the Japanese media, were offering their support to the South Korean team [which did advance] is a positive sign that the future will be better," Oh Koo Sak, a Korean resident of Osaka, told a reporter for the *Japan Times*.[15]

There were other, more important reasons for optimism. Economic and people-to-people exchange increased rapidly during this period. Merchandise trade between Japan and South Korea reached $72 billion in 2005—nearly double the amount from a decade earlier.[16] Corporations from the two countries forged strategic partnerships to take advantage of different strengths, especially in technology and distribution. For example, Japan's Kyocera and Korea's Hanaro Telecom teamed up on high-speed data communications, while LG Electronics of South Korea joined forces with Homac of Japan to sell home electronics in Japan.[17] And many more Korean and Japanese tourists began to visit the other country: 4 million in 2004—up from 2.7 million in 1994 (Ku 2008: 31).

Younger Koreans began to import Japanese popular culture, especially manga and anime. J-pop groups such as Chemistry broke through in South Korea. Meanwhile, in Japan, the Korean TV drama, *Winter Sonata* (and its ruggedly handsome star, Bae Yong-joon—known in Japan as "Yon-sama"), became a smash hit, launching a new cross-national matchmaking business for Japanese women interested in Korean men. Other cultural exports did almost as well. *Dae Jang Geum*, a court drama, triggered Japanese interest in ancient Korean cuisine. And musical performers such as BoA (Kwan Bo-ah), the "Queen of K-Pop," attracted fans from Sapporo to Fukuoka.

Japanese journalists and scholars (Kuwahara 2014) hailed this deepening interest in Korea as *hanryû*—the Korean wave.

It was not long, however, before the boom generated a backlash. One manifestation was the popularity of a Japanese manga, *Ken Kanyrû* ("I Hate the Korea Wave"), which on the cover features the young protagonist declaring, "We do not need to apologize or pay compensation to Korea anymore!" The book of cartoons sold more than 300,000 copies in the first three months after its release in 2005. Other signs of backlash were evident on social media, particularly the online bulletin board "2-channel," which routinely lit up with racist, xenophobic posts attacking South Korea (or North Korea or China).[18]

In Japanese academia as well, nationalist voices became much more vocal. Conservative historians complaining that the nation had become dangerously "masochistic" banded together to write a new, purposefully patriotic history textbook for junior high school students. The book omitted or downplayed allegations of Japan's military aggression or war crimes, such as the forced recruitment of "comfort women." In 2001, when the Japanese Ministry of Education authorized the textbook, Korean (and Chinese) nationalists took to the streets and the Web in angry protest, even though only a tiny number of schools actually adopted it. Representatives of 90 Korean NGOs formed a new coalition, the Movement for Correcting Japanese Textbooks, to mobilize against what they viewed as a revisionist trend in Japan.[19] And the South Korean government issued an official document demanding that Tokyo correct thirty-five "erroneous, distorted, and abbreviated or omitted" items in this and seven other approved textbooks.

In the wake of this controversy, Seoul and Tokyo did agree to establish a panel of experts from each country to jointly examine the history of interactions between Korea and Japan. But this effort did not yield a breakthrough. Although the panel produced reports in 2005 and 2010, it was unable to come up with a joint history textbook. In fact, it was best known for bitter disputes that mirrored the bilateral disagreement over how to remember the past.[20]

Koizumi Jun'ichiro was Japan's prime minister for the first five years of the new millennium (2001–2006). It didn't seem to matter that, only six months after assuming office, the nationalist, neoliberal leader of the Liberal Democratic Party visited the site of a former prison in Seoul, where Japanese colonial authorities had imprisoned, tortured, and executed Korean dissidents, and expressed his "heartfelt remorse" for Japan's brutal behavior during the occupation.[21] Or that he also visited Pyongyang and offered a similar apology there. What Koreans (and Chinese) angrily noticed during Koizumi's tenure was that he visited the Yasukuni Shrine every year, fulfilling a campaign promise he had made during his bid for leadership of the Liberal Democratic Party.

Thus, despite a promising start, the first decade of the new millennium ultimately brought a gradual deterioration in relations between Japan and its closest neighbor. In addition to renewed conflict over history textbooks and Yasukuni visits, the simmering disagreement over Dokdo/Takeshima reached a full boil. In May 2004, right-wing activists in southwestern Japan organized a flotilla to "take back Takeshima." The Japanese Coast Guard, fearing a military response from South Korea, repelled the expedition— but only after Tokyo issued a ringing endorsement of its sovereignty claim. Local politicians in Shimane Prefecture, where fishermen once enjoyed access to the resource-rich waters around the islands, then called on the central government to join them in recognizing the 100th anniversary of the day (February 22, 1905) that Japan had incorporated the islands into its budding empire. Tokyo was officially silent on "Takeshima Day," but allowed the local celebration to proceed and, once again, backed the underlying claim.

South Korea exploded in nationalist fury. Ordinary citizens rallied daily and defiantly in front of the Japanese embassy in Seoul, where one middle-aged man set himself on fire, while a mother and her son simultaneously hacked off their little fingers to protest what they viewed as an unforgiveable revival of Japanese imperialism. Newspapers, as well as television and radio stations, enthusiastically covered the demonstrations, featuring interviews with angry protesters and equally outraged politicians, as well as commentary by only marginally more dispassionate pundits arguing that Dokdo still belonged to Korea. In the midst of all this upset, President Roh Moo-hyun, writes Dudden (2008: 4), demanded that Japan "learn the truth" about the islands. Later, when Prime Minister Koizumi dispatched a survey ship to Dokdo/Takeshima, the Korean president responded by vowing to block it, even if doing so meant sinking the vessel (Kimura 2019: 163). President Roh warned Tokyo it would wage a "diplomatic war" over the islands.[22]

In the hot summer of 2006, when citizens, journalists, and politicians in South Korea were venting their anger at Japan, I reconnected with Lee Jung-bok, a professor at Seoul National University who studies Japanese politics. We had known each other for years, and I expected to receive a friendly but academic lesson, a cool-headed analysis that blamed populists in each country for the diplomatic breakdown. But what I actually heard was quite different: "On the history issue, Japan has failed to act responsibly," Lee told me over lunch. "If you want to understand why the relationship between our countries has gotten so bad, you have to take into account the increasingly revisionist, nationalist attitude in Japan. This attitude is quite dangerous."[23]

One could argue that Dokdo, textbooks, and Yasukuni conspired to reverse a warming trend in Korea-Japan relations. A poll conducted by *Dong-a Ilbo*, one of South Korea's leading newspapers, did show that national opinion about Japan cooled significantly between 2000 and 2005. However, a closer look at the data reveals that this was actually a return to the status quo ex ante of the 1990s. Long-standing resentment and deep-seated hostility may have abated—but only for a brief moment at the turn of the century.[24]

After Koizumi left office in 2006, Japan–South Korea relations did not improve significantly, despite Japanese efforts to tread lightly on the past. Until 2013, succeeding prime ministers stayed away from Yasukuni. All have embraced the Murayama statement of 1995, repeating in general terms the apology for Japan's occupation of Korea and its behavior in World War II. Government officials who failed to follow the diplomatic line generally have been punished. For example, General Tamogami Toshio was dismissed from his post as head of the Japanese Air Self-Defense Force after he wrote a revisionist essay suggesting that Japan entered World War II to liberate Asia from Western imperialism.[25] Even the late Abe Shinzo, the nationalist prime minister who questioned whether "comfort women" were ever coerced to become prostitutes, pledged to follow the 1993 Kono statement that became the basis for Japan's apology for its wartime policy and practice of sexual slavery.

None of this broke the diplomatic ice. In 2012, ROK President Lee Myung-bak faced a political crisis after announcing he would sign an agreement with Japan to share military intelligence. Opposition politicians accused him of betraying the nation and threatened a no-confidence vote in the National Assembly. Lee not only canceled the General Security of Military Information Agreement (GSOMIA), he spent the rest of his term demonstrating his anti-Japanese bona fides. For example, he became the first South Korean president to ever visit Dokdo, trumpeting his country's claim to the islands. A few days later, he stated that Emperor Akihito would not be welcome on the peninsula until he had issued a *new* apology to the victims of Japanese colonialism. (The emperor and his father already had delivered two formal statements of contrition.) Then he demanded that Japan adopt "responsible measures" for the sex slaves whose human rights had been violated by the Japanese military.[26]

Lee's equally conservative successor, Park Geun-hye (daughter of the former military dictator) was, at least at first, even more truculent. She edged diplomatically closer to Beijing and distanced herself further from Tokyo. After entering the Blue House in early 2013, she waited almost three years (until November 1, 2015) before agreeing to meet her Japanese counterpart in a summit. She repeatedly demanded that Prime Minister Abe acknowledge responsibility for Japan's brutal occupation of the Korean Peninsula and renounce its claim to Dokdo/Takeshima.

Phase Four (2015–): A Thaw or Another False Hope?

A month after the long-awaited Park-Abe summit meeting, the two countries reached a major breakthrough on the "comfort women" controversy. The Japanese government promised to directly provide compensation to surviving women, and the Korean government promised to quit complaining. This was followed by another controversial agreement signed in November 2016—a modified version of the GSOMIA that had bedeviled the Lee administration four years earlier. South Korea's defense ministry vowed to limit its cooperation with Japan to the sharing of information regarding North Korea's military, which had recently carried out its fifth nuclear test. But the agreement clearly represented a warming of diplomatic ties.

President Park did not last long. A bizarre corruption scandal led to her impeachment (and eventual imprisonment), and new elections brought to power a center-left government headed by Moon Jae-in. The new president initially was critical of both agreements with Japan. But in January 2018, he announced he would not seek to renegotiate the deal regarding "comfort women." And President Moon allowed the GSOMIA, which requires annual renewal, to remain in force—at least for another year.[27]

By late 2018, hopes were high for a new, more positive trend in Korea-Japan relations. But then everything seemed to fall apart. First the ROK Supreme Court ordered a Japanese steel producer to compensate Koreans forced to work under Japanese colonial rule. From Japan's perspective, the decision violated the terms of the 1965 normalization treaty. Then Seoul chose to shut down the Reconciliation and Healing Foundation established as part of the 2015 agreement with Japan to provide assistance for the surviving "comfort women." Although President Moon did not pull the plug on the agreement itself, his decision effectively killed it, jeopardizing the bilateral relationship. Prime Minister Abe responded by imposing export controls on chemicals needed by Korea for its semiconductor industry, and threatened further trade sanctions.[28]

The back-and-forth restored a frosty status quo in bilateral relations. And it led to one particularly scary moment. In December 2018, Tokyo lodged a formal complaint with Seoul, alleging that a South Korean warship had signaled hostile intent by locking its fire-control radar onto a Japanese patrol plane. The Korean military responded by accusing the Japanese plane of flying dangerously low. A former ROK ambassador to Tokyo offered this blunt assessment: "The relationship between South Korea and Japan is suffering a compound fracture unprecedented in the five decades since the two countries established diplomatic relations."[29]

In March 2022, a conservative, Yoon Suk-yeol, won the Korean election for president and immediately criticized his country's frosty relationship with Japan. He highlighted the "strategic importance" of warmer Seoul-Tokyo ties.[30] Optimism bloomed like a spring flower—again.

Factors

Discourse/Gestures of Contrition

Since 1965, when Foreign Minister Shiina visited Seoul to secure a normalization treaty, Japan has repeatedly apologized to Korea for past misdeeds. These expressions of contrition have evolved over time. Indeed, in her masterful study of Japanese apologies for World War II, Yamazaki (2006: 38, 52, 53) suggests that early statements proved "inadequate" and subsequent statements, while ultimately unsuccessful in satisfying the Korean public, represented significant rhetorical progress.

In 1984, when Korean president Chun visited Tokyo, Prime Minister Nakasone acknowledged in broad strokes that Japan had committed "wrongs" that resulted in "great suffering," while Emperor Hirohito spoke even more vaguely about an "unfortunate past" that was "regrettable," according to Wakamiya (1998: 243–46). The Korean government and media appeared to welcome and even accept these apologies, but the history controversy remained. Yamazaki (2006: 38) notes that, on apologies, "[m]ore specifics, less genteel euphemism, and a more heartfelt expression of regret were required."

All of that came in the 1990s, when Japanese apologies tended to identify specific crimes or offenses, used plain language, and conveyed greater sincerity and emotion. A new prime minister (Kaifu) and a new emperor (Akihito) apologized to President Roh (1990) for the horrible suffering Koreans experienced during the Japanese occupation of the peninsula. Most significantly, Kaifu went beyond previous statements of "regret," explicitly using the Japanese word (*owabi*) for "apology." He acknowledged "frank feelings of remorse" for the "unbearable grief" that Japan had inflected on Korea.

In a speech to the ROK National Assembly (1992), Prime Minister Miyazawa built on this rhetorical foundation by apologizing for the "unbearable suffering and grief" experienced in the past by Korea, the colonized "victim" (*higaisha*), at the hands of Japan, the colonial "perpetrator" (*kagaisha*). This was an unequivocal acknowledgment of responsibility. But Miyazawa did not stop there. He also condemned the "inexcusable" treatment of Korean women serving, often against their will, as prostitutes for Japanese troops during World War II, saying his government's policy was "painful to the heart" (*kokoro ni itamu*).

Prime Minister Hosokawa issued a statement in 1993 apologizing for the nation's "aggression" in Asia as well as its "colonial rule" in Korea. He was even more contrite in a summit meeting that year with President Kim Young-sam, acknowledging that Japan, as a perpetrator, had caused "unbearable suffering" by forcing colonized Koreans to use the Japanese language, adopt Japanese names, and serve as prostitutes for the military.

Prime Minister Murayama held a press conference in his home (1995) to apologize even more profusely for Japan's "colonial rule and aggression." At a state dinner (1996), Emperor Akihito expressed "deep sorrow" over the "great sufferings" Korea experienced during the period of Japanese colonization. Prime Minister Obuchi included a written apology, modeled on the Murayama statement, in a joint communiqué with President Kim Dae-jung (1998).

But these apologies, by themselves, had little impact. Although they were "better" or "stronger" statements of contrition, they did not move the needle of public opinion in South Korea. During the 1990s, polling conducted by *Dong-a Ilbo* never showed even 10 percent of Koreans harboring a "favorable" view of Japan. Meanwhile, as figure 4.1 demonstrates, those with an "unfavorable" view represented nearly 70 percent of respondents in 1995, the year Japan issued its most heartfelt apology.[31] This newspaper's polling reveals three exceptions over the longer term: a brief moment of relative "warmth" in 1984, when "only" 39 percent of respondents said they disliked Japan; a slightly longer period in 1999 and 2000, when more than 42 percent reported such feelings; and another brief moment in 2010, when 36 percent reported that they viewed Japan unfavorably. It is, of course, possible that these departures from an otherwise consistent pattern of hostile public opinion reflect the Korean public's short-term response to Emperor Hirohito's oblique comment on the past, Prime Minister Obu-

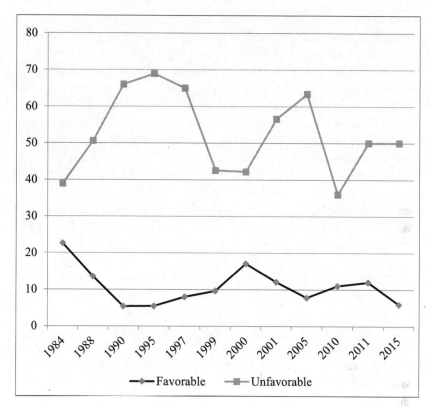

Fig. 4.1. Korean Views of Japan
Source: Data from *Dong-a Ilbo.*

chi's written apology, and the rise to power of a Democratic Party led by more contrite or at least Asia-friendly politicians such as Hatoyama Yukio. To be sure, these rhetorical gestures were widely noted, and mostly welcomed, in Korea. But it seems more likely that anomalous survey results reflect growing appreciation for bilateral and trilateral agreements reached with Japan during these exceptional moments. I discuss these below.

It also is useful to recognize that Koreans, while demanding more apologies from Japan, are themselves openly skeptical about the impact of such statements. In one poll, for example, Kim, Friedhoff, and Kang (2012: 4), researchers at the Asan Institute for Policy Studies, found strong opposition among South Koreans to a proposed agreement on military information-sharing with Japan. It then asked those opponents whether they might feel differently if Japan first apologized more robustly for its colonization of the Peninsula. More than 70 percent said no, an apology would not soften their position.

Thinking comparatively, we should note that Japan, unlike Germany in its postwar outreach to France, *did* apologize to South Korea. We can, of course, debate the quality of Japan's various statements of contrition. But one fact is clear: The statements did not help Japan reconcile with South Korea. Germany, on the other hand, was able to reconcile with France, even without uttering a single apology.

Like Germany in its postwar dealings with France, Japan did not formally compensate South Korea for any material or psychological damages. As noted earlier, it provided $800 million in grants and soft loans to its neighbor as the initial price of diplomatic normalization (and provided additional funding, as noted, in subsequent years, including 1984 and 1998), but always insisted on calling this "aid" rather than "reparations." And in negotiations over the 1965 treaty, it persuaded Seoul to give up any future claims, including those from individuals. Despite this, aggrieved Koreans (now angry at their own government, as well as Japan's) pushed hard for compensation—only to be rebuffed in 2007 by the Japanese Supreme Court. Tokyo nonetheless chose to tap public and private resources to build the Asian Women's Fund, a pot of cash to compensate individual "comfort women." In the end, this only generated additional resentment because it circumvented a demand from the Korean Women's Council for direct government payments to victims. Following a 2015 agreement, Tokyo did set aside 1 billion yen (about $10 million) in government funds. But the pact was controversial, challenged by the Women's Council and other citizen groups as miserly.

The comparative point remains: Japan was *not* less generous toward South Korea than Germany was toward France after World War II, and yet it failed to achieve reconciliation, while Germany succeeded.

In trying to measure the effect of discourse on the level of reconciliation between South Korea and Japan, we must include an evaluation of high-profile "denials." As noted in chapter 1, public apologies always generate a certain amount of domestic backlash. Nationalists all over the world respond angrily when political leaders acknowledge, even vaguely, a country's past foreign-policy mistakes. So it is fair to say that Japan is not alone in hosting what Dudden (2008: 34) calls a "multimillion-dollar denial industry."

But right-wing Japanese politicians, upset by official apologies or pronouncements, often have stoked the fires of public outrage in Korea by challenging accepted wisdom about history. In 2013, Hashimoto Toru, the mayor of Osaka and cofounder of the short-lived Japan Restoration Party, questioned the claim that the Japanese military had forcibly rounded up women to serve as sex slaves in "comfort stations." If South Koreans believe this, he declared, "they should show us the proof." Hashimoto later defended the use of "comfort women" during the war, saying they were necessary to "provide relaxation for those brave soldiers who had been in the line of fire."[32]

Do "anti-apologies" like this one help explain Japan's ongoing failure to achieve reconciliation with South Korea? My answer is no. While I agree with Lind (2008, 2013) that such heterodox statements, and the international media's fascination with them, do undermine Japan's official discourse of contrition, I think they are too isolated and episodic to cause lasting political damage. Koreans, especially educated elites, must know that Japanese "deniers" are swimming against a strong current.

This was not always so: In the 1950s and early 1960s, "deniers" were more firmly in the mainstream. Japan's early postwar leaders tended to believe that colonial policies had been justified and appropriate. They also thought those policies proved beneficial, in the end, for the fledgling economy of South Korea. In 1953, Japanese diplomat Kubota Kenichiro outraged negotiators across the table by arguing that Japan's massive investment in its colony more than offset any Korean claims for compensation. Far from being chastised, Kubota was backed up by Foreign Minister Okazaki Katsuo. Unsurprisingly, negotiations collapsed.[33]

But in more recent times, Japanese "deniers" are rebuked not only in Korea but at home, by a politically powerful mix of progressives, business leaders, and mainstream politicians. When Education Minister Fujio Masayuki told a reporter in July 1986 that Japan's annexation of Korea was "perfectly proper" (i.e., "legal"), he triggered a domestic as well as international crisis that led to him apologizing and resigning.[34] And in 2013, during the media scrum over Hashimoto's comments on the "comfort women," even Prime Minister Abe, a nationalist who shared some of the mayor's skepticism about the Kono statement, took pains to distance himself from those comments.[35] Korea's ambassador in Tokyo noted with satisfaction that Hashimoto's views are not widely shared among Japanese.[36]

In addition, we should recognize that Japanese deniers, including a very prominent one (ex–prime minister Abe), have continued to be active even as Korea-Japan relations enjoyed some improvement in more recent years (2015–18). Discourse and gestures seem to have had little impact here.

Economic Interdependence

Both Kimura Kan (2013, 2019) and Koo Min Gyo (2005), using a neoliberal institutionalist perspective, claim that relations between Japan and Korea are shaped by trade and investment ties, or by the overall level of economic interdependence. This is the commercial-peace theorem: As economic ties strengthen, diplomatic relations improve, and vice versa. But the evidence does not support this claim in the Japan-Korea case—for three reasons.

First, economic interdependence between Japan and South Korea has been highly asymmetrical. The latter relies far more heavily on the former, importing Japanese goods and technology at a much higher rate than the other way around. In 2020, South Korea faced a $21 billion merchandise trade deficit with Japan—up from $4 billion in 1988.[37] This is generally a condition that does not engender warm feelings. In fact, Koreans have long complained that Japan reproduces domination through trade and investment flows.

Second, the period of growing economic closeness between the countries coincides with growing political distance. In 1980, Japan-Korea trade intensity (the share of global trade by the two countries that consists of bilateral trade between them) was 2.85 percent; by 1989, it was 5.05 percent (the highest level it ever reached). At the same time, though, Korean views of Japan soured (see fig. 4.1).

Third, as economic interdependence between these countries has weakened, especially in recent years, diplomatic relations have not deteriorated commensurately. In fact, they improved marginally, though perhaps just temporarily, in recent years. The correlation between commercial and diplomatic ties, then, appears to be negligible, or perhaps even negative.

In the late 1980s, Japan accounted for about 30 percent of Korea's global imports and about 20 percent of its exports. But as figures 4.2 and 4.3 reveal, those shares fell steadily over time, to less than 20 percent of global imports and about 10 percent of exports in the late 1990s, and to less than 12 percent of global imports and about 5 percent of exports by 2016. In other words, Korea has become far less dependent on trade with Japan (and the U.S.) over the past three decades.

Instead, as the figures show, it has become increasingly dependent on trade with China. And yet polling data suggest that Korean views of Japan have not changed very much. Figure 4.1 shows some fluctuation between 1984 and 2015, but not a long-term decline in Japan's favorability. And figure 4.4, using results from polling conducted by the East Asia Institute in Seoul, actually shows a significant improvement between 2015 and

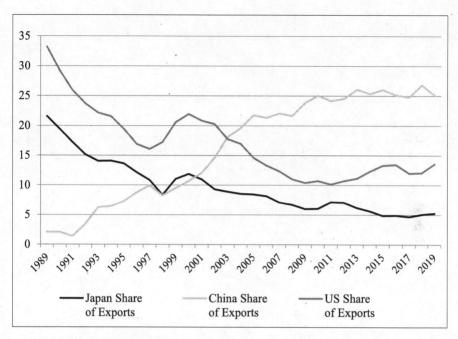

Fig. 4.2. Where Do Korean Exports Go?
Source: Data from World Bank, WITS.

2019. (Korean views of Japan turned sharply negative again in 2020, before regaining some lost ground in 2021.)

That four-year trend of improvement undermines the commercial-peace thesis. If Japan is being eclipsed by China as a vital trade partner, how can we explain the fact that, at least for a time, South Koreans came to have an increasingly positive image of their former overlord? I try to answer that question next.

Formal Cooperation

There is one causal variable that did not change much between 1990 and 2015, when we witnessed a continuing trend in strained diplomatic ties between Korea and Japan: The two countries did not cooperate in any regional or even bilateral regimes of significance. Over the years, state leaders have noted, sometimes with sadness, that Northeast Asia (China, Japan, South Korea) is unique in the world for its dearth of political cooperation. Some of them have even called for change. In his 2003 inauguration speech, for example, Korean president Roh Moo-hyun confided that he

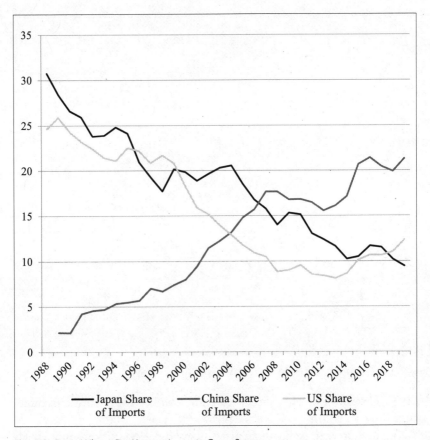

Fig. 4.3. From Where Do Korean Imports Come?
Source: Data from World Bank, WITS.

had long dreamed of a Northeast Asian "order of peace and prosperity like the one that now exists in the European Union."[38] And when he became prime minister of Japan in 2009, Hatoyama Yukio proposed an East Asian Community, also modeled on the European Union, which would promote *yûai* (or fraternity) between Asian trading partners.[39]

But these schemes never materialized. South Korea and Japan did participate jointly in the East Asia Summit, launched in 2005, as well as in the annual meetings of ASEAN Plus Three (the 10 members of the Association of Southeast Asian Nations, plus the otherwise unaffiliated three: China, Japan, and South Korea). But the two countries remained, for the most part, estranged.

This changed, marginally, in 2015 and 2016, when the two countries

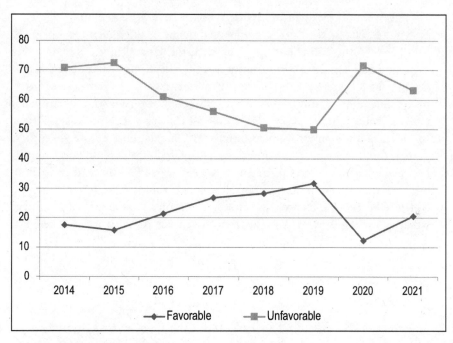

Fig. 4.4. Korean Views of Japan
Source: Data from East Asia Institute.

forged agreements on "comfort women" and military information-sharing. The first deal was significant enough. Korean activists and politicians had never been impressed by Japan's 1993 commitment to create a mostly private fund to compensate the Korean women who had worked as prostitutes or sex slaves for the Japanese military; they wanted the government of Japan to demonstrate national responsibility.[40] So when Prime Minister Abe changed his tune in 2015 and agreed to invest public money in a compensation fund, many Koreans were pleasantly surprised. At the same time, they were not ready to rally behind a pact that required South Korea to drop the comfort women issue once and for all by, for example, removing a bronze statue of a female victim in front of the Japanese embassy in Seoul. The statue in Seoul, like similar statues being erected around the country and in several places around the world, was financed with private rather than public funds—giving Seoul some distance from the controversy. Nevertheless, the center-left government that came to power in 2017 did not block the bilateral peace process. As a candidate, Moon Jae-in had called the Japan-ROK pact "seriously flawed;" as president of the nation, however, he agreed to let it stand.

The second agreement, GSOMIA, could have been groundbreaking. Reached in late 2016, it was accompanied by deepening defense cooperation between the two countries along with the United States (Heginbotham and Samuels 2018). In recent years, they have jointly participated in the Red Flag exercise, with Korean fighter jets escorting a Japanese cargo plane, defending it from simulated attacks. They also have jointly participated in the Pacific Dragon missile exercises, sharing technical data. Did this foreshadow an improvement in Japan-ROK relations? Figure 4.4 suggests it did, for a while. But other events—including the tense encounter between a Japanese patrol plane and a Korean warship in December 2018, as well as a trade conflict that began to escalate in summer 2019—eventually conspired to block such progress. President Moon announced in August he would allow the GSOMIA to lapse in November 2019. (It was rescued a year later, but only after U.S. intervention.)

Summary

Superficially, this case looks a lot like Germany-France: two liberal states, longtime trading partners, and Cold War allies of the United States. But unlike Germany and France, Japan and South Korea have not yet reconciled, although relations improved, at the margins, between 2015 and 2018.

It is undeniably true that Japan's colonization of Korea in the first half of the 20th century left bitter feelings on the peninsula. One tastes this bitterness on a sign for visitors to the restored Gyeongbokgung, the imperial palace from the Choson Dynasty, which was, we are told, "cruelly destroyed by Japan's wicked policy of aggression." One also sees it throughout a tour of the red-brick Seodaemun, a former prison in Seoul turned national(ist) museum that graphically documents the brutality of the Japanese colonial regime. And one hears it in conversations with local people.

In three different visits to South Korea, I interviewed dozens of people. Only a few expressed positive feelings about Japan. More common was this comment from Shin Gil-sou, a Korean diplomat who participated in the Northeast Asian History Foundation, a tripartite effort (China, Japan, and South Korea) to develop a common understanding of the history of this region: "We'd like to leave the past behind, but Japanese attitudes—their distorted sense of victimization—constantly trigger our own feelings of anger. It is very difficult for us to look ahead, to be positive, when they [Japanese elites] constantly defend or even glorify their own misbehavior in the past."[41]

The ghostly presence of the past continues to haunt Japan-Korea relations today. It has not been erased by Japanese apologies, or by economic interdependence between the two countries. Regional or even bilateral cooperation, which transformed Germany-France relations, would probably tame the past, making it less haunted or ghostly. But that is, by comparison, still underdeveloped in the case of Japan and Korea. In 2015, we began to witness some incipient cooperation between these countries, especially with the 2016 military information-sharing pact. But that cooperation did not last, and the longer-term trajectory of bilateral relations seems unchanged.

FIVE

Germany and Poland

Enlarging the Tent

If Franco-German reconciliation is surprisingly robust, progress toward rapprochement between Poland and Germany is perhaps even more stunning. As we saw in chapter 2, Europe's long-standing continental power—first as Prussia and then as imperial Germany—had tormented its eastern neighbor for centuries, three times cleaving Poland into ever-smaller pieces and later slaughtering its citizens in war.

In 1993, the first year they were asked in a reliable survey, 53 percent of Polish respondents indicated that they flatly disliked Germany; only 23 percent clearly liked it. Nearly three decades later, in 2022, the numbers were much better: only 24 percent of Poles now indicated that they held a starkly negative opinion of Germany, while 44 percent were decidedly positive. And this was during a period of sometimes strained relations.[1] Several years ago, I met with an adviser to the Polish prime minister while her boss was visiting the German chancellor in Berlin. She was quite upbeat. "The past is now where it belongs—in the past. We have created a new normal, a new reality between our countries."[2]

Germany's earlier reconciliation with its western neighbor was the model for its more challenging effort to repair relations with its eastern neighbor. Poland is "our France in the east," declared Friedbert Pflüger (1996), foreign policy spokesman for the then-ruling Christian Democratic Union (CDU). German-Polish reconciliation, he suggested, required a bilateral bond that is embedded in a broader [European] community. The two nations "cannot just be casual friends but must be like a married couple."

Unlike German-French rapprochement, however, this one has unfolded slowly and often painfully. The Cold War initially stood in the way. Then, in 2015, a right-wing populist party, Law and Justice (PiS), came to power in Warsaw, pursuing anti-immigrant and antidemocratic policies that earned an official rebuke from European (including German) leaders. The criticism angered PiS leaders, who renewed claims that Germany still owes Poland compensation for its 1939 invasion and subsequent occupation. But Poles seem ambivalent on the question of reparations, and do not share their government's occasional resentment toward Germany (or the European Union).[3]

In the mid-1990s, Poland desperately wanted to join the EU and NATO; Germany quickly emerged as its sponsor in this process. Germany earned widespread credit for serving in this role, and has continued to work closely with Poland in both institutions, especially the EU. This, as we shall see, has been the key to success in (mostly) taming the ghosts of history. But let us first understand the process.

Getting to "Tak"

Phase One (1945–1990): A Cold, Cold War

For two decades after World War II, West Germany (the Federal Republic of Germany, or FRG) and Poland had little to do with one another—at least officially. Poland was allied with the Soviet Union and East Germany (German Democratic Republic, or GDR). There was, to be sure, increasing interaction between representatives of civil society. In the most significant example, clergy bridged the divide, leading in 1965 to a famous letter from Polish Catholic bishops inviting their German counterparts to a millennial celebration of Christianity, recognizing the suffering of both Poles occupied and assaulted by Nazi Germany and Germans expelled from Poland at the end of World War II, and simultaneously bestowing and begging forgiveness. But the two states remained for the most part aloof and mutually suspicious. They were, after all, Cold War rivals: West Germany was a member of the U.S.-led North Atlantic Treaty Alliance (NATO); Poland was a member of the Soviet-led Warsaw Pact. Leaders in Bonn were focused on integrating with the capitalist West, while those in Warsaw were beholden to the Red Army for their grip on power.

The ice melted a bit in 1969 with the inauguration of Willy Brandt and the launch of *Ostpolitik*, his policy of outreach to Germany's neighbors

across the "Iron Curtain" to the east. The new chancellor, a Social Democrat (SPD), was especially eager to improve ties with Poland, much as his
more conservative predecessors in Bonn had managed to do with France.
In December 1970, he visited that country's capital and fell to his knees
in sorrow at the monument honoring Jews murdered by SS units during
the Warsaw Ghetto Uprising. "I was convinced," Brandt (1992: 164) wrote
later in his memoir, "that the same historical rank had to be accorded to
reconciliation between Poles and Germans as to the friendship between
Germany and France."

Two months before that fateful trip to Warsaw, Brandt and his Polish counterpart had agreed to restore trade relations, including scientific
cooperation and tourism, between their countries. Then, in December,
they signed the Treaty of Warsaw, setting the stage for diplomatic normalization in 1972 and provisionally recognizing the Oder-Neisse Line
as Poland's western border. This was the line drawn by the Allied Powers
at the end of World War II to divide Germany and Poland at the Oder
and Lusatian Neisse Rivers. The conservative governments in Bonn in the
1950s and 1960s had explicitly rejected the Potsdam Conference's decision
to not only reverse territorial claims during the Nazi invasion of 1939 but
to move Poland's border even further west, allowing it to absorb nearly all
of Silesia, more than half of Pomerania, the eastern part of Brandenburg,
a small piece of Saxony, the former Free City of Danzig, and the districts
of Masuria and Warmia in what had been East Prussia. (The Allied Powers
did this westward remapping to compensate Poland for the loss of some of
its eastern territory to one of their own, the Soviet Union.) Brandt's decision to sign the treaty did not settle the dispute once and for all; Potsdam
required a peace settlement between the Allies and a unified Germany. But
it was a major concession by his government and cost the Social Democrats support at home. German nationalists, including many of the residents expelled from those lands at the end of the war, still considered them
German territory.

Under Brandt and his successor, Helmut Schmidt, the SPD-led government of West Germany apologized to Poland and began paying compensation to victims. It also authorized German historians to begin discussions with their Polish counterparts on how textbooks in the two countries
might more accurately describe painful events from the past.[4] But this
progress toward reconciliation was constrained by the international logic
of the Cold War, especially after a conservative coalition led by Helmut
Kohl of the CDU regained a majority in the German Bundestag in 1982.
The new chancellor was, in those days, an adamant opponent of de jure

recognition of the Oder-Neisse Line. He also was aligned closely with the anticommunist policies of the United States, which under Ronald Reagan had renewed its nuclear showdown with the USSR. The change in Bonn set off alarms in Warsaw, where General Jaruzelski had already imposed martial law to quell political and labor unrest that had spilled over from the Lenin Shipyards in Gdansk. When Kohl not only joined the Western chorus of condemnation against Poland's crackdown on the Solidarity movement, but suspended aid payments to West Germany's deeply indebted neighbor, Warsaw responded angrily, accusing the FRG of neofascism and revanchism.

Although the New Cold War of the 1980s undermined Polish-German relations, it did not completely set back the clock. Kohl was determined to achieve German unification, and realized that positive relations with Erich Honecker, his counterpart in East Germany, depended in large part on FRG cooperation with Poland. So he sent his commerce minister to Warsaw in 1985 to upgrade economic ties between the two countries. West Germany agreed to restore export credit guarantees, thereby boosting trade, and it pledged to back Poland's bid to join the International Monetary Fund. Two years later, Kohl sent his commerce minister back to Warsaw to negotiate yet another extension on the time period for repaying Polish debts to West Germany.

A dramatic breakthrough came in 1989, when the communist leadership in Warsaw was defeated in Poland's first free elections. Tadeusz Mazowiecki, the new Polish prime minister, reached out warmly to West Germany, calling for "real reconciliation."[5] But for strategic reasons (as well as some political opposition from older conservatives), he was reluctant to grant Bonn's most ardent wish: Polish support for German unification.

Kohl understood that Poland wanted two things in exchange for such support. First, it sought a final resolution to the lingering question over its western border, and second, it coveted membership in Western regional institutions, particularly the European Communities (the EC, the precursor to the European Union), but also NATO. As fate would have it, the chancellor was traveling in Poland when the Berlin Wall collapsed in November 1989. After returning briefly to Bonn, where he issued his Ten-Point Plan for Unification, Kohl resumed his official visit and seized the moment. He signed 11 agreements with Mazowiecki on everything from regular meetings between the two foreign ministries to cultural exchange between the two countries.[6]

From that point on, negotiations over unification proceeded in tandem with discussions over the border. Poland watched closely as the two

Germanys joined the U.S., the U.K., France, and the Soviet Union in the "Two Plus Four" talks on unification in July 1990. Those talks concluded in September, and a month later, East Germany was formally absorbed into West Germany. Poland and the newly unified Germany quickly concluded a frontier treaty in November that confirmed the Oder-Neisse Line, obligated the two countries to respect each other's sovereignty, and called for "mutual understanding and reconciliation."

Phase Two (1991–2003): An Invitation to Cooperate

For Polish-German relations, the last decade of the 20th century began inauspiciously. In April 1991, after removing visa restrictions on Poles, the German government organized a welcoming ceremony at the Bridge of Friendship over the Oder River. About 150 neo-Nazis from the former East Germany crashed the party, chanting ultranationalist slogans and throwing rocks at vehicles crossing the river with Polish visitors. The demonstrators represented only themselves, a tiny minority, but they voiced a more nuanced, nagging concern among the wider population about embracing a poor neighbor at a time when Germany was already struggling to finance unification. And they reminded Poles that history does not disappear overnight: "Friendship? Hah! These people still have Hitler in their souls," an older Polish woman told a reporter that night.[7]

Despite the misgivings of some citizens, political elites in both countries persevered. In June 1991, they signed the Treaty on Good Neighborly Relations and Friendly Cooperation, which created new bilateral institutions, including the German-Polish Commission on Cross-Border Cooperation and the German-Polish Youth Office (modeled on the Franco-German Youth Office). In August, Germany and Poland went even further, teaming up with France to establish the Weimar Triangle, a collaborative effort to, first and foremost, secure Polish accession to the EC.

Over time, negotiations between Polish and German elites paved the way for dramatically improved relations between the two nations. But this happened in a multilateral, European context. As early as 1993, the two states took baby steps toward security cooperation. First, each resolved to open its military academies to the other; Polish officers soon began receiving training in Germany. Before long, soldiers from the two countries were engaged in joint military exercises. This represented a sea change, according to German defense minister Volker Rühe: "Anyone who knows even a little bit about history knows this is not a routine event when Polish and German soldiers are working together. It shows how well German-Polish relations are developing."[8] This breakthrough occurred under the protective cover of NATO enlargement. Among members of the alliance, Germany was the earliest supporter of Poland's bid to join.

Likewise, the two countries devoted themselves to strengthening economic cooperation. Bilateral trade increased rapidly, while foreign direct investment from Germany flowed heavily into Poland, especially its manufacturing sector. This form of cooperation, too, occurred under a regional umbrella. Poland had an obvious interest in joining the European Communities. Not only did it want freer access to the rich, integrated markets of Europe, it wanted to use the EC as a lever to transform itself into a more effective, productive, and market-oriented economy. But Germany also had a strong interest in Poland's accession. It wanted a stable and prosperous neighbor to the east, an economy that could become a consumer of German goods, and a source of cheap but semiskilled labor for German manufacturers. So Germany emerged as Poland's champion in the enlargement process.

"When it came to Poland entering the EU, we showed that we were Poland's best friend," says Angelica Schwall-Düren, an SPD member of the Bundestag from 1994 to 2010.[9] "We made it clear that Poland had to enter in the first round. And we provided more material support than anyone else."

Phase Three (2004–2014): Overcoming Nationalist Histories

When you listen to Hubert Knirsch, a German diplomat, you are quickly reminded that history doesn't move in a straight, unwavering line. Knirsch had worked at the embassy in Warsaw in the late 1980s, helping to negotiate the terms of the friendship treaty between Germany and Poland. "We thought we had solved everything," he told me with a sigh of sadness or frustration.[10] "But we were terribly mistaken." When he returned to Warsaw in 2004, the same year Poland joined the EU, the diplomat was surprised to find cracks in the relationship—a result of what he called "bad vibrations."

The past, as it turned out, was continuing to violently shake the ground. For several years, conservative politicians in Germany had been pushing to establish a Center Against Expulsions, a museum to honor the Germans who had been displaced from their homes in what became western Poland at the end of World War II.[11] Erika Steinbach, a member of the Bundestag and the head of the Expellees' Association, recast the issue as one of human rights rather than nationalism, comparing her members to the Bosnian and Albanian victims of "ethnic cleansing" in the 1990s. At the same time, a subset of the expellee community had established the Prussian Trust to pursue claims for German property expropriated by Poland after the Potsdam Declaration of August 1945. These unofficial initiatives won some public support in Germany—a fact that outraged many Poles, who generally viewed themselves, for very good reason, as victims, not perpetrators, of war crimes.[12] The Polish Sejm (lower house of the Parliament) responded in September 2004 with a resolution not only dismissing German demands for compensation, but demanding its own war reparations, even though Poland had renounced such claims in a 1953 agreement with the GDR and in the 1970 treaty with the FRG.

Chancellor Schröder addressed the crisis during his 2004 visit to Poland. In a speech commemorating the 60th anniversary of the Warsaw Uprising, he reassured his hosts: "We Germans are very much aware who started the war and who its first victims were. As such, there can be no room for restitution claims from Germany that turn history on its head."[13] The Polish government, in turn, backed away from its call for reparations.

Then came the election, in 2005, of right-wing nationalist Lech Kaczynski as Poland's new president. Kaczynski and his PiS used the history issue as a tool to stir up populist support, darkly warning that the EU had become a Trojan Horse for renewed German might. In a 2006 visit to Berlin, he hectored Chancellor Angela Merkel about the past, demanding that she distance herself from the movement on behalf of German expellees. Then, after being lampooned by a German newspaper, Poland's president skipped a second meeting with the chancellor. At about the same time, Germany and Russia agreed to collaborate on a pipeline that would bring natural gas under the Baltic Sea to Western Europe, bypassing Poland. Embittered, the Polish defense minister likened the deal to the 1939 Ribbentrop-Molotov pact that invited a Nazi invasion from the West and a Red Army encroachment from the East.[14]

But even as Polish political elites grew increasingly testy with their German counterparts, Polish citizens did not really sour on their neighbors. One public opinion survey commissioned by the Institute of Public Affairs in Warsaw in November 2005 showed remarkable stability in Polish-German relations. Asked to identify the country with which Poland should cooperate most closely, 37 percent named Germany for economic matters (ahead of all other countries) and 32 percent named Germany as the leading political partner (ahead of all but the U.S.). "We were quite surprised by the results," acknowledged the young leader of the study. "The perspective of Polish people has not been significantly influenced by the rhetoric of our politicians."[15]

It was about then that I met Professor Klaus Ziemer, who was director of the German Historical Institute in Warsaw. He spoke proudly of the progress being made on a history textbook jointly authored by German and Polish academics. "In the middle of all this political noise, I am sometimes amazed at how easily we are able to cooperate with our Polish partners."[16]

The right-wing political establishment suffered major setbacks as the first decade of the new millennium came to a close. First, the Law and Justice Party lost control of the Sejm in the 2007 elections, and then its standard-bearer, President Kaczynski, died in a plane crash in 2010. Civic Platform, which became Poland's ruling party, proved to be more pragmatic, less populist. It also was much friendlier to Germany and the EU.

In 2011, in the midst of the Greek financial crisis and growing anxiety about the future of the euro, Poland's minister of foreign affairs, Radoslaw Sikorski, pleaded with Germany to play a stronger, not weaker, role in Europe. "I will probably be the first Polish foreign minister in history to say this, but here it is: I fear German power less than I am beginning to fear its inactivity. You have become Europe's indispensable nation. You may not fail to lead: not dominate, but to lead in reform."

The statement, an official endorsement of German leadership in Europe, was unprecedented. But the domestic reception was even more stunning in that there was no backlash. No apparent discomfort. "I think the public understands that Germany is our most important partner," explained a prominent Polish diplomat.[17]

Phase Four (2015–): The Ghost Returns, but Less Hauntingly

Law and Justice returned to power in 2015, securing an outright majority of the Sejm. Like Hungary's ruling Fidesz party, PiS adopted antiimmigrant and antidemocratic policies that alarmed the European Union. First, it refused to follow an EU mandate to accept a larger number of refugees, especially Syrians, to relieve the burden on frontier states such as Greece and Italy. At an election rally, party leader Jaroslaw Kaczynski, twin brother of the former president, warned that Muslim migrants would bring cholera, dysentery, and other diseases into the country, as well as "all sorts of parasites and protozoa."[18] The EU responded by asking the European Court of Justice to sanction Poland, Hungary, and the Czech Republic. Then PiS moved to pack Poland's highest court by forcing the retirement of older jurists and filling those positions with younger, friendly ones. The EU threatened to penalize Poland, perhaps by restricting its voting rights or simply reducing the flow of benefits from the European

"Cohesion Fund." Poland has been the biggest beneficiary of that program, which is designed to redistribute income to poorer countries in the EU.

If the conflict deepens, Poles—especially older and more conservative ones—may choose nationalism over Europatriotism. And they may come to blame the EU's leading member. We did see a small increase in anti-German sentiment among the Polish population, as evidenced by the renewed call for war reparations. And there have been other, admittedly anecdotal sources for concern. On its cover, a popular Polish weekly magazine has shown EU leaders, including ex-German Chancellor Angela Merkel and the former German president of the European Parliament, Martin Schulz, dressed in Nazi uniforms and studying a map of the continent.[19] History remains an irritant (again) in the manipulative hands of political entrepreneurs.

But two forces are helping to tame the ghosts of the past and sustain the process of German-Polish reconciliation. First, Russia's invasion of Ukraine in February 2022 reunited a somewhat fractured Europe. Germany and Poland have collaborated closely with fellow EU members, imposing sanctions on Russia and providing arms to an embattled Ukraine. Second, German efforts to include and embed Poland in Europe have paid dividends with Polish civil society. Unlike their right-wing leaders, Poles are clearly *not* anti-EU; in 2018, a public opinion survey indicated that a record 92 percent of Poles wanted to remain in the European Union.[20] And they have not turned against Germany. As noted in the introduction, Poles in 2022 were far more favorable than unfavorable toward their neighbor. Trust, the most important ingredient in reconciliation, has not collapsed.

What is holding this relationship together, despite the countervailing tug of right-wing nationalism in Poland? Let us carefully consider the competing explanations (discourse and economic interdependence) before analyzing the all-important role of formal cooperation (especially regionalism) in fostering reconciliation between the two countries.

Factors

Discourse and Gestures of Contrition

As we saw in chapter 3, Adenauer and the other conservative politicians who led West Germany between 1949 and 1969 apologized publicly for the Holocaust and paid compensation to Israel, but were otherwise mum about German aggression against neighboring states not only in World

War II, but in earlier conflicts.[21] Despite this, they managed to achieve reconciliation with France by the mid-1960s. The same cannot be said for Poland, where communist leaders still branded their counterparts in Bonn as fascists, and Polish citizens continued to view Germans as bullies.[22] But between 1969 and 1982, the Social Democratic Party—led first by Brandt and then by Schmidt—made a concerted effort to change all that.

Ostpolitik was directed at the eastern bloc as a whole, but Brandt felt a special obligation to reach out to Poland. As noted earlier, the chancellor stunned the world in December 1970 when he suddenly knelt in front of the monument honoring Jews murdered during the Warsaw Ghetto Uprising. The *Kniefall*, an apparently spontaneous gesture, became an iconic image of contrition; it is commemorated with its own monument today.

Under Brandt and his SPD successor, Schmidt, West Germany also began paying compensation to Polish victims. In 1972, West Germany agreed to pay DM100 million to Polish victims of Nazi medical experiments. Three years later, it signed a "cash for people" deal, providing DM1 billion in low-interest credit and a DM1.3 billion payment for unrealized Polish pensions during the occupation in exchange for the migration of 120,000 ethnic Germans from Poland.

Civil-society groups also began meeting during this time. For example, the German-Polish Textbook Commission, established in 1972 under the auspices of UNESCO, brought together German and Polish historians to try to develop a common understanding of the past.[23] Although *Ostpolitik* clearly created new opportunities for transnational collaboration, it did not push the countries down a sustainable path toward reconciliation.

Indeed, West Germany became quieter and less generous in the 1980s, a function of the CDU's return to power, the demise of détente (the rise of a second Cold War), and the repression of the Solidarity movement in Poland. With the exception of President Richard von Weizsacker's address to the Bundestag on May 1, 1985, an address that focused on the "guilt" of all Germans,[24] West German politicians avoided public statements of contrition and declined to make additional compensation for war crimes against Poles.[25] In fact, Chancellor Kohl even appeared to thumb his nose at victims of Nazi aggression by paying a visit, along with U.S. president Ronald Reagan, to a military ceremony at Bitburg, where 49 members of Hitler's Waffen-SS had been buried.

But once Poland renounced communism and expressed its desire to join Western institutions, German conservatives changed their tune. In 1991, as part of its treaty obligations, the government of unified Germany invested 256 million euros into the Foundation for Polish-German Rec-

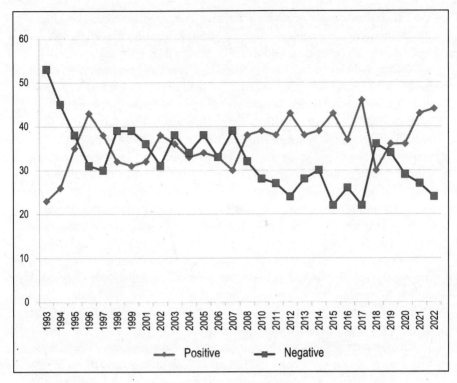

Fig. 5.1. Polish Views of Germany
Source: Data from CBOS.

onciliation, which it created to compensate victims of Nazi aggression and war crimes.[26] In 1994, President Roman Herzog of the CDU traveled to Poland for the 50th anniversary of the Warsaw uprising and asked for for-giveness. "It fills us Germans with shame that the name of our country and people will forever be associated with pain and suffering which was inflicted on Poland a million times." This sudden outpouring of euros and words did not, however, produce a quick payoff: A year later, in 1995, only 35 percent of Poles had a positive view of Germany, while 38 percent con-tinued to harbor negative feelings (see fig. 5.1). Polish attitudes about its neighbor eventually did warm up—but not for some time.

When the Social Democrats returned to power in 1998, they rededi-cated themselves to the discourse of contrition and gestures of compensa-tion. Chancellor Schröder delivered two dramatic statements to Poles. The first came in December 2000, when he told the Sejm that "no nation in his-tory was forced to suffer so heavily under the German pursuit of hegemony and tyranny as Poland." The second came in August 2004, when he became the first German head of state to help commemorate the Warsaw Uprising. At that ceremony, he apologized for the "immense suffering caused by German aggression."

The SPD regime also teamed up with German industry in 2000 to create a foundation ("Remembrance, Responsibility and the Future") to compensate European individuals who had been victims of forced labor or even slavery. About a half-million Poles received a total of nearly 1 billion euros.[27] But this new round of public statements and payments, like the earlier one, did not seem to move the needle. In 2001, as in earlier years, Poles still expressed negative feelings (36%) more often than positive ones (32%) about Germany (see fig. 5.1).

With public remorse firmly established as part of the political elite's discursive tradition, Chancellor Merkel, leader of the CDU, traveled to Gdansk in August 2009 and apologized for Germany's invasion of Poland 70 years earlier. That invasion "brought immense suffering to many people," she declared. German troops leveled cities and murdered people. "Brute force and violence permeated everyday life. Barely a Polish family was spared." But Merkel's speech apparently did not sway many Poles; by December 2008, eight months before, they had already come to have relatively positive feelings about Germany (38%). Five months later, in January 2010, that level of goodwill remained steady (39%) (see fig. 5.1).

Economic Interdependence

West Germany and Poland traded very little with one another during the first two decades of the Cold War. *Ostpolitik* changed that. Two-way trade increased sevenfold during the 1970s, albeit from a very low base. Likewise, tourism expanded rapidly; during that decade, the number of West Germans traveling to Poland climbed to more than six times the previous level, while the number of Polish visitors to West Germany increased to more than three times the earlier level.[28] These flows plateaued during the 1980s, a decade of increased Cold War tension.

But bilateral trade tripled again in the 1990s following the unification of Germany and the diplomatic breakthroughs.[29] And by the end of that decade, German multinational corporations (MNCs) accounted for nearly 20 percent of the total stock of foreign direct investment (FDI) in Poland.[30] This growing economic exchange did coincide with increasingly positive views of Germany by Poles.

While the two economies have become closer in the post–Cold War era, they have not become truly interdependent. In 1991, bilateral trade between Germany and Poland represented only about 1 percent of

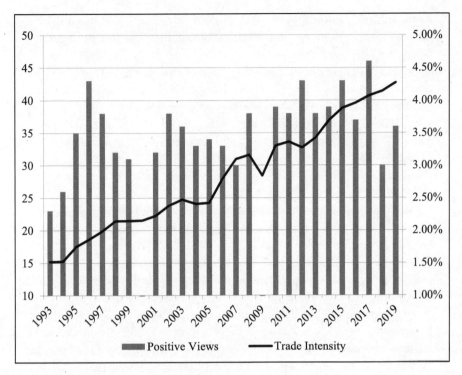

Fig. 5.2. Polish Views of Germany (%) vs. Trade Intensity
Source: Data from CBOS and World Bank, WITS.

total trade by the countries. By 2017, that share had increased—but still remained only moderate at about 4 percent.

Figure 5.2 reveals that this variable (trade intensity) is not correlated with fluctuations in public opinion. Between 1993 and 1997, for example, trade intensity grew at a tepid rate while Polish views toward Germany improved dramatically. Likewise, between 2002 and 2007, Poles became significantly less enamored with Germany, even as trade intensity strengthened.

German firms, especially auto-parts manufacturers such as Daimler, have continued to invest heavily across the Oder-Neisse. As of 2019, they had pumped about $45 billion into the Polish economy, accounting for almost 20 percent of the cumulative stock of FDI.[31] But Germany is no longer the leading source of new FDI in Poland; the Netherlands now is. By contrast, Polish FDI in Germany is miniscule.

Importantly, the interdependence between Poland and Germany is not only low, but quite asymmetrical. Germany buys more than a quarter (27%) of the exports from its eastern neighbor, making it the number-one export market for Poland; likewise, it generates more than a fifth (21%) of its neighbor's imports, making it the number-one supplier. Poland, by contrast, is not even among Germany's top five trading partners.

Poles are acutely aware of this imbalance. "It is a very close relationship, but not an equal one," says Jan Truszczyński, Poland's former ambassador to the EU.[32] "For young Poles, Germany is a big, important country that beckons to them. But when they go there, they quickly realize that they know much more about Germany than their counterparts know about Poland."

Formal Cooperation

After nearly a half century under communism, Poland looked west and saw greater freedom and prosperity. Polish elites coveted membership in Western institutions such as NATO and the European Communities, but came to accept a truism: "The road to Europe goes through Germany."[33] In those early days, Krzysztof Skubiszewski (1992), Poland's foreign minister, called for a "Polish-German community of interests that will be an important component of the international order in a uniting Europe." Hyde-Price (2000: 217) breaks this down: "At the heart of this 'community of interests' is the dual enlargement of NATO and the EU—a goal which has been championed by both countries. The dual enlargement process is also important because it provides a multilateral context for German-Polish relations."

So while Poland was looking west and seeing opportunity, Germany was looking east and seeing the same: Europeanization could facilitate reconciliation with its potentially important neighbor. "The nearer Poland gets to the EC, the more intensively we can use this framework also for German-Polish cooperation," declared Hans-Dietrich Genscher, Germany's foreign minister.[34]

It worked once, so why not implement the strategy a second time? Chancellor Kohl, speaking in Chicago in 1997, cited precedent in describing his vision: "We want to create with our eastern neighbor Poland what was possible with . . . France. This is all the more important as German-Polish history and the German-Polish border are linked on both sides with bitter experiences. . . . [W]e must draw a decisive lesson . . . that there will never again be border problems in Europe. . . . For this reason, we want Poland . . . to become a part of the European Union."[35]

As early as 1989, West Germany pushed the European Communities to create a new aid program—PHARE (Poland and Hungary Assistance for the Restructuring of their Economies), which was designed to help those countries become viable members of the community. Between

1990 and 1998, the EC paid Poland about 1.251 billion euros through
PHARE.[36] West Germany also lobbied its European partners to unilaterally extend the community's customs agreement, the Generalized System
of Preferences, to Poland. Then, in 1990, it persuaded the EC to establish
a new fund, INTERREG, designed to promote cross-border cooperation
between existing and prospective members. By 1993, 68 percent of the
program's funding was devoted to projects for Polish-German integration.[37] One such project is European University Viadrina, which is located
in Frankfurt-Oder, but reserves a third of its space for Polish students coming across the border. "We have been part of a historic process, a process
of disaggregating or de-homogenizing memory," says Gesine Schwan, the
former president of the university, who served as coordinator of Germany's
foreign relations with Poland under both Chancellor Schröder and Chancellor Merkel.[38] "Young people, naturally, are leading this effort. They are
more willing to challenge the old 'truths,' especially as they become familiar with individuals from the other country."

Germany quickly emerged as Poland's chief advocate for EC membership. In the 1990–91 negotiations over the Association Agreement, it
quietly but consistently encouraged more recalcitrant members, such as
France, to welcome enlargement beyond the EC-15. And Germany, more
than any other member, backed an accelerated timetable for an accession
process that, by necessity, included Poland. In 1994, Chancellor Kohl used
his position as president of the EU Council to help shape the criteria for
evaluating membership applications. A year later, in a speech to the Sejm,
he raised Polish expectations about Europeanization: "It is my desire, our
desire, that in the nearest future—and I am thinking primarily about this
decade—Poland should find its way to the European Union and to the
security structures within NATO."[39]

Yoder (2008: 5) argues that the EU served as "a school for improving
relations between German and Polish elites, because the EU imparts common values, norms, patterns of political and economic activity—and in so
doing, breeds familiarity, trust and a sense of linked destinies." It was a
political foundation for reconciliation between the two countries.

As noted earlier, Germany was the first NATO member to embrace
Poland's bid to join the security alliance. "Without our neighbors from
central and eastern Europe, the strategic unity of Europe will remain an
illusion," declared defense minister Rühe in a 1993 speech in London.[40]
Although he wanted to avoid upsetting Russia, which firmly opposed
NATO enlargement, Chancellor Kohl publicly but cautiously took up the
cause—especially on behalf of Poland, which he called "the most impor-

tant" candidate. He and U.S. president Bill Clinton became the leading advocates for expanding the alliance. At a 1997 summit in Madrid, they insisted—over the objections of French president Chirac—that Poland, Hungary, and the Czech Republic be invited to enter negotiations over accession.[41]

It was at about this time that Germany's favorability peaked in Polish public opinion surveys. In 1996, 43 percent of Poles told pollsters that they had a positive view of their former enemy—and only 31 percent had a negative view (the first year CBOS recorded a net favorable rating) (see fig. 5.1). In 1997, 73 percent of survey respondents said it was possible for their country to reconcile with Germany (only 25 percent said it was impossible).

While the debate over NATO enlargement came to an end in 1999 with the dramatic accession of Poland and two other refugees from the Warsaw Pact, negotiations over EU enlargement dragged on. Among other things, Germany's new ruling coalition of the SPD and Green Party began to worry about a possible influx of cheap labor from new members of the Union. At the same time, Germans began to voice an unrelated concern about the plight of countrymen and women expelled from their homes in post-Potsdam Poland. As noted, the noise next door irritated Poles, and Polish affection for the EU flagged in public-opinion surveys. Berlin paid notice; indeed, it responded by renewing its commitment to Europeanization. In 1999, Joschka Fischer, Chancellor Schröder's foreign minister, made an unequivocal statement of support: "Germany believes that measures must be taken to ensure Poland's entry into the European Union at the soonest possible date."[42] In 2000, Schröder went to bat for Poland at a summit meeting in Nice, insisting that it be awarded 27 votes in the Council of Ministers—just shy of the 29 votes held by each of Europe's most populous members (Germany, France, Italy, and the UK).[43] And in 2002, he endorsed Poland's demand for direct payments to its farmers under Europe's Common Agricultural Policy, despite Germany's desire to dramatically trim the CAP budget.[44]

Until the bitter end of a long process, Germany insisted that Poland remain among the candidates for early admission to the EU, even though it had fallen behind other countries, such as the Czech Republic and Slovenia, in the race to meet the criteria.[45] And after it gained entry in 2004, Poland often won German support on issues about which it cared strongly. For example, the former head of the central and east Europe division in the German foreign ministry recalls that Germany cast the deciding vote in the EU for Warsaw's bid to host the center for a new program on

Europe's external borders, "even though Budapest submitted the stronger proposal."[46]

It is impossible to prove, categorically, that German support for Polish Europeanization paved the way for reconciliation, but most scholars agree that it made a big difference. For example, Freudenstein (1998: 53) offers this assessment: "Germany's role as Poland's advocate within NATO and the EU has had profound positive effects on its image in Poland." And Polish opinion leaders make similar claims. Dariusz Rosati, an ex–foreign minister turned economist, says German deeds were even more helpful than German words. "They took very real, very tangible steps to close the door on the past. They welcomed us into European institutions, made us a genuine partner in the peace-building process."[47]

Just as regionalism fostered Polish-German reconciliation, a lack of European (and trans-Atlantic) cooperation undermined it. In 2003, for example, European members of NATO divided sharply over the U.S. invasion of Iraq to topple Saddam Hussein's regime. U.S. Secretary of Defense Donald Rumsfeld referred to opponents, led by Germany and France, as "old Europe," and praised newer members of NATO, especially Poland, which sent troops to join the U.S.-dominated "coalition of the willing." This coincided with a cooling of Polish-German relations from 2003 through 2007 (see fig. 5.1). Likewise, in 2018, the EU, including Germany, began threatening Poland with sanctions over its refusal to absorb refugees and its efforts to pack the courts. This also led to a cooling of Polish-German relations.

One could argue that, having gained membership in both NATO and the EU, Poland in the new millennium no longer needed Germany as much as it previously had. This would suggest that reconciliation requires deeper integration in Europe, including greater cooperation on fiscal and monetary policy. Even if it decides not to abandon the złoty and join the Eurozone, Bledowski (2018) believes Poland would benefit if it cooperates further with Germany to stabilize the regional economy, as it did between 2012 and 2015. For example, he says it should join the European Banking Union. This would not only help the Polish economy; it would help the European economy and Polish-German relations. "Poland," writes Bledowski, "should abandon old grievances against Germany and embrace its neighbor as a friend and ally. The German political class will appreciate and welcome Polish advice and may even stomach occasional admonitions. This will be possible once the goodwill is well ensconced and the relationship is free from recriminations."

Summary

As Pękala (2016) notes, reconciliation is a long-term process; it does not happen overnight, and typically does not proceed in a straight line. In the case of Germany and Poland, we have witnessed progress and retreat over the past three decades, a nonlinear process that is still ongoing—but generally moving forward.

Two factors—apologies and economic interdependence—have not played a central role in driving this process. Although Catholic bishops in West Germany and Poland promoted reconciliation in the mid-1960s through messages of contrition and forgiveness, the two nations remained divided by geopolitical interests. Once the Cold War ended, leading to the collapse of the USSR and the GDR, German officials did set up a fund to compensate victims of Nazi aggression and war crimes (1991) and then another to provide reparations to Europeans forced to work for the Reich (2000). They also issued significant public statements of apology (1994, 2000, 2004, 2009). But these did not really shift public opinion. Likewise, economic flows between the two countries have not shaped political relations. Bilateral trade has grown at a fairly steady rate, while diplomatic ties have improved most dramatically in two moments: 1993–96, and 2007–17. And the two economies are asymmetrically interdependent: Poland relies heavily on Germany as a market for exports and a source of imports; Germany relies marginally on Poland, except as a manufacturing export platform for German MNCs.

This case study suggests that formal cooperation has been the driving force between German-Polish reconciliation. The EU and NATO served as anchors, securing a newly democratic Poland's place in Western Europe, the region to which it long hoped to belong.[48] Germany sponsored Poland's entry into both organizations, vouching for the new member and winning concessions for it.

In Europe, the Polish-German partnership became as important as (or perhaps more important than) the Franco-German partnership—at least for a while. "Poland today has already largely replaced France as a German tandem partner, when it comes to institutional ideas for Europe," declared Gebert and Guérot (2012: 5). Between 2011 and 2015, Berlin and Warsaw collaborated closely to bolster European institutions. Frustrated with NATO for its frequent interventions in dangerous, relatively distant countries such as Afghanistan and Libya, they agreed to strengthen the EU's Common Security and Defense Policy.[49] And they jointly maintained

a hard line in the Euro crisis, demanding that Greece and other finan-
cially strapped members undertake austerity measures before receiving big
bailouts from Europe.[50] As they cooperated on these regional initiatives,
German-Polish relations warmed and reconciliation appeared irreversible.

Then, as noted previously, PiS returned to power in Warsaw; in addition, Donald Trump became president of the United States. This chapter,
like the next one, demonstrates that domestic and global politics matter
dearly in interstate relations. In the case of the former, Law and Justice
Party leaders have used history—including a renewed call for reparations
from Germany—to curry favor with nationalists in their political base.
Polish-German relations have suffered as the EU, led by Germany, has
criticized PiS policies that defied European rules and norms on immigration and the rule of law. In the case of the latter, Trump drove a wedge
between the two central European neighbors on a host of issues, from
the Iran nuclear agreement to the Intermediate-Range Nuclear Forces
Treaty (both of which the U.S., under Trump, abandoned, to the chagrin
of Germany); from the Nord Stream 2 pipeline designed to carry natural
gas between Russia and Germany (which Poland and the U.S., except for
a brief time in 2021 under newly elected President Joe Biden, strongly
oppose) to bilateral Polish-U.S. military cooperation (including, perhaps,
a permanent U.S. base in Poland, known colloquially as "Fort Trump,"
which Germany and France feared might undermine efforts to strengthen
European defense autonomy through, for example, Permanent Structured
Cooperation, or PESCO, and the European Intervention Initiative, or
E2I). "Trump's behavior has undoubtedly driven Berlin and Warsaw further apart on a range of issues," according to Buras and Janning (2018: 27).

But neither domestic nor global politics has blocked Polish-German
progress toward reconciliation, which is largely a function of formal cooperation on regional affairs. The behavior and rhetoric of political entrepreneurs such as Jarosław Kaczyński and Donald Trump did threaten
German-Polish relations for a time, but did not turn Poles completely
against Germany (or European institutions). Even after elections that
brought PiS back to power in Warsaw and put Trump in the White House,
Polish citizens in 2017 expressed their most positive views of Germany in
a quarter century of polling by CBOS (see fig. 5.1).

What seems increasingly clear is that Poles no longer view Germany
exclusively through the dark lens of history. "Our relationship today is built
on shared interests, shared values," says Rosati.[51]

SIX

Japan and China

Can't Buy Me Love

Like (West) Germany and Poland, East Asia's leading powers were rivals during the Cold War. Before that, Japan treated China about as horribly as Germany treated Poland: The former tributary state, which industrialized and "Westernized" first, conquered its one-time mentor in 1895, repeatedly intervened in its domestic affairs in the first part of the 20th century (with, for example, the "21 Demands" of 1915), carved a Manchurian puppet state out of China in 1931, and invaded the rest of the country again in 1937. The second Sino-Japanese War is infamous for the cruelty of imperial troops, notably the massacre and rape of civilians in Nanjing and the medical experiments on live Chinese patients in Harbin, where Japan's Unit 731 was acquiring clinical data for the nation's biological and chemical warfare programs.

Knowing this history, one could be forgiven for assuming that the People's Republic of China (the PRC, established under Mao Zedong in 1949) has always resented Japan. But as I stated in chapter 2 and will demonstrate more carefully below, it has not. In fact, the country's hostility toward Japan is relatively new. This bitterness emerged in the 1980s, a decade in which Japan began apologizing rather openly for its past aggression. And it grew dramatically in the 1990s and the first decade and a half of the new millennium, despite even more sincere and specific statements of contrition, despite billions in Japanese bilateral aid that served as a substitute for official reparations, despite the communist party-state's deepening integration into the global capitalist order, and despite strengthening economic ties between Japan and China.

Chinese antipathy toward Japan appeared to peak in 2005 with the publication of a revisionist history textbook whitewashing Japanese war crimes, and with yet another visit to the Yasukuni Shrine by Prime Minister Koizumi Jun'ichiro, a nationalist. But after a very short period of relative thaw, Sino-Japanese relations became even frostier than before. By 2013, nearly 93 percent of respondents to a *China Daily* poll indicated they had an unfavorable view of Japan (see fig. 6.2). Although the level of hostility declined over the next seven years (to "only" 53 percent in 2020, before rising again to 66 percent in 2021), mistrust remained. Many Chinese continue to view Japan as a serious military threat. In 2019, more than 75 percent of respondents told *China Daily* they saw Japan this way—marking it as the PRC's greatest threat (according to the public). This apprehension temporarily abated in 2020, when 48 percent of Chinese respondents identified Japan as a menace, but rose again in 2021, when 61 percent did. Today, a Chinese person praising the country's former aggressor is rare, and likely to invite suspicion.

In 2006, when I first began exploring the problems addressed in this book, I sat down in a Beijing coffee shop with Jin Xide, then a Chinese diplomat and researcher at the Chinese Academy of Social Science. He wasted no time in advancing the Communist Party line: "History education in Japan is very bad. The postwar generation in Japan knows little or nothing about what really happened in World War II." In addition, the new leaders in Tokyo "have abandoned the country's postwar pacifism." With China rising to become the world's second-largest economy, Japanese elites "have become dangerously aggressive."

After an hour of chatting, though, Jin relaxed visibly and began to share his fond memories of living in Japan and his hopeful vision for improved Sino-Japanese relations. "I love Japan," he told me. "I spent nearly six years there, and learned a lot about postwar politics and society in that country. I still have a lot of Japanese friends." Jin told me the Chinese party-state is actually far more moderate about Japan than a significant cross-section of the Chinese public. The government, he said, "is walking a fine line between saying too much, which stirs up nationalism, and saying too little, which attracts criticism from the nationalists." Chinese leaders, he confided, "are very concerned that anti-Japanese feeling will jeopardize our economic ties with Japan. So we focus on things like Yasukuni and textbooks, because we really have no choice there. On other issues, like technology trade and military cooperation, I think we can build a better, even closer relationship. More and more people in the government agree with me about this."[1]

I remained in touch with Jin for some time after that initial meeting, but then realized he was no longer responding to letters and emails. When I returned to China in 2009, I could not find him. It appeared that Jin had fallen off the grid. Then I was told he had been accused of espionage and sent to prison.

Why have Sino-Japanese relations devolved to the point where a nuanced view about Japan might cost a Chinese diplomat not only his job but his freedom?[2] I will examine the same set of factors considered in other case studies. We shall see that Japan has apologized to China as much as, or probably more than, Germany has apologized to Poland for past misdeeds. Likewise, we shall see that the two economies are even more interwoven than Germany's and Poland's. What makes this case of Sino-Japanese relations so different from the European case is the lack of institutionalized regionalism fostering cooperation between the two states.

From Courtship to Demonization

Phase One (1949–1981): Wooing the "Hijacked" Japanese People

When Mao declared the birth of a new nation in October 1949, his overarching objective was to consolidate political power under the Chinese Communist Party (CCP). Two major obstacles stood in the way. One was the Guomindang (the GMD, or KMT, better known as the Nationalist Party under Chiang Kai-shek), which had, for the most part, retreated to the island of Taiwan after losing its civil war with the communists, but still claimed some loyalists on the mainland. The other was the United States, which supported the KMT and identified the CCP-led government in Beijing as its enemy in the Cold War.

To win over the Chinese public, Mao pursued a historiography emphasizing communist victory in the struggle against Japanese imperialism rather than national humiliation at the hands of invading forces. Under this narrative, the CCP was heroic and the KMT was inept, even traitorous. The Maoist approach had the effect of minimizing the significance of historical events such as the massacre at Nanjing, which had been, after all, the capital of KMT-led China at the time. Xu and Spillman (2010: 116) contend that middle-school textbooks in China did not mention the massacre until 1979, and then only briefly. Alexander and Gao (2007) found that, between 1946 and 1982, the *People's Daily*, the CCP mouth-piece, used the phrase "Nanking Massacre" only 15 times, and usually just in passing. But the most dramatic example of the government's effort to downplay Japanese atrocities came in 1962, after historians at Nanjing University completed a lengthy manuscript documenting the massacre. It included new statistics on the number of casualties, photos of the bru-tal violence, and interviews with survivors. Beijing chose to classify the manuscript as top secret, allowing it to be shown by the city of Nanjing only to Japanese visitors.[3]

Mao also rallied the Chinese public against "American imperialism," noting that the U.S. was working to contain and isolate the CCP regime in Beijing while propping up the KMT government in Taipei. History text-books in the 1950s praised Soviet aid to a new and revolutionary China, contrasting it with U.S. aid to the "reactionaries" in Japan.[4] In 1950, an editorial in the *People's Daily* claimed the United States was "taking the opportunity that the forces of Japanese people have not yet been well orga-nized" to transform Japan into its colony and military base for aggression against the rest of Asia.

> The U.S. oppresses Japanese democratic forces, pampers Japanese war criminals, and supports the revival of Japanese aggression forces in an attempt to use them as its tools for launching new wars. All these U.S. policies are against the Potsdam Declaration, against the policies of the two main nations that defeated Japan—the Soviet Union and China—and are against the interest of Japanese people and the people in various Asian countries.[5]

Mao viewed Tokyo as a potential ally, along with other, smaller Western powers and socialist states, in a united front against U.S. hegemony. His slogan then was "Oppose America, Support Japan."[6] So Beijing, eager to break out of its isolation, launched a campaign of "People's Diplomacy" to foster closer ties with Japan, or at least the Japanese Left (which enjoyed relatively strong support at home in the 1950s and 1960s) and weaken the U.S.-Japan Security Alliance. This is not to suggest that the CCP exoner-ated Japan for its past aggression on the mainland—not at all. Rather, it is to note that the party-state specifically blamed Japanese militarists rather than the Japanese people. This distinction was evident in history textbooks that focused narrowly on the brutality of the Rijun (Japanese military), which controlled Tokyo in the 1930s and early 1940s.[7] Likewise, official rhetoric treated the Japanese people as victims of war—not much different from the Chinese people. Thus, Hiroshima and Nagasaki emerged as important symbols, for the CCP, of U.S. aggression and Japanese suffering. "Don't forget this terrible holocaust ['*haojie*']," exhorted the *People's Daily*.[8] By remembering the past in this way, the "New China" ironically embraced a cornerstone of the mainstream Japanese narrative about World War II, a narrative in which Japan itself was largely innocent, but had been hijacked by a "militarist clique."

The PRC extended an olive branch even to alleged war criminals and other Japanese nationals in China at the end of the war. Of the more than 1,000 Japanese detained at a special prison in Fushun on suspicion of participating in atrocities against China, only 45 were indicted. The others were pardoned and immediately released. The PRC gave fairly light sentences to those who did appear in court, and—by 1964—had released and returned all of them to Japan. Likewise, Beijing moved swiftly to repatriate about 29,000 Japanese nationals who had become stranded on the mainland at war's end. Significantly, it did so before Japan reciprocated on repatriating Chinese nationals.[9]

Cold War alliances began to shift in the 1960s, first with the rupture in Sino-Soviet ties and then with the dramatic rapprochement between China and the United States. Officially, Beijing and Tokyo moved closer. The big breakthrough came in 1972, when Prime Minister Tanaka Kakuei visited China, offering a weak apology for his country's past behavior, and Premier Zhou Enlai warmly responded. The two signed a bilateral agreement to normalize diplomatic relations. It formalized Beijing's pledge to not ask Tokyo for reparations to cover damages from World War II, and opened the door for commerce between the two nations. But China was still very poor, and wracked by political convulsions. Although manufactured goods began to flow from Japanese ports, mostly in exchange for coal from China, capital did not budge. Japanese industry was not yet ready to invest on the mainland.

Mao died in 1976, ending the Cultural Revolution and breathing new life—yet again—into a politically comatose reformer. By 1978, when Deng Xiaoping was able to consolidate power, China was beginning to open up its economy and liberalize some of its markets. It quickly signed a Treaty of Peace and Friendship with Japan, focusing on common cultural roots. And the new "paramount leader" visited his country's longtime enemy, telling Emperor Hirohito that "the past is behind us . . . we must move forward actively and constructively."[10] A year later, in a politically sensitive decision, Deng agreed to accept Japanese foreign aid (Official Development Assistance, or ODA), which came primarily in the form of cheap loans for infrastructure. He eventually established special economic zones, laboratories for private investment. Japanese manufacturers, encouraged by Deng's pro-market policies and by their own government's ODA, began to build factories in coastal China.

Under Deng, capitalism was afoot, and the Communist Party, desperate for a new source of legitimacy, eventually turned to anti-Japanese nationalism.

Phase Two (1982–2005): Utilizing "Patriotic Education"

Goodwill between the countries continued, at least for a while and at the level of civil society. China began to import more Japanese products—from food and toys to automobiles and television sets. It even imported TV shows that nurtured sympathy for the Japanese. In 1985, 200 million Chinese viewers feasted on *Ôshin*, a Japanese drama about a local woman who overcomes poverty through hard work, perseverance, and dedication to family.[11] The blockbuster drama reinforced an earlier theme, promoted by communist officials before Deng, that ordinary Japanese citizens were not unlike the Chinese.

But the official narrative was changing—for reasons rooted in domestic politics. As the "iron rice bowl" cracked, transforming fabled proletariats into market-vulnerable *precariats*, communism began to lose its "stickiness" as an ideological glue binding the Chinese people to the party. Deng understood this, and moved to rally the nation behind a modernization campaign to overcome a century of humiliation at the hands of outsiders, but especially the "wicked" Japanese. History took on a radically different meaning. It wasn't enough to simply hail the heroism of the CCP; now it also was necessary to highlight the barbarity of Japan, the country that had occupied Manchuria in 1931, and tried to conquer the rest of the country in 1937.

In the early 1980s, Deng launched ambitious projects to build museums highlighting Japanese war crimes in places such as Nanjing and Harbin. The mother of such projects, the Museum of Chinese People's Resistance Against Japanese Aggression, was built outside Beijing at the site of Japan's ill-fated attempt to subjugate all of China. It resembles a grand palace, with a garden of bronze statues illustrating Japanese cruelty, a giant flagpole reflecting national pride, and a red-carpeted entrance inviting Chinese citizens to contemplate the horrors they faced and the victory they claimed (all by themselves, without any American effort, according to this account).

Nearly in tandem, Japanese also turned more patriotic in the 1980s, especially under Prime Minister Nakasone Yasuhiro. He wanted to reject the post–World War II pacifist paradigm that constrained Japanese foreign policy. He pushed, mostly without success, for higher levels of military spending. He became a strident supporter of Japan's Cold War alliance with the U.S. And for a while, he tried to advance a more triumphant inter-pretation of Japan's modern history, one that emphasized "glory."

China responded angrily to this turn. In 1982, after the Ministry of Education in Tokyo authorized the publication of history textbooks that appeared to whitewash Japanese war crimes,[12] the official CCP organ, *Ren-min Ribao* (People's Daily) condemned Japan, writing in a series of fiery editorials that it "distorts history and beautifies invasion."[13] In 1985, as noted in chapter 4, Nakasone triggered even more upset when he made an official visit to the Yasukuni Shrine, which now housed not just the spirits of rank-and-file soldiers, but also 14 notorious criminals from World War II. Chinese students took to the streets to protest what they characterized as Japan's unrepentant attitude about the past. These may have been the first public demonstrations allowed by the communist regime since the birth of the People's Republic in 1949.

After each of these ruptures, Japan tried hard to restore otherwise peaceful relations with China. Leaders of the ruling Liberal Democratic Party (LDP), as well as the Ministry of Education, assured their Chinese counterparts that they understood Japan had "invaded" China in 1937, engaging in "aggression," despite what mealy-mouthed textbooks initially might have suggested. Nakasone even told the ministry to require right-wing writers to revise textbooks downplaying wartime atrocities such as the Nanjing Massacre. And perhaps most importantly, the prime minister promised he would not rub salt in old but still raw wounds by revisiting the private yet still controversial Yasukuni Shrine.

For more than a decade, Japan tried to maintain this conciliatory pos-ture toward China. Sure, there were notable exceptions, when some LDP politicians tried to curry favor with the far Right by denying evidence of Japanese misdeeds. Most opinion leaders, however, were consistently frank and open about the country's military past. Japanese history text-books suddenly acknowledged wartime atrocities. Courts finally agreed to hear tort cases brought by Chinese citizens demanding compensation for being dragged from their homes and forced to work under terrible, slave-like conditions in Japan.[14] And Japanese political elites began to issue truly profound statements of contrition. The August 1995 apology from Prime Minister Murayama Tomiichi, a socialist, was the most compelling of these; it set a standard that nearly all of his successors followed.

The Chinese, however, were not impressed by these gestures. They hungrily consumed anti-Japanese books such as *The China that Can Say No* (1996) and *Japan: A Country that Refuses to Admit Its Crimes* (1998).[15] And they eagerly watched critical films such as *Hong Gao Liang* (Red Sorghum) and *Guizi Lai Le* (Devils at the Doorstep), both of which portrayed Japanese soldiers as uniquely depraved or simply evil.

Some scholars insist that this virulently anti-Japanese nationalism originates in Chinese society, not with the party-state. They note that the latter has censored some of the books and films attacking Japan, and has curbed some of the protests criticizing China's former enemy. For example, Austin and Harris (2001: 62), highlight the party-state's decision to jail prominent dissident Bao Ge in 1994 for mobilizing a campaign to secure a stronger apology, as well as war reparations, from the Japanese state. Xu and Fine (2010) also emphasize calls by Chinese citizens for tougher diplomacy with Japan.

This analysis is useful because it reveals that Chinese political movements are not always driven by elites. At the same time, though, it tends to discount the influence of the Chinese party-state's Patriotic Education Campaign, which emerged in the 1990s after the Tiananmen Square massacre and even deeper market reforms conspired to further undermine the ideological salience of communism. Jiang Zemin, general secretary of the CCP and president of the PRC, wanted to give Chinese youth more reason to rally behind the ruling party. Chinese textbooks, museums, and monuments became even more explicit, telling shocking stories of Japanese treachery and brutality—how they slaughtered civilians in Nanjing and dissected live Chinese patients in Harbin. This became the shared Chinese narrative of World War II, and the Communist Party was the dominant narrator.

In 1998, Jiang visited Tokyo a month after Korea's Kim Dae-jung had come and gone. Japanese prime minister Obuchi Keizo issued similar statements of regret and contrition to the two leaders. But while Kim chose to accept Obuchi's apology for Japanese colonial domination of the Korean Peninsula, President Jiang continued to point an accusing finger at "Japanese militarism" and "the painful lessons of history" during his summit meeting with the prime minister.[16] Two years later, Chinese premier Zhu Rongji tried to calm the waters, promising that he would not "stir up the Japanese people over issues regarding history" in a pending visit to Tokyo.

Chinese antipathy toward Japan found a fat target in the new millennium, when Japanese prime minister Koizumi Jun'ichiro pursued a stubbornly nationalist program. Koizumi, backed by Japan's Izokukai, the

Bereaved Families Association, visited the Yasukuni Shrine every year during his time in office (2001–2006). Also on his watch, the education ministry authorized a new textbook drafted by a group of right-wing historians (Tsukurukai) opposed to mainstream historiography they viewed as unnecessarily "masochistic" because it openly acknowledged Japanese misdeeds during World War II.

Chinese leaders had no affection for Koizumi, vowing never to participate in a summit meeting with the prime minister. But Chinese citizens grew increasingly hostile. In April 2005, anti-Japanese anger spilled from the web, where millions of social media users signed a petition to deny Japan a coveted permanent seat on the UN Security Council, to the streets, where protesters rallied in front of diplomatic outposts and threw garbage and rocks at Japanese shops. The demonstrations became so charged that Chinese officials felt obliged to intervene. They dispatched riot police to hot spots throughout the country, and even blocked internet and cell-phone communications used by protest organizers. Signaling that it not only understood but also shared the sentiment of angry citizens, the Chinese party-state ultimately took its own bold stand. In May 2005, after members of the Koizumi administration insisted that Japan had a right to honor its war dead as it saw fit, Vice Premier Wu Yi dramatically aborted a state visit to Tokyo.

Escalating conflict over history adversely impacted other areas of Sino-Japanese relations, including Senkaku-Diaoyutai. China became more vocal in asserting its claim to islands controlled by Japan. In September 2005, five Chinese military vessels entered disputed waters around the islands, and one of them took aim at a Japanese coast-guard plane called to the scene. Although the showdown ended without any shots being fired, both sides realized just how close they had come to triggering an actual war.

Phase Three (2006–): From Bad to Worse to Maybe Better

Koizumi paid his last visit to Yasukuni in August 2006 before retiring. Although his successor, Abe Shinzo, was just as nationalistic, he revealed an eagerness to improve relations with the country that had recently become Japan's number-one trading partner. The new prime minister pledged that he would not make a pilgrimage to Yasukuni. Upping the ante, he also announced that he would make his first diplomatic foray to Beijing, not—as is customary—to Washington. One result of his October 2006 mission was the creation of a Sino-Japanese history task force charged with, among other things, writing a joint textbook. Another was the launch of a Japan-China 21st Century Exchange Program, which enables high school students from each country to visit the other. More than 1,000 Chinese students visited Japan in that first year.[17]

Abe was largely responding to domestic pressure for reconciliation. Japan's business community was unhappy with the freeze in Sino-Japanese relations, which threatened exports and investments. Even the center-right *Yomiuri* newspaper had begun publishing articles designed to remind its readers about Japan's wartime behavior, and its responsibility for making amends.[18]

Relations did thaw—for a time. When Chinese premier Wen Jiabao visited Tokyo in 2007, he praised Japan for grappling with its own history and thanked it for donating large amounts of foreign aid to China.[19] A year later, when Chinese president Hu Jintao met in Tokyo with his business-minded counterpart, Prime Minister Fukuda Yasuo, the two sides issued a joint statement that recognized Japan's commitment to peace since World War II.[20] Even the Nanjing Massacre Museum features a photo of the two leaders shaking hands, as well as a plaque extolling the large amount of foreign aid Japan has given to China over the years.[21] A major diplomatic breakthrough appeared to come in 2009, when the Democratic Party of Japan (DPJ) seized power from the conservative (and more nationalist) LDP. Hatoyama Yukio, DPJ leader and new prime minister, had campaigned as a pan-Asianist, promising warmer relations with China. On the eve of that election, Zha Daojiong, a political scientist at Beijing University, told me he was suddenly optimistic: "Yasukuni is just one issue. We have a lot of other things to talk about and seek cooperation on."[22] History appeared passé.

But that expectation soon was dashed. In 2010, a Chinese fishing trawler collided with two Japanese coast-guard vessels in waters off Senkaku. In response to Japan's arrest of the trawler captain, China imposed strong sanctions, including a ban on the export of rare earth minerals and the cancellation of cultural-exchange programs. Tensions between the countries mounted. Then, in 2012, after Japan purchased three of the five islands from a private owner, China exploded. Vice Premier Li Keqiang bitterly criticized Japan's action, according to Gustafsson (2015: 130), as "an outright denial of the outcome of victory in the war against fascism" and "a grave challenge to the postwar international order." A new round of citizen protests erupted in more than 100 Chinese cities, where demonstrators chanted anti-Japanese slogans, set fire to Japanese cars, and looted Japanese stores.

In his second round as prime minister, beginning in late 2012, Abe—the proud grandson of Kishi Nobusuke (an architect of Japan's puppet state in Manchuria, who survived the Tokyo War Crimes Tribunal to become a hawkish prime minister)—proved to be the nationalist leader everyone thought he was all along. He identified China as a potentially destabilizing force in the region, and called for a more "proactive" Japanese military that can engage in "collective self-defense" with the United States. Although Abe endorsed the 1995 Murayama statement on World War II, he also equivocated by challenging the claim that the imperial army had *forced* Asian women to serve as prostitutes and questioning whether Japan had actually "invaded" China in the 1930s.[23] Compounding the history problem, Abe changed his policy about Yasukuni, opting to visit the shrine in December 2013.

Beijing responded frostily to the political reincarnation of Abe Shinzo. Chinese officials bitterly criticized the Japanese prime minister for his historical "revisionism"; Xi Jinping, the new leader of the Chinese party-state, flatly refused to meet his counterpart until the Asia Pacific Economic Cooperation (APEC) summit in November 2014, and even then could not muster a smile. "Obviously, Mr. Xi did not want to create a warm or courteous atmosphere," concluded Togo Kazuhiko, a Japanese diplomat turned academic.[24] China also took a hard-line position on the territorial dispute with Japan. In 2013, it established an Air Defense Information Zone over the Senkaku/Diaoyu islands, warning Japanese planes to stay out. They did not. The East China Sea became the scene of frequent and often frightening showdowns between Japanese and Chinese fighter jets in what the *New York Times* (March 8, 2015) called "a test of wills."

Tension between the two countries also rose in the wake of lawsuits filed by some of the 40,000 Chinese citizens brought to Japan under duress to work in Japanese factories during the Pacific War. The Japanese Supreme Court rejected those claims in 2007, noting that China renounced any right to collect damages under its normalization treaty with Japan. Beijing has encouraged citizens to seek damages in Chinese courts, and at least one large Japanese firm (Mitsubishi Materials) has established a $56 million fund to compensate victims of forced labor.[25]

In recent years, conflict between the two countries appears to have waned, if not disappeared entirely. But a bloody past continues to haunt the present. In 2017, for example, Chinese officials blasted a Japanese hotel operator for distributing a book that downplays the extent of the Nanjing Massacre. Written by Motoya Toshio, CEO of the Tokyo-based APA hotel group, and shared in the chain's guest rooms, the book calls

Chinese accounts of the 1937 killings "absurd." A Chinese foreign ministry spokeswoman complained that the book "again shows that some forces within Japan refuse to squarely face history and even attempt to deny and distort history."[26]

Despite continued tension, Sino-Japanese relations also have enjoyed some warming. In October 2018, Prime Minister Abe paid a high-profile visit to Beijing that aimed for cooperation rather than competition. The two sides reached important agreements on everything from currency swaps to the development of advanced technologies. In addition, the Japanese government indicated that it would terminate its Official Development Assistance program in China, which had provided $32 billion in aid over 40 years—but less and less recently. Instead, it signaled that it would collaborate with China by jointly funding infrastructure projects in the region. The first major collaboration could be a high-speed rail project in Thailand.

Factors

Discourse/Gestures of Contrition

This case study suggests that, contrary to conventional wisdom, bilateral relations between these nations have worsened, not improved, as Japan demonstrated greater contrition toward China. In other words, Japanese apologies and compensation have not had the anticipated (beneficial) effect.

Japan generally avoided specific and heartfelt statements of contrition during the halcyon days of Sino-Japanese relations (1949–1981). Beijing happily accepted this, and did not demand more.

In 1972, Prime Minister Tanaka expressed "regret" (*hansei*) for the trouble (*meiwaku*) caused by Japan's military when he signed the joint communiqué on normalizing relations with China. Likewise, Emperor Hirohito, visiting Beijing in the same year, also expressed "regret."

These statements were relatively superficial. Tanaka, for example, spoke vaguely about "an unfortunate period over dozens of years in the past" and avoided any use of the word "apology" (*shazai* or *owabi*). (In a subsequent speech to the Diet, he admitted he was not even personally convinced that Japan's invasion of China represented an act of aggression.[27]) But the Chinese premier was apparently satisfied with this statement, hailing the "friendship between our great nations," blaming Japanese "militarists" (as opposed to Japan itself) for any bad, bilateral blood, offering to postpone the debate over ownership of the Senkaku/Diaoyu islands in the East China Sea, and renouncing, once again, any claim to war reparations. He only insisted on Japan's ambiguous embrace of a "one China" policy.[28]

It is impossible to know exactly what Chinese citizens thought in those days; the communist party-state did not use or allow scientific polling. But it is safe to assume that the public was just as satisfied with Japan's super-ficial gestures of contrition. No anti-Japanese protests erupted in China until 1985, after Beijing revised its historiography and adopted a more critical view of Japan's wartime behavior.

In the 1980s and early 1990s, Japanese apologies remained relatively weak. Prime Minister Nakasone, speaking at the United Nations in October 1985, said he "regretted the unleashing of rampant ultranationalism and militarism that brought great devastation to the people of many coun-tries around the world and to our country as well" (Yamazaki 2006: 141). He did not mention China by name, and did not apologize for invading Japan's neighbor and carrying out war crimes. Seven years later, in the first visit of a Japanese monarch to Beijing, Emperor Akihito went a bit further in addressing communist leaders: "In the long history of relations between our two countries, there was an unfortunate period in which my country inflicted great suffering on the people of China." He expressed "deep sad-ness" over this history, but did not apologize.[29]

This lack of contrition did not seem to upset the relationship. A 1988 poll (Jiang 1989) found that 53.6 percent of Chinese respondents had a favorable view of Japan, compared to 38.6 percent who were negative or even hostile.[30] During this period, Chinese writers such as Feng (1992) and Xiao (1992) often portrayed Japan in a positive light, noting that it served as a model for economic development, Deng Xiaoping's paramount goal. Rozman (2002) and Ross (2013), among others, describe the late 1980s and early 1990s as the calm before the storm that hit Sino-Japanese relations.

It was in the mid-1990s that Japan ramped up its rhetoric of contrition. Prime Minister Hosokawa Morihiro, the first non-LDP state leader in sev-eral decades, used specific language at an August 10, 1993 press conference to condemn Japan's "mistaken" or "wrong" (*machigatta*) war of "aggres-sion" (*shinryaku sensô*) against China.[31] Less than a year later, during a visit to Beijing, he clearly apologized for these "acts of aggression . . . which caused unbearable suffering and sorrow." The prime minister capped his statement with a powerful gesture, laying flowers at the Monument to the People's Heroes in Tiananmen Square.[32]

This groundbreaking apology was followed, and surpassed, almost immediately by another. In August 1995, the 50th anniversary of Japan's surrender in World War II, Prime Minister Murayama, a socialist, expressed his "deep remorse" and delivered a "heartfelt apology" (*kokoro kara no owabi*) for its "mistaken national policy, advanced along the road to war," causing "tremendous damage and suffering to the people of many countries, particularly to those of Asia."

The Murayama statement became the gold standard, repeated by nearly every prime minister who followed him. Prime Minister Hashimoto Ryutaro invoked it enthusiastically in 1997, when he paid a visit to China and visited a war museum in Shenyang. His successor, Obuchi Keizo, recited Murayama's words in 1998, when his counterpart, Chinese president Jiang Zemin, visited Tokyo. Even Koizumi Jun'ichiro, perhaps the Japanese leader most reviled by the Chinese in recent times, drew on the statement in 2001 when he visited China and placed a wreath on the statue of a Chinese soldier outside the grandiose Memorial Museum of the Chinese People's Anti-Japanese War in Lugouqiao (the Marco Polo Bridge, where the imperialist violence began in 1937). In a summit meeting with President Jiang, Prime Minister Koizumi expressed a "heartfelt apology" over Japanese aggression, adding that his country must "learn a lesson" from it.

Prime Minister Abe, another nationalist, also embraced the Murayama statement. In 2015, on the 70th anniversary of the end of World War II, he expressed continued remorse for Japanese "aggression" and acknowledged that his country had "inflicted immeasurable damage and suffering" on "innocent people."

But these supposedly improved Japanese apologies did not move the needle toward reconciliation. Chinese leaders continued to hector their Japanese counterparts about the past. (This was especially evident in 1998, when President Jiang used various opportunities to lecture his Japanese hosts on history.) And Chinese hearts grew harder, not softer, according to polling. A 1994 survey by *China Youth Daily* found that 97 percent of respondents felt "indignation" toward Japan.[33] Two years later (December 1996), fewer than 15 percent indicated that they liked Japan. Another year later (1997), that share had fallen to 10 percent.[34]

Indeed, even a cursory examination of public opinion polls shows that Chinese views of Japan generally soured, not sweetened, in the years following the "breakthrough" Murayama statement. Figure 6.1 shows the results of surveys conducted by the Chinese Academy of Social Sciences between 2002 and 2010, when anti-Japanese feeling grew.

Figure 6.2 shows the results of polls conducted by *China Daily* and Genron, a Japanese nonprofit group, between 2005, a particularly bad

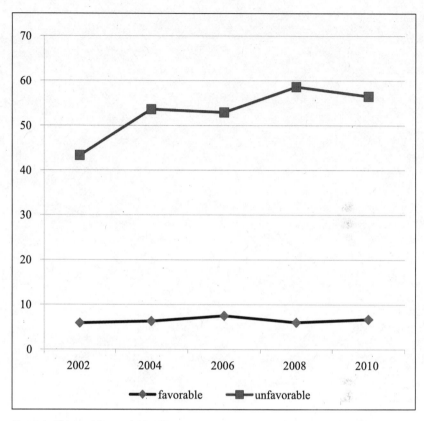

Fig. 6.1. Chinese Views of Japan
Source: Data from CASS.

year in Sino-Japanese relations, and 2021. Again, the results show lingering resentment. Despite softening since 2013, when a shocking 93 percent of Chinese respondents expressed an unfavorable view of their neighbor, anti-Japanese hostility in 2020 and 2021 remained at a level comparable to that of the dark days of 2005–10. The Pew Center (2016) found a deterioration in Chinese attitudes toward Japan between 2006, when 70 percent of respondents were negative, and 2016, when 81 percent expressed hostility.

What about nonverbal gestures of contrition? In lieu of war reparations, Japan agreed in 1979 to begin providing ODA or bilateral aid to China. Both sides understood that this represented a kind of public apology (see, for example, Lu 1998: 18–22), even though there was no formal document referring to aid as compensation for past wrongdoing. Wu (2008), an economist at Liaoning University of Technology, documents the

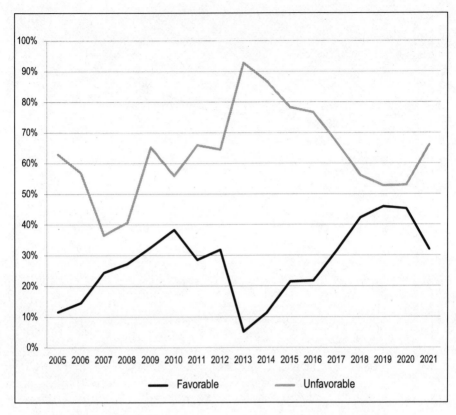

Fig. 6.2. Chinese Views of Japan
Source: Data from *China Daily.*

many Chinese development projects funded by Japanese ODA. He notes
(p. 1) that it "made a great contribution to China's social and economic
development, as well as the peoples' living level improvement."

Japanese aid came mostly in the form of yen loans with concessional (or
below-market) interest rates, and it helped finance major investments in a
large number of infrastructure projects (roads, railway lines, airports, elec-
trical facilities, dams, irrigation systems) and even manufacturing plants
(such as the Baoshan steel mill in Shanghai). Technical assistance accompanied the capital; by 1986, about 40 percent of foreign experts in China
were Japanese.[35]

Japan gave a much smaller share of its aid in the form of grants for
social programs, but its overall ODA to China remained substantial. By the
1990s, the annual flow usually exceeded $1 billion—easily making Japan

the largest bilateral donor to its rapidly growing neighbor. In one year (1999), it accounted for 67 percent of all bilateral aid given to China.[36]

Japanese ODA to China, which totaled about $32 billion over four decades, apparently failed to purchase anything close to reconciliation. Aid peaked in the 1990s, just as Chinese hostility toward Japan began to accelerate. Komori (2018), a conservative journalist in Tokyo, finds "no evidence [that] the Chinese government ever promoted friendly policies or improved its attitude toward Japan on account of ODA." Despite receiving an unprecedented volume of assistance, Communist Party leaders increasingly invoked history to criticize Japanese foreign policy, and strongly opposed Japan's bid to acquire a permanent seat on the United Nations Security Council. Aid slowed and then ended entirely in 2018, just as relations between the countries began to improve.

We must acknowledge that a variety of factors, other than statements and gestures of contrition (such as ODA), have influenced Sino-Japanese relations since the early 1990s. For one, as noted earlier, conservative politicians chafing over public apologies have managed to build a kind of "denial industry" in Japan. In 1994, for example, Justice Minister Nagano Shigeto called the Nanjing Massacre a "fabrication," arguing that China had exaggerated the scale of murder and rape. He was forced to resign. And in the same year, Sakurai Shin, director of the Environmental Agency, claimed that Japan had not engaged in "aggression" against China, embracing revisionist historiography about Japanese efforts to liberate East Asia from Western colonialism. He too was forced to resign. In 2008, Tamogami Toshio, then chief of staff of Japan's Air Self-Defense Force, wrote an essay arguing that Japan had not engaged in a war of aggression against China and the United States. Yes, he too was promptly pushed out of office.

In addition, Japanese officials frequently engaged in public practices that appeared to undermine official apologies and certainly rubbed salt in old wounds in China. Although Koizumi was not alone (Hashimoto also visited the Yasukuni Shrine in 1996; Abe, as noted, visited in 2013), the LDP maverick upset the Chinese (as well as the Koreans, as noted in chapter 4) more than any other Japanese leader by making a "pilgrimage" every year he served as prime minister (2001–2006). He was fulfilling a campaign pledge he had made to the Izokukai. Another irritant was the decision by the Education Ministry to approve history textbooks, especially the revisionist one authored by the Tsukurukai, that appeared to diminish or even ignore Japanese war crimes.

Finally, territorial disputes—especially the one over Senkaku-Diaoyu—have complicated the bilateral relationship. In 1996, a right-wing group in Japan constructed a lighthouse on the island, inflaming Chinese passions. Tension intensified again when Chinese gunboats (2005) and then a Chinese fishing trawler (2010) entered waters near the islands claimed by Japan. China reacted with even greater hostility in 2012, when Japan decided to "nationalize" some of the Senkaku islands. Ironically, the DPJ regime pursued this policy in an effort to calm the waters; it wanted to pre-empt Ishihara Shintaro, then the right-wing governor of Tokyo and an unrelenting critic of all things China, who had signaled his intent to purchase the islands and thereby rattle the Chinese.

Even after acknowledging these complicating factors, it remains impossible to conclude that Japanese apologies and compensation (indirectly via ODA) helped produce any genuine reconciliation with China. Communist leaders in Beijing, and ordinary people throughout the country, continued to complain bitterly about the past. The polling is especially clear: Chinese citizens became increasingly grumpy about Japan from the late 1990s into the second decade of the new millennium, despite the growing number and quality of apologies, and despite the increased flow of Japanese ODA to China. This only moderated recently, when the discourse and gestures of apology actually became more muted.

In 2015, Prime Minister Abe signaled his own impatience with the endless calls for Japanese contrition. "We must not let our children, grandchildren, and even future generations to come, who have nothing to do with [World War II], be predestined to apologize."[37] It is important to note that this apparently hard-hearted statement did not seem to hurt Japan's standing with China.

Economic Interdependence

Advocates of "commercial peace" (Pax Mercatoria) argue that economic interdependence fosters stable, warm relations between countries. In other words, diplomatic ties should grow stronger as economic linkages strengthen. But the evidence here completely contradicts that hypothesis, supporting instead the work of contrarians such as Barbieri (2002). The Chinese and Japanese economies are well integrated by commodity and capital flows, a process that has accelerated over the past three decades—even as relations between the two countries have frayed.

Bilateral trade between China and Japan has blossomed, expanding 38 times between 1980 (when it was valued at $9 billion) and 2011 (when it was valued at $346 billion); it nearly quadrupled between 2001 and 2011.[38] Japan, then Asia's only economic power, was China's number-one trading partner in the 1960s, and continued to serve as its leading source of imports until 2013, when Korea assumed that role. China became Japan's number-one trading partner in 2007, and has continued to occupy that role. It supplies a large share of Japan's imports (24% in 2019), especially machinery and electronics.

Trade between the two economies is driven in part by Japanese foreign direct investment in China. In 2021, Japan accounted for 33,000 multinational corporations operating in the Middle Kingdom—more than any other country.[39] Japanese multinationals such as Matsushita have built major production facilities in China, especially along the eastern seaboard, importing high-tech components from Japan and exporting finished goods as well as lower-tech components back to Japan. Japanese foreign direct investment (FDI) to China swelled from $177 million in 1987 to $14.4 billion in 2019.[40] Chinese FDI to Japan has grown dramatically in recent years, but remains far lower ($1.9 billion in 2019) than direct investment flowing in the opposite direction.

Increased capital flows between the two economies have not brought closer diplomatic ties. FDI flows from Japan to China have been, on average, 10 to 100 times higher in the new millennium, when bilateral ties were strained, than they were in the 1980s, when those relations were warmer. Likewise, FDI flows from China to Japan jumped by an order of magnitude between 2007 ($15 million) and 2013 ($140 million), and yet relations worsened over those years.

Tourism is yet another form of economic exchange. The number of Chinese visitors to Japan, and to many other developed countries, continues to grow as personal incomes rise in China. But the flow of Japanese tourists to China peaked in 2007 with nearly four million visitors (15% of the total). This followed several years of weak diplomatic relations.[41]

One simple way to evaluate economic interdependence is by measuring trade intensity, the share of bilateral trade (exports and imports between two countries) in the overall trade of those countries. Sino-Japanese trade intensity was less than 3 percent in 1980, when bilateral relations were still warm, but more than 7 percent in 2005, when bilateral relations became especially cold. Indeed, as figure 6.3 shows, the two economies became ever more tightly integrated between 1990 (2.64%) and 2009 (7.64%), a period of deteriorating diplomatic relations. This suggests that economic interdependence appears to be *inversely* correlated with reconciliation—at least in the case of these two nations. More recently, the share of bilateral trade in the overall trade of the two countries has not changed significantly, despite sharp fluctuations in political relations.

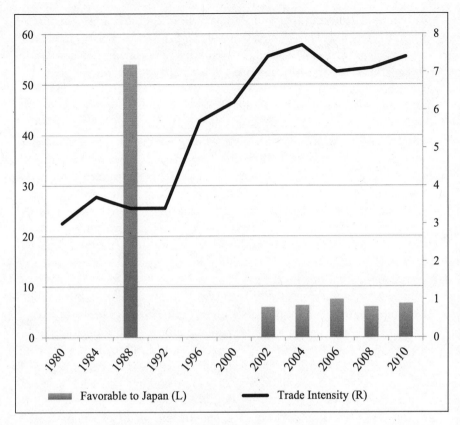

Fig. 6.3. Chinese Views of Japan vs. Trade Intensity
Source: Data from CASS and World Bank, WITS.

If we look more narrowly at China's trade dependence on the Japanese economy (see fig. 6.4), we find a long-term decline that is not correlated with fluctuations in Chinese views of Japan. Since the mid-1990s, when China relied on Japan for more than 20 percent of its imports and exports, China has become less and less dependent on the Japanese market; indeed, by 2013, it relied on Japan for only about 8 percent of its imports and only about 7 percent of its exports. We can isolate specific periods to compare Chinese dependence on the Japanese economy with Chinese views of Japan. Between 2002 and 2010, for example, we see (fig. 6.4) a sharp and steady decline in China's trade dependence on its neighboring economy, but (fig. 6.1) a relatively consistent (and unfavorable) view of Japan on the part of Chinese respondents, according to Chinese Academy of Social Sciences polling. Likewise, in the recent period between 2013 and 2019,

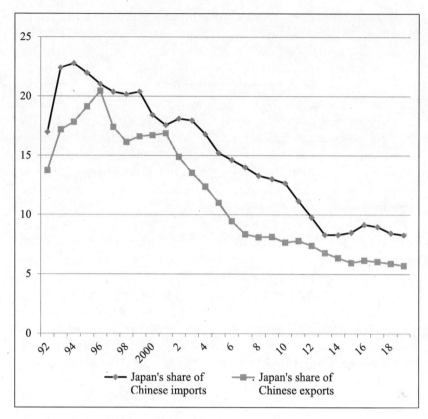

Fig. 6.4. China's Dependence on Trade with Japan (% by year)
Source: Data from World Bank, WITS.

we see (fig. 6.4) little change in China's trade dependence on its neighbor but (fig. 6.2) a marked improvement in Chinese attitudes toward Japan, according to *China Daily* polling. In other words, we find no evidence of the positive correlation between economic ties and diplomatic relations that is presumed by advocates of Pax Mercatoria.[42]

Even as China improved its bilateral economic position, Chinese views of its partner became more negative. In polling conducted by the Chinese Academy of Social Sciences, favorable opinions about Japan fell from nearly 54 percent in 1988 to less than 6 percent in 2002.[43]

This analysis demonstrates that, in the case of Japan and China, growing economic exchange actually coincides with a souring political relationship. Observers such as Dreyer (2014) have described this as "hot economics, cold politics." Just as the two economies were becoming closer, diplomatic ties were weakening. In other words, economic interdependence has not produced a "commercial peace"; it has not, in any fashion, served as a balm on otherwise injured ties between the two states.

Formal Cooperation

One factor that appears to correctly explain the outcome, just as it did in the three previous case studies, is regionalism (or, in this case and in the Japan–South Korea case, a relative *dearth* of regionalism for most of the case study). As noted in chapter 4, Northeast Asia represents the one and only corner of the world conspicuously missing meaningful agreements promoting security and economic cooperation.

There have been two exceptional moments in which Japan and China did manage to negotiate successfully over regional issues. These also happen to be the only moments in contemporary history when Sino-Japanese relations have appeared to be relatively warm.

One such moment was in the late 1970s and early 1980s, after the two states normalized relations. They agreed to shelve their dispute over ownership of the Senkaku/Diaoyu islands in the East China Sea, allowing boats from both countries to fish the waters around the archipelago. And they shared concerns about Soviet influence in Asia, especially Southeast Asia, where USSR-backed Vietnam had invaded Cambodia. As noted already, the earliest poll revealing Chinese public opinion about Japan is from 1988, and it suggests that warm feelings (54%) overwhelmed cold ones (39%)—a sharp contrast from later polls. On top of polling, some observers, including Lam (2006: 15), have described the late 1970s and the 1980s as the "golden years" in the Sino-Japanese relationship.

The other moment is the current one (at least as of this writing in 2022). After reaching a nadir in 2013, Chinese attitudes toward Japan have continued to improve (with some deterioration in 2021). As figure 6.2 shows, a little more than 45 percent of respondents in the *China Daily* poll indicated they had favorable views of their former enemy in 2019 and 2020—by far the rosiest results recorded since 2005, when this annual series began. One might attribute this improvement to the fact that, in recent years, only minor dustups have occurred in the official relationship, including Prime Minister Abe's 2013 pilgrimage to the Yasukuni Shrine. More significantly, though, China and Japan have agreed to cooperate on a range of big and mostly regional issues.

In Southeast Asia, the two states have moved forward with the Japan-

China Policy Dialogue on the Mekong Region, a joint initiative to improve living standards along the river—especially in Cambodia and Laos, where both governments have provided substantial foreign aid. Bi (2017: 199) calls this a "win-win formula" for donor and recipient countries.

But the 2018 summit between Abe and Xi was the major breakthrough, yielding a number of important agreements.[44] Japan and China renewed a plan that had expired in 2013 to swap currencies, creating a reserve pool of $30 billion to help their own companies facing trade-related complications and rescue Asian economies facing future financial stress. They signed a pact to establish the "China-Japan Innovation Cooperation Mechanism" to promote joint research on advanced technologies, including artificial intelligence. After hesitating for several years, Japan also signaled that it would join China's "Belt and Road Initiative," collaborating on infrastructure projects such as a high-speed railway connecting Thailand's major airports. Japan, the primary sponsor of the Asian Development Bank (ADB, based in Manila), even indicated it might consider joining China's Asian Infrastructure Investment Bank, long considered a political challenge to the ADB and the World Bank. Kawashima Shin (2018), professor of international relations at the University of Tokyo, wrote that the Abe-Xi summit reflected a new effort to "normalize relations," emphasizing "cooperation between equals."

What triggered this new interest in Sino-Japanese cooperation? We probably have to credit the surprising outcome of the 2016 presidential election in the United States. Donald Trump, in his capacity as nationalist leader of the most powerful country on earth, managed to foster closer relations between Japan and China by targeting both countries with harsh rhetoric and new tariffs.[45] Beijing and Tokyo "responded to the Trump administration's provocations . . . by trying to resurrect their troubled relationship," claims Stephen Nagy (2018). But he does not believe the two countries are ready to reconcile, as Germany has done with its European neighbors: "the difficult security, economic and political issues that have divided the two Asia giants remain and they cannot be easily resolved."

Nagy is right: The conditions in Asia are quite unlike those in Europe, where Germany made up with France by the early 1960s and began to achieve rapprochement with Poland in the 1990s. On that continent, regionalism has provided a solid foundation for interstate trust-building; in Asia, by contrast, regionalism has remained underdeveloped, despite the end of the Cold War. Japan is still locked into a bilateral security alliance with the United States, and has been mostly unable or unwilling, until perhaps recently, to pursue formal agreements to cooperate with Northeast

Asian neighbors like China that do not include the United States. In the lurch, diplomatic ties have frayed.

Granted, China and Japan do share some defense information through the ASEAN (Association of Southeast Asian Nations) Regional Forum, or ARF; both have participated in Six Party Talks, now in limbo, on North Korea's nuclear weapons program; Beijing, which had opposed Tokyo's proposal for an Asian Monetary Fund, has supported the more modest Chiang Mai Initiative for bilateral currency swaps in the region; and representatives of the two countries do meet every year at the annual ASEAN summit in an arrangement now known as the APT (ASEAN Plus Three, with the latter being China, Japan, and South Korea). But there is no NATO in Asia, as Hemmer and Katzenstein (2002) have noted. And while there is a complex patchwork of generally weak institutions promoting greater trade and investment in the region, including APEC and the East Asia Summit, there is nothing remotely as strong as the European Union in Asia. These groups have diluted their potential influence by adding new members on both sides of the Pacific.

On the security front, Japan is legally allied with the United States in what China views as an effort to block or slow its emergence as a regional or even global power. Beijing is increasingly anxious about U.S.-Japan defense guidelines, as well as a Japanese policy of "collective self-defense." On the economic front, Japan and China seem locked in a contest for leadership in Asia.[46] Each has signed a major trade deal with ASEAN, but not with one another. One of the two powers (Japan) has been committed to an ambitious trade liberalization plan, the Trans-Pacific Partnership, that initially included the U.S. and excluded China, while the other (China) is the architect behind a rival plan, the Regional Comprehensive Economic Partnership, which excludes the U.S.

Geopolitical concerns, especially Japan's loyalty to the United States, may have stymied efforts to achieve significant regional security or trade agreements. Feng Zhaokui (2006), a researcher for the Chinese Academy of Social Sciences, believes the U.S. promotes a basic level of tension between China and Japan. To defend this bold claim, he paraphrases former U.S. Secretary of State Henry Kissinger, a master of realpolitik: "The United States should see that U.S.-Japan relations and U.S.-China ties are better than China-Japan relations so that the United States is placed in the optimum strategic position."

A leading social scientist in Shanghai shares Feng's vision. Sino-Japanese relations, he told me, "can only be improved through building regional, multilateral institutions. If East Asia can come together like Europe has, if it can form a more stable unit by cooperating on a variety of issues, everyone will benefit. To speak bluntly, the biggest obstacle to the peace and stability in our corner of the world is the United States, which wants to preserve its hegemony."[47]

Even some Japanese intellectuals express a similar perspective, even if they don't blame the U.S. directly. Tsugami Toshiya, who served as a high-level bureaucrat in the Ministry of International Trade and Industry before becoming a business consultant and best-selling author, told me in 2011 that Japan must "rebalance" its relations with the two superpowers. "I'm a patriot, so I am not arguing that we should adopt a pro-China position only to secure greater independence from the United States. But now that China is rising and the U.S. is declining, it makes perfect sense for us to secure a better relationship with our most important neighbor. We can build trust with China without completely sacrificing our ties with the United States."[48]

Summary

Unlike Germany, which has mostly vanquished the ghosts of the past in its relations with a former Cold War enemy (Poland), Japan remains haunted in its dealings with China. The bilateral relationship began auspiciously, thanks to Mao Zedong's desire to focus on the Communist Party's victories rather than China's past humiliations, as well as his interest in driving a wedge between Japan and its patron-state, the U.S. And that relationship has improved in recent years, thanks largely to new agreements between two states targeted by the United States. In between, though, Sino-Japanese relations have been fraught.

Diplomatic ties hit rock bottom in the first decade of the new millennium, after the Japanese government authorized a revisionist textbook for junior high school students and after its nationalist prime minister made several pilgrimages to a controversial shrine for Japan's war dead. They recovered slightly, only to collapse again in 2010, following a maritime incident in the East China Sea, and in 2012, when the Japanese government nationalized the Senkaku islands. Polling confirms that Chinese citizens have seethed with resentment and hostility toward Japan since at least 2000. This happened despite Japanese apologies for its wartime behavior that became, in the 1990s, increasingly pointed and heartfelt. And it happened despite economic flows (trade and investment) that pulled the two economies closer together just as the two states seemed furthest apart.

The best explanation for the diplomatic distance between China and Japan until recently is the lack of regional institutions fostering cooperation between the two states. This began to change in 2017 and 2018, as Japan and China forged agreements in the face of threats from a new U.S. president who targeted both of them as unfair traders.

SEVEN

Janus-Faced Superpower

The U.S. Role in Different Regionalisms

The case studies in this book demonstrate that the European project of political cooperation yielding closer and closer integration helped Germany reconcile with neighbors it had mistreated in the past, while a lack of similar regionalism in Asia left Japan isolated and distrusted by its history-hugging neighbors. But this critical finding merely begs another question: Why did strong regional institutions arise in Europe but not in Asia? The simple answer is that, beginning in 1945, the United States promoted multilateralism in Europe and U.S.-dominated bilateralism in Asia.

More specifically, American officials used the Marshall Plan at the end of World War II to prod old enemies such as France and West Germany to collaborate on rebuilding their ravaged economies through the European Coal and Steel Community (ECSC) and similar organizations. They also established the North Atlantic Treaty Organization (NATO), a multistate military bloc designed to deter Soviet aggression in Europe.

In Asia, by contrast, the U.S. insisted on occupying a central position in commercial and military relations. It gave large amounts of bilateral aid to capitalist allies, and—with the exception of the Association of Southeast Asian Nations (ASEAN), an anticommunist bloc—opposed fledgling regional institutions that did not include the U.S. This position has remained constant. For example, in 1990, when the prime minister of Malaysia called for an East Asia Economic Group (EAEG) made up of ASEAN members along with Japan, China, and South Korea, the

U.S. blasted the proposal as exclusionary. EAEG's leading member, Japan, demurred, and the proposed organization became a largely irrelevant "caucus." And in 1997, when Japan called for an Asian Monetary Fund to bail out fiscally distressed economies in the region, the U.S. again protested loudly. It worried that the Asian Monetary Fund would undermine the International Monetary Fund, a global but Washington-based organization controlled by the United States.[1] Japan bowed to U.S. pressure and abandoned its idea.

For regional security, American officials have insisted on maintaining a set of bilateral alliances with Japan, South Korea, Taiwan (at least until 1979, when the U.S. finally established diplomatic ties with the People's Republic of China), and the Philippines. This hub-and-spokes pattern,[2] dominated everywhere by the U.S. military, also sets Asia apart from Europe, where states cooperate in a multilateral defense alliance.

Here, too, we are compelled to dig deeper: Why did the U.S. adopt such a Janus-faced policy orientation? Why did it pursue multilateralism in Europe and bilateralism in Asia?

The answer has to do with cultural identity and political power. U.S. officials felt a cultural affinity, even a racial identity, with Europeans, and thus trusted them to collaborate on economic and security affairs. In addition, the U.S. had never enjoyed asymmetrical power over that region. It was content to exercise a relatively gentle hegemony *across* a connected Europe. By contrast, American leaders felt no such affinity for or identity with Asians, whom they viewed as "backward." They did not trust their counterparts across the Pacific to manage their own affairs. Plus, they had dominated different parts of Asia for decades. So they insisted on playing a central role in almost all regional economic organizations, and opted for a hierarchical hub-and-spokes system of mostly bilateral defense alliances.[3] As a result, the U.S. was able to maintain a steep hegemony based on disproportionate power *over* other states in the region. This is not to suggest that Asian leaders have been puppets of a grand puppeteer in D.C.; rather, I mean that, on the most contentious issues, they have not enjoyed much autonomy.

In this chapter, I present these two claims separately and then fuse them in a conclusion. I operate with the presumption that constructivism and realism are not contradictory but can in fact complement one another, with the former emphasizing cultural norms (the ideas, values, and beliefs that constitute a community's identity) and the latter emphasizing power (the capacity of a dominant or influential state to compel other states to act in the former's interest, or perhaps realign their interests to accommodate the former). The first section draws heavily on the work of Hemmer and Katzenstein (2002), who say they are "analytically eclectic" but are primarily constructivist in orientation. The second section is influenced by realism, especially the critical realism of Beeson (2005).

The Civilized and the Backward

Europe: From Mother to Brother

On Ellis Island, in New York Harbor, a national museum documents the role of the U.S. as a "distant magnet" for immigrants from England, Ireland, the Benelux countries, Germany, Scandinavia, the Mediterranean, Central Europe, and Eastern Europe. One has to study the exhibits much more closely to learn anything about the unwilling immigrants who came on slave ships from Africa, or the more recent immigrants who came in significant numbers from Asia and now, in the largest numbers, from Latin America. One won't find much about the Native Americans who already lived here.

The United States is increasingly multicultural, but most Americans, especially older Americans, trace their lineage to Europe. They could call themselves "European Americans," but usually do not. Instead, they describe themselves as "normal" Americans. They unconsciously identify with the Mother Continent.

In ideational rather than merely racial or geographical terms, these unhyphenated Americans reflexively align themselves with "the West" or "Western Civilization."[4] They fancy themselves members of a complex but mostly mythical lineage extending from the Mediterranean to Western Europe to the New World.

In fact, of course, this cultural solidarity (Occidentalism) is relatively new. It didn't always include the Irish, who escaped poverty and famine in the mid-19th century to find work on railroads and in factories in a sprawling, industrializing America. Those "bog trotters" or "Paddies" were not "normal" Americans in those days; they faced fierce hostility from earlier settlers, who were predominantly white, Anglo-Saxon Protestants. Later, as the century turned, immigrants from southern, central, and eastern Europe—Italians, Poles, and Russian Jews—suffered similar discrimination, even though they, too, eventually became "white" and "Western." Congress responded to these rolling waves of humanity by imposing restrictions designed to freeze the ethnic composition of the United

States. In 1924, it went further to defend a threatened racial homogeneity, severely curtailing immigration by Africans and flatly banning immigration by Arabs and Asians. That legislation was encouraged by U.S. social scientists, including Raymond Leslie Buell (1923: 307), who argued that Japanese in-migration, if left unchecked, would "wipe out American standards of living, eventually reduce us to the economic level of the Oriental, and implant an alien and half-breed race on our soil that might make the negro problem look white."[5]

Occidentalism emerged gradually. It first expressed itself in the late 19th century through the writings of social Darwinists such as John Fiske. The influential historian, who lectured for a time at Harvard, trumpeted the "Manifest Destiny of the Anglo-Saxon race," and suggested that continental Europe had been weakened by "Asiaticization," the assimilation of inferior races (barbarians). Fiske (1885: viii–ix) argued that the U.S. had a combination of optimal political institutions and superior racial stock, and thus had a natural duty to flex its muscles and expand—just as England had done. "The [Anglo-Saxon] race which gained control of North America must become the dominant race in the world, and its political ideas must prevail in the struggle for life." Racism thus informed foreign policy as the United States emulated European states and became an imperialist power, declaring its commercial influence over Latin America through the Monroe Doctrine and by establishing colonial mastery over territories such as Puerto Rico and the Philippines.

During World War I, political and business elites in the United States came to distinguish themselves from what they viewed as quasi-Asiatic "barbarians," including the central European "Huns."[6] President Woodrow Wilson, for example, spoke acidly of "hyphenated Americans," especially German-Americans, who might harbor dual loyalties. In 1917, the U.S. entered the war on the side of Western Europe (and, by extension, Russia), propelled at least in part by concern over the fate of long-time allies with whom it culturally identified. That is, Americans felt greater affinity for (and less threat from) those nations. Stephen Walt uses this case to defend his heterodox or "balance of threat" realism, noting that, contrary to the prediction of structural realism, the United States teamed up with Great Britain and France, even though those two states possessed greater material resources than their enemies, imperial Germany and Austria-Hungary.

Over time, "Western" identity came to function as a counterpoint to "Eastern" ideologies such as Bolshevism and anarchism. In 1919 and 1920, the federal government rounded up and deported hundreds of immigrants, especially Russians, associated with the radical labor movement. The Palmer raids linked anticommunism and nativism in a campaign to "purify the body politic against foreign invasion" (Jackson 2006: 156).

Like World War I, World War II in Europe does not conform neatly to a cultural narrative, in that the United States joined forces with an "Eastern" power (the Soviet Union) as well as traditionally "Western" powers such as the U.K. But American leaders drew on Occidental tropes to rally the troops. President Roosevelt called the invasion of Normandy an effort to preserve "our civilization," and General Eisenhower told Allied forces they were engaging in a "Great Crusade" on behalf of "liberty-loving people everywhere." In these and other rhetorical flourishes, U.S. elites ignored the inconvenient fact that they were allied with a brutal dictator (Stalin).

It was during the Cold War, of course, that the West-East divide became reified with the drawing of what Churchill called an "Iron Curtain" across Europe, and the building of the Berlin Wall. In 1945, American elites looked across the Atlantic and saw—for the second time in a half-century—a region in tatters. They felt deep sympathy for their cultural siblings on the continent. In the emerging superpower rivalry with the USSR, the United States closely identified with West European states, including a defeated one that had been led by a fascist party and organized around a murderous ideology of Aryan nationalism. It viewed its allies (old and new) as "responsible" partners in a global capitalist order, even if junior ones. So the United States used diplomacy and dollars to encourage regional cooperation that began with the European Coal and Steel Community and continued through the Lisbon Treaty. And it forged a multilateral security alliance designed to contain Soviet communism.

In their early Cold War discourse, U.S. elites routinely touted a "common civilization" or long-standing "community" of shared ideals and interests that linked their newer nation to "the Old World." For example, in promoting the NATO treaty, U.S. diplomat W. Averell Harriman told the Senate Committee on Foreign Relations in 1949 that "there is a spiritual emotion about this which is hard to overemphasize . . . free men are standing shoulder to shoulder."[7] An otherwise vocal critic of the Truman administration's overall foreign policy, Walter Lippmann (1947: 24–25), referred to European members of the proposed "Atlantic community" as "natural allies of the United States" who shared "the common traditions of western Christendom, and their economic, political, legal, and moral institutions which, with all their variations and differences, have a common origin and have been shaped by much the same historic experience."[8] Assistant Secretary of State Will Clayton was more explicit. He testified to Congress that prospective members of NATO should share American "ideals of freedom" and be "composed of the white race."[9]

As Jackson (2006: 133) notes, the project of rebuilding the region, and especially West Germany, was steeped in discourse about "Western civilization," a white, Christian transnational community that encompassed both Europeans and Americans. He quotes James Eastland, the Mississippi Democrat, who told his Senate colleagues in December 1945 that the United States was bound by a civilizational duty to take more aggressive measures to help Europe recover from the ravages of war: "It is not to the interest of America that oriental, atheistic philosophies prevail in the heart of Europe, the cradle of Western Civilization; and yet, if these policies are pursued, this will be the result, to the grave detriment of America."

Jackson documents how rapidly U.S. elites, not just Eastland, moved to add West Germany to their inventory of "the West," casting the Soviet Union even more starkly as an Eastern "other." This became clear in their marketing of the $17.6 billion scheme to help European allies rebuild their devastated economies. U.S. Secretary of State George Marshall, the architect of the bailout plan, used this language in pleading to Congress:

> There is convincing evidence that the peoples of western Europe want to preserve their free society and the heritage that we share with them. To make that choice conclusive they need our assistance. It is in the American tradition to help. In helping them we will be helping ourselves—because in the larger sense our national interests coincide with those of a free and prosperous Europe. (U.S. Senate 1950: 1277; quoted in Jackson [2006: 161])

The West vs. East trope persisted throughout the Cold War. In fact, it reached a new height of discursive bravado in the 1980s under President Ronald Reagan, who castigated the Soviet Union as "the evil empire" and called on Americans to embrace "the self-evident truths of Western civilization" that "have been passed down like precious heirlooms from generation to generation since the generations began."[10] These consisted of various political liberties, Reagan proclaimed. In this grandiose formulation, Russians were not potential allies momentarily pressed under the thumb of a communist regime; they represented a horde, perhaps a Slavic horde, of the perpetually unfree.

With the collapse of the Soviet Union in 1991, one might have expected the edifice of "the West" to crumble, too. But this trans-Atlantic identity

survived even what Francis Fukuyama saluted as "the end of history"—
the triumph of liberalism (democracy and capitalism) over authoritarian-
ism. A new non-Western "other" soon emerged. Sometimes it was called
"radical Islam," sometimes "political Islam," and sometimes just "Islam."
In the United States, an oppositional stance was pushed by virulently anti-
Muslim organizations such as the American Freedom Defense Initiative
and viciously anti-Muslim publications such as *Jihad Watch*. Some U.S.
academics used more sophisticated discourse to advance this framing. For
example, in a seminal analysis of contemporary international relations,
Samuel Huntington (1996) claimed the world was embroiled in a "clash
of civilizations," where the pivotal conflict pitted "the West" against "the
Rest" (and especially traditional Islamic culture). As before, white Americans viewed Europeans as allies, next of kin, in an existential struggle to
preserve "Western Civilization."

This pattern continues. When terrorists blow up buildings in Baghdad
or Nairobi, Americans tend to shrug. Distant violence against brown and
black people may be unfortunate, but it feels somehow normal or at least
tolerable. Those people come from what then–president Trump called
"shithole countries." But when terrorists attack white cartoonists in Paris,
Americans tend to react passionately. They are moved to change their
Facebook profiles to the French flag and post memes declaring "Je Suis
Charlie." Empathy reigns.

Asia: The Less-"Civilized" Child

Opinion leaders in the U.S. have never felt such kinship with Asia. This is
not to say they have never felt a close connection to that region. In fact,
the U.S. has often behaved as though it faces a kind of noblesse oblige to
instruct, "civilize," and, as I argue below, rule the region.

In the "Made in America" imagination, Asians (or "Orientals") tend to
be children or inscrutable aliens, not peers and partners.[11] They might be
cute, or perhaps exotic, but they are generally immature and less "civilized."
They are beneath or behind Westerners. Racism informs this attitude
toward what many have called (Eurocentrically) "the Far East," a region
that is actually west of the United States and that includes important U.S.
allies such as Japan, South Korea, Taiwan, the Philippines, and Thailand.

This has been evident at different moments of history. For example,
while they claimed to be "liberating" Filipinos from the yoke of Spanish
colonialism, U.S. officials used a narrative inspired by what one historian
(Miller 1982: 137) has called "paternalist racism" to justify their decision

to retain control of the islands for half a century. William Howard Taft, who was the first governor-general of that U.S. colony before becoming president, told Congress in 1902 that "our little brown brothers" in the Philippines would need "fifty or 100 years" of American tutelage before they acquired "anything resembling Anglo-Saxon political principles and skills."[12] The natives, he argued, were "utterly unfit for self-governance," but could be subdued and managed "as we govern the Indian tribes."[13] In a similar tone, Franklin Delano Roosevelt used to talk about the "brown people of the East" who, like all children, require the supervision of more mature "trustees" (Hunt 1987: 162–64).

At about the same time, the United States began to view itself as the patron of China, which it came to regard as perilously fragile and in need of American patronage. The U.S. first pushed an "open door" policy toward that country, hoping to keep any single great power from gaining political control (while ensuring that large U.S. corporations had economic access to a promising Chinese market). In 1915, Washington ordered Tokyo to roll back its "21 Demands" on China, which had been designed to consolidate Japanese power on the mainland. And in 1940, it imposed an embargo on exports of oil and scrap iron to Japan, protesting Tokyo's escalating war of aggression against China.

All of this reflected paternalism, or what Thomson, Stanley, and Perry (1981) call "sentimental imperialism"—an almost religious zeal to protect and promote (or, as some suggested, "civilize") Asia, especially China, while also dominating it. Although American support for this policy was widespread, it was perhaps strongest among a group of Republican politicians, Christian missionaries, Asia-oriented business people, and Western and Midwestern pundits who became known, pejoratively, as the "China Lobby." Henry Luce, born to U.S. missionaries in China, emerged as the titular head of this informal group and exercised tremendous influence on U.S. policy as the publisher of *Time* magazine. He was enamored with Chiang Kai-shek's corrupt and otherwise unpopular regime, which he referred to as "Free China" as opposed to Mao Zedong's "Red China." Luce and fellow Sinophiles seemed especially fond of Chiang's wife, featured on the cover of *Time* three times. She was an elegant and charming woman who studied English at Wellesley and conjured up fantasies (and stereotypes) among American men about "Oriental beauty." In 1943, when nationalists and communists were putatively united in fighting Japanese imperialism, she spoke to an enraptured U.S. Congress as well as a live audience of 17,000 at Madison Square Garden. Madame Chiang's speeches were broadcast live on radio to millions more across America.

Cosmopolitan Americans, according to Thomson (1967: 56), had become obsessed with mainland China, much like a wealthy patron becomes fixated on a needy client.

No other nation in Asia had been on the receiving end of so much American goodwill, good works, and philanthropy. No other nation had been the focus of more persistent and grandiose American illusions. . . . An "Open Door" to China came to mean . . . 400 million potential Christians—our special receptacle for the outflow of our altruism, and our special protectorate against the obvious greed of the European and Japanese predators. We admired Chinese culture, liked the Chinese people, delighted in Chinese food, and deplored China's patent incapacity for effective self-government. China made us feel good: it fed our sense of benevolence and moral superiority.

But in 1949, the Communist Party won the civil war and captured Beijing. Bewildered and devastated, U.S. elites blamed one another for "losing" China, as though it had been a child running away from its parent. For the next three decades, they doted on their remaining, Mandarin-speaking dependent—the Republic of China (Taiwan).

U.S. political elites frequently referred to Asians with condescension and even outright contempt. These were not "natural allies." For example, an internal U.S. State Department memo from regional planner Charlton Ogburn (1953: 262) flatly proclaimed that "we do not take the Asians very seriously and in fact regard them as inferiors." Likewise, General Douglas MacArthur famously said that the Japanese, "measured by the standards of modern civilization . . . would be like a boy of twelve compared with our development of 45 years."[14] (By contrast, he claimed that the Germans were "quite as mature" as the Americans.)[15] In a conversation with a friend, American diplomat Dean Acheson apparently explained his opposition to staying the course in Vietnam by saying "too much blood already has been spilled for those little people just out of trees."[16]

Political elites weren't unique in making such racist remarks. Scholars, too, frequently resorted to the teleological logic of modernization theory to describe the region's presumed backwardness. Kenneth Young (1965: 45) was just one of many writers who believed Asia was still in the midst of a painful process of becoming more "developed."

The ancient-modern societies, states or nations of Asia are going through a cycle of political and social metabolism in their struggle for development and modernization. There is a constant interaction of build up and break down in the political-social-psychological sphere at the local level of the countryside and the city level of urban aggregation.

Beckmann (1962: preface) was more explicit. Unlike its giant neighbor, Japan managed to modernize, he wrote, "because Japanese feudal society was receptive to innovations based on Western ideas and institutions, [while] China, on the other hand, resisted change."

During the Cold War, American scholars celebrated the fact that the United States, which called itself the "Leader of the Free World," was available to help Asian countries through this messy process of development, a process of "growing up" or becoming "civilized." As Harvard sinologist John Fairbank (1966: 124) told Congress, Americans uniquely understand that "contact, open society, pluralism, the international trading world" are the most effective means of modernizing.

Fairbank did not mention violence, but Americans came to view this, too, as sometimes a necessary tool for fostering "civilization" in Asia. Fighting in Vietnam, U.S. troops often referred to the Vietnamese, both their enemies in the North and their supposed allies in the South, as "gooks"—a derogatory term perhaps used first during the Philippine-American war and certainly later in Korea. The jungle, these soldiers implied, was filled with uncivilized, savage peoples. Baritz (1985: 37) notes that Americans referred to dangerous areas in Vietnam as "Indian country," and a U.S. veteran of the My Lai massacre reported that American soldiers took scalps— "like from Indians" (Drinnon, 1990: 456–57).

Although American troops long ago exited Vietnam, thousands remain in South Korea and Japan—a fact that upsets some host-country citizens, especially residents near U.S. military bases who complain about noise, pollution, accidents, prostitution, and more than a trivial loss of sovereignty. In response to these complaints, American officials sometimes sound like grumpy parents. At other times, they adopt racialized rhetoric to criticize their hosts. For example, in 2003, a Pentagon official noted that South Korea relies heavily on the United States for its security, and perhaps should begin to do more on its own. "It's like teaching a child how to ride a bike," the official grumbled. "We've been running alongside South Korea, holding on to its handlebars for 50 years. At some point you have to let go."[17]

In December 2010, the head of the U.S. State Department's Japan Desk expressed frustration with anti-base agitators in Okinawa, the sparsely populated set of islands in the East China Sea that hosts a majority of American soldiers in Japan. He allegedly referred to Okinawans as "masters of extortion" for demanding compensation for the environmental and social impacts of the U.S. military. This official apparently also dubbed Okinawa "the Puerto Rico of Japan," suggesting that its thankless residents have "darker skin" than their counterparts on the main islands and that they are "lazy."[18]

Military minders are not the only Americans who haughtily look down on Asians. The former president of the United States referred to the leader of North Korea as "Little Rocket Man," characterizing him as a petulant child during a rally in 2017. He later suggested that the U.S. might have to "totally destroy" that country, much like it wiped out Hiroshima and Nagasaki in August 1945. There is little empathy here.

Leadership and Domination

Europe: American Hegemony

For a very long time, the modern world was multipolar. The United States was a major power, but it shared that status with states such as France, Germany, England, Japan, and the Soviet Union. It was not until 1945 that the U.S. could clearly be viewed as the world's one and only superpower. It emerged from World War II with economic and military supremacy, having built manufacturing industries that could produce steel, chemicals, autos, and ships for its own market and for export, and having created the most powerful land, naval, and air force ever seen. It controlled nearly half of the world's gold and reserve currencies. It was the only nuclear power, and possessed more than 100 aircraft carriers—twice as many as Britain, the only other country with a sizable fleet.

But despite its overwhelming power, the U.S. did not treat Europe imperiously. Even before the war ended, the U.S. was collaborating with the U.K. on a redesign of the global financial architecture. Bretton Woods, the new regime established in 1944, was a joint Anglo-American project, though it cannot be denied that John Maynard Keynes, the British economist, played second fiddle to his American counterpart, Harry Dexter White, in negotiations over the dollar standard. The United States also worked closely with five European allies (the U.K., France, Belgium, the Netherlands, and Luxembourg), plus Canada and Australia, in laying the foundation for the General Agreement on Tariffs and Trade (GATT) in

1947. On military matters, too, the United States emerged as a leader, but did not try to dictate. Lundestad (2003: 49), for example, notes that European officials, especially British foreign secretary Ernest Bevin, took the first steps in launching NATO. In the early 1950s, alarmed by the prospect of Soviet expansionism, officials in Western Europe also pushed Washington to dramatically expand U.S. troop deployments on the continent.[19]

This is why Lundestad suggests that American hegemony in Europe was a case of "empire by invitation," rather than empire by imposition. The Marshall Plan, which led to regional schemes for economic integration, would not have come about "if the Europeans had not wanted it," he writes (p. 59). The same goes for the military alliance: "Considering Washington's initially lukewarm response to Bevin's pleas for an Atlantic security system, it seems likely that the setting up of NATO would at least have been substantially delayed if it had not been for the European invitations."

With one important exception, European allies have chosen to follow U.S. leadership rather than contest it.[20] This is only surprising if one relies on a mechanical calculation, mapping state resources onto interests. European states came to enjoy both peace and prosperity via transatlantic cooperation. And they rarely had to comply with unwelcome directives from Washington, which exercised what Ikenberry (2001) calls "strategic restraint"—especially in its dealings with Europe.

In 1945, when the fighting finally ended, the United States had an overriding strategic interest in Europe. It wanted a friendly and more united zone of stability, a region that would not reboil, ensnaring the U.S. in yet another violent conflict. Accordingly, it promised a massive plan to rebuild economies in ruin. Access to bailout funds came with only one condition: Recipient countries had to demonstrate they could cooperate with one another through the new Organization for European Economic Cooperation, which would administer the reconstruction dollars.

Before long, the U.S. interest in "Team Europe" acquired a new urgency. The Soviet Union was extending its reach across Eastern and even Central Europe, where communist leaders seized power in places such as Budapest and pro-Moscow insurgencies threatened to do the same in such places as Athens. Indeed, procommunist regimes soon forged a Warsaw Pact under the Kremlin's leadership. The U.S. quickly tweaked its transatlantic plan. It no longer wanted just a zone of stability; it now sought an economically prosperous and militarily powerful region, a strong, capitalist bloc that could stand together and halt what it presumed to be Moscow's ambition: westward expansion.

The U.S. leaned on West Germany's neighbors to accept the incipient state's economic and political recovery. It pushed Paris especially hard because it realized that, without a Franco-German rapprochement, "there will be no possibility of peace in Europe" and it could not achieve its vision of a pro-American union of European states.[21] Unsurprisingly, the French, having suffered a century-long string of Teutonic conquests, initially resisted. But they were compelled (or, according to revisionist historians such as Hitchcock [1998], "induced") to abandon a policy of dominating Bonn and embrace a collaborative approach reflected first in Schuman's call for the European Coal and Steel Community. The 1951 Treaty of Paris was a giant leap toward regional integration, establishing most of the institutions that would eventually constitute the European Union. At the same time, the U.S. pulled its European allies, along with Canada, into a transatlantic military alliance to combat Soviet aggression.

With prodding from the U.S., NATO expanded in 1954 to include West Germany, which was so eager to repair its reputation that it accepted a number of conditions on its entry.[22] Under these conditions, demanded by France and brokered by the United States, the new member of the alliance agreed that it would not reestablish a general staff for its armed forces; it would leave its air defense system under NATO command even during peacetime; it would curb its ability to independently produce powerful weapons; and it would allow the United States to maintain troops on its territory (Gould and Krasner 2003: 63–65). West Germany thus became more firmly embedded in a multilateral framework that satisfied European concerns about a possible resurgence of German power, a framework that bound the region together more tightly than ever.

The Treaty of Rome followed, turning the European Coal and Steel Community into the European Economic Community, a customs union that encouraged freer trade among members of the region. Nearly three decades later, the Single European Act built on this foundation by seeking to harmonize regulations. Throughout this period, West Germany demonstrated a credible commitment to the deepening of European integration. In the late 1980s, as the Cold War waned, it even championed the idea of a common currency (the Euro) to replace the badly strained European Monetary System, which had allowed its own Bundesbank to emerge as the de facto central bank of Europe. West Germany's commitment to regionalism, its so-called "Europatriotism," eased its neighbors' long-standing fears and weakened opposition to German reunification, which came about rather suddenly in 1990.

But none of this could have happened without U.S. support. From the outset of the Cold War, Washington dedicated itself to rebuilding Europe through multilateralism. It energetically sought to balance Soviet power without overextending itself.

This proactive position was outlined in a 1949 briefing paper by the U.S. State Department's Office of German and Austrian Affairs: "So long as we are occupying Germany, and particularly in view of our insistence on a controlling voice in German foreign economic matters, we have a direct responsibility for action in Europe. Furthermore, any movement toward strengthening Europe and resolving the German problem would further the objectives of the North Atlantic Pact. Such a movement will need all the impetus that can be given it" (134).

It is true, of course, that American enthusiasm for the European project has wavered from time to time, especially in the post–Cold War era, when economic concerns have regained their salience. The U.S. has, for example, complained about Europe's protection of farmers through the Common Agricultural Policy as well as its export subsidies for Airbus. But since Washington employs similar trade policies, its criticism has never been too loud, except during the Trump interregnum.

On the security front, too, the U.S. has renewed its support for multilateralism in Europe, including NATO, after a dramatic break between 2017 and 2021. Not only did the "Western" alliance survive the collapse of the Soviet Union, it actually expanded to include former members of the Warsaw Pact as well as Baltic and Balkan states. The U.S. pushed for enlargement to its current roster of 30 members, and it routinely encouraged joint leadership. In the late 1990s, the alliance led a campaign of "humanitarian bombing" against Serbia to aid Muslim separatists in Kosovo. U.S. General Wesley Clark was the NATO commander at the time, but he relied heavily on a multilateral committee of generals chaired by Klaus Naumann, a German.

Even outside the transatlantic alliance, the U.S. has generally supported European efforts to integrate defense programs. To be sure, it was ambivalent about the Franco-German move in 1992 to establish a unified military force, Eurocorps. American policymakers would have preferred that the new force operate under NATO command, but ultimately welcomed the heightened cooperation between continental Europe's leading powers. Indeed, the U.S. has been remarkably positive about other forms of military cooperation beyond American control, such as the Common Security and Defense Policy in the Maastricht Treaty and the European Defense Agency in the Lisbon Treaty—so positive, in fact, that some conservative groups, such as the Heritage Foundation, have expressed concern about a diminution of NATO's authority. Luke Coffey (2013), the Margaret Thatcher Fellow at Heritage, noted with alarm that then-president Obama, attending his first NATO summit in 2009, praised Europe for developing "more robust defense capabilities" on its own.[23]

Former President Trump, who campaigned on an "America First" platform, threatened to renegotiate U.S. relations with Europe. Early in his term, he shocked regional allies by calling NATO "obsolete" and suggesting that European members were not shouldering their military burden. He also attacked the European Union as a "vehicle for Germany," applauding British citizens for voting to leave the regional organization and encouraging other member states to follow suit. But these statements, representing a repudiation of well-established norms of trans-Atlanticism, never really fostered a coherent change in policy. And then Trump was replaced by a traditional "Atlanticist." Joe Biden, the new president, spent 2021 shoring up frayed ties with Europe and then, in 2022, worked closely with those old allies to help Ukraine and punish Russia. After the Kremlin launched a massive invasion of its pro-Western neighbor, the U.S. and Europe supplied weapons to Ukraine and imposed new and stiffer sanctions on Russia.

Between 1945 and today, the story of U.S.–Western European relations has been one of brokered multilateralism. American power prevailed, stipulating the parameters of "acceptable" foreign policy among allies in this period. But it did not overwhelm or coerce Europe. The United States was influential, even hegemonic, but it was not imperious in its relations with Europe. For the most part, it has promoted horizontal cooperation with, and within, the region.

Asia: American Imperialism

Unlike their conduct toward European powers, American political elites have long been arrogant in their treatment of Asia. They often have viewed themselves as the rightful rulers or at least as natural guardians of the region. And they repeatedly have undermined efforts at multilateralism, as evidenced by the failure of initiatives such as Malaysia's East Asia Economic Group and Japan's Asian Monetary Fund (outlined earlier in this chapter). "In East Asia," argues Beeson (2005: 982), "American power has either made regionalism difficult because of the essentially bilateral strategic architecture it has created or—until recently at least—actively opposed regional initiatives that threaten to undercut its influence."

This imperious view of the region first emerged in the very late 19th century, when the U.S. began to gobble up territories in the Pacific: Hawaii, Wake, Midway, Guam, Samoa, and the Philippines. U.S. imperialists believed their nation had a clear, perhaps even divine mandate to expand across the Pacific, which they increasingly referred to as an "American Lake," or in the ethnocentric discourse of MacArthur, an "Anglo-Saxon Lake."[24] U.S. domination, they argued, was necessary for Asian development, modernization, and liberation.

In the most dramatic case, U.S. soldiers teamed up with Filipino nationalists to end Spanish rule over the Philippines—but then chose to remain, succeeding the Spaniards as colonial overlords. The battle against nationalist guerrillas was brutal and bloody, extinguishing the lives of more than 4,000 Americans and at least 250,000 Filipinos. Karnow (1989: 191–92) notes that U.S. commanders, many of them veterans of Indian wars, directed their troops to "burn and kill the natives." After overwhelming the resistance, U.S. officials spent nearly a half-century ruling the Philippines. As noted earlier, they did not trust Filipinos to govern themselves.[25]

If U.S. behavior in the Philippines represented typically ruthless imperialism, others have suggested that American elites adopted a kind of "sentimental imperialism" in their relations with China. They tried (and sometimes failed) to defend that embattled nation from other predators, especially the Japanese.

At the conclusion of World War II, U.S. defense planners called for absolute domination of Asia. American security, according to the Joint Chiefs of Staff, "rests on the ability . . . to control the Pacific Ocean and since no such control can be effective unless it is complete," any breaks in the system of military bases "tend greatly to weaken if not vitiate the effectiveness of the system as a whole."[26] Likewise, American diplomats sought exclusive, top-down relations with junior partners in the region.

The U.S. carried out its occupation of Japan in the name of the "Allied Powers," but did not in reality share power with them as it did in Germany. The occupation authority, the Supreme Commander of the Allied Powers (SCAP), was a strictly American body led by General MacArthur. It ruled through Japan's civilian bureaucracy, but tolerated little dissent. In addition to censoring literature, newspapers, magazines, and film, rejecting flattering narratives of the Japanese military and unflattering depictions of the U.S. military, SCAP wrote a new constitution for Japan after rejecting a proposal from Japanese politicians and legal scholars.

On the Korean Peninsula, the U.S. had to contend with another occupying authority, the Soviet Union—at least until 1948, when Syngman Rhee, the U.S.-based expatriate favored by Americans, became the president of a new Republic of Korea in the south. In China, the U.S. aligned itself with Chiang's pro-capitalist regime from 1945 to 1949, and continued to back the nationalists even after they lost the civil war on the mainland and retreated to Taiwan.

In sharp contrast to their alliance-building methods in Europe, American leaders forged essentially bilateral rather than multilateral pacts in Asia. The 1951 U.S.-Japan Security Treaty (ANPO to the Japanese), revised in 1960, was the central axis in the so-called "hub-and-spokes" pattern in Asia. But similar bilateral deals were arranged with the Philippines in 1951, South Korea in 1953, and the Republic of China/Taiwan in 1954.[27] Although they supported greater economic exchange and political cooperation, Washington bureaucrats in 1957 decided that "the U.S. should not initiate efforts to form new regional economic organizations in Asia." Rather, it should pursue closer relations with individual countries through selective projects; in other words, it eschewed multilateralism.[28]

It is true that the U.S. brokered the Southeast Asia Treaty Organization (SEATO) in 1954, but this was a geographically incoherent grouping that included only two Southeast Asian nations (the Philippines and Thailand) while encompassing European states (the United Kingdom and France). More importantly, it specifically reserved unilateral authority for the United States. This was spelled out in the Rusk-Thanat (1962: 498–99) statement, in which the U.S. emphasized that its military duty to Thailand "does not depend upon prior agreement of all the other parties to the treaty, since the obligation is individual as well as collective."

Likewise, Hemmer and Katzenstein (2002) note that SEATO's structure was markedly different from NATO's. There was, for example, no unified command, no multilateral allocation of defense resources. U.S. authorities even tried to avoid the widespread use of the SEATO acronym because they feared such usage would invite inappropriate comparisons to NATO. As the U.S. State Department (1954: 740) argued, "the SEA pact is not conceived [by the United States] as a parallel to NATO."

Even now, decades after the Cold War's end, the U.S. military seeks to dominate the region and contain a rising China with its overwhelming firepower. Pacific Command, based in Hawaii, still oversees an extensive system of bases with about 90,000 soldiers and sailors from Yokosuka to Darwin, and with state-of-the-art defense technology. Retired Adm. Harry Harris, ex-Pacific Command commander, has boasted that "everything that's new and cool is coming to the region," including a new fleet of Zumwalt-class stealth destroyers.[29]

Organizationally, U.S.-led bilateralism continues to undergird the regional security architecture of East Asia, minus China. Strengthening this system of alliances will secure a "free and open Indo-Pacific," according to Washington, which today counts on loyal support from Tokyo, Canberra, and New Delhi—all of which are very anxious about Beijing's growing influence in Asia.[30] The U.S.-Japan Security Alliance remains the cornerstone of this system, "the basis for stability and prosperity in the region," according to Joseph Nye (2010), who helped write the Pentagon's 1995 East Asian Strategy Report.

The alliance has survived changes in domestic politics. In 2009, when the Democratic Party of Japan toppled the long-ruling Liberal Democratic Party, the new prime minister in Tokyo, Hatoyama Yukio, called for a dramatic reorientation of Japanese foreign policy: a strengthening of "fraternal" bonds with Japan's neighbors, including China, which seemed to imply less dependence on the country's long-standing military patron. Among other things, he proposed an "East Asia Community" modeled on the European Union. Japan's sudden policy shift rattled those in charge of "alliance maintenance" in Washington. They were especially upset by a Democratic Party of Japan proposal to reduce the size of the U.S. military footprint in Okinawa, which is currently dotted with more than 30 different American bases—almost 15 percent of the main island's land mass. Defense Secretary Robert Gates quickly traveled to Tokyo to tell the Hatoyama administration in no uncertain terms that it could not abrogate an agreement to maintain the level of troops in Okinawa by relocating a controversial U.S. Marine Corps base to a different site on the island.

No one should be surprised by the outcome: The Democratic Party of Japan eventually buckled, reneging on its campaign promise to base-weary Okinawans and maintaining the previous Liberal Democratic Party regime's commitment to the U.S. troop deployment policy.

In the U.S., too, presidents come and go—but the alliance system remains firmly intact. Barack Obama, elected in 2009 and re-elected in 2012, promised a "rebalancing" of U.S. power in Asia. This brought additional troops to Australia, Singapore, and Guam, as well as a new trade pact with countries on both sides of the Pacific, excluding China. However, immediately on taking office in 2017, Donald Trump withdrew from the Trans-Pacific Partnership. He also threatened to reduce U.S. troops in Japan and South Korea, but ultimately left them in place. Security advisers persuaded him that troop deployments extend U.S. power in what they now ritually call a "free and open Indo-Pacific."[31] Joe Biden, who became president in 2021, has vowed to strengthen the alliance system in East Asia, building on existing bilateral ties.

Christopher Hughes (2004: 13) notes that fledgling multilateral arrangements, a "noodle bowl" of different forms of regionalism, have emerged in East Asia. These have ranged from relatively weak bilateral and plurilateral trade agreements to six-party talks on North Korea's nuclear weapons program. Like me, however, Hughes does not envision a major change in East Asia's status quo: "The U.S. makes it clear that it tolerates multilateral frameworks only so far as they supplement and do not supplant its existing hub and spokes system; if they challenge it, then it demonstrates no interest."

Conclusion

Why has the United States approached Europe and Asia in such starkly different ways? My answer to this puzzle has drawn on realism and constructivism. The U.S. has treated the mother continent as an equal, or almost equal, player in the world, in part because it did not enjoy a surfeit of power vis-à-vis European states, but also because it felt an affinity toward "Westerners." It trusted those states, and those citizens, to cooperate with the U.S., and with one another. By contrast, the U.S. looked down on its Asian allies. Structurally, the U.S. was far more powerful, especially in the first three decades after World War II. But it also viewed Asians, culturally, as subordinates, as "little brown brothers" requiring adult supervision. This Janus-faced view of the two regions is rooted in power and identity—and remains largely unchanged over the past century and a half.

Realism points us to the disparate configurations of power and geopolitics in these two regions at the start of the Cold War. In Europe, the U.S. enjoyed the support of crippled but rebuilding powers of roughly equal size resisting an apparently looming threat of Soviet expansion. It pursued "empire by invitation"—for its own sake, of course, but also on behalf of insecure states such as the United Kingdom, France, Belgium, the Netherlands, and West Germany. The situation in Asia was different. Except for Japan, which would redevelop quickly to become an unparalleled economic power, the region was—at least initially—characterized by weakness. The U.S. had long played an outsized role here, and it continued to dominate. In addition, capitalist allies in Asia faced a more diffuse set of communist threats—from other states, including the People's Republic of China, but also from communist insurgencies within their own borders.

The U.S., then, enjoyed unparalleled power in Asia, and chose to "rule" the region through a hub-and-spokes pattern. Indeed, one cannot understand this initial choice of bilateralism over multilateralism without taking gross asymmetries in power into account. But this power-based explanation, as previously noted, fails to explain the remarkable continuity in U.S. policy in Asia despite changing geopolitical conditions. In the 1990s, when Japan was still the largest economy in Asia, Washington leaned hard on its subordinate ally to refrain from joining the East Asia Economic Group, which was popular with Japanese business, and to abandon the Japanese bureaucracy's own proposal for an Asian Monetary Fund to bail out the region's distressed economies. In the new millennium, after China eclipsed Japan in economic clout, American leaders continued to favor bilateral trade deals or multilateral ones (like the short-lived Trans-Pacific Partnership) that excluded Asia's new powerhouse. As before, they frowned on regional initiatives centered on Southeast Asia's established grouping (Association of Southeast Asian Nations) plus the three Northeast Asian powers (China, Japan, and South Korea).

We can only understand the continuity in U.S. backing for a hub-and-spokes pattern of alliances in Asia by adopting a hybrid approach that highlights identity as well as power. U.S. officials pursued this series of bilateral ties in Asia because they *could*, but also because, as constructivism informs us, they did not trust their allies in Asia to act "appropriately" on their own. Although they felt a special connection, maybe even a "kinship," with their European partners, they did not identify as equals or even associates with Asian states.[32]

EIGHT

The Healing Power of Institutions

Masuda Masayuki, an analyst for the National Institute of Defense Studies in Tokyo, has heard this question too many times: How has Germany managed to achieve reconciliation with its neighbors, while Japan has not? On this day, I am apparently piling on, joining an annoying scrum of inquisitors. "I am so tired of trying to compare these cases," he tells me with an exasperated look on his face.[1]

It has indeed become de rigueur to contrast Japan's experience with Germany's. Academic conferences have explored the subject. In 2009, for example, the American Institute for Contemporary German Studies at Johns Hopkins University hosted a workshop, "Reconciliation or Resentment? Honoring the Past or Minimizing It in the Foreign Policies of Germany and Japan."[2] Likewise in 2011, the Shorenstein Asia-Pacific Research Center at Stanford hosted another, "Colonialism, Collaboration and Criminality," that used the same comparative framework.[3]

Japanese scholars, in particular, have been wracking their brains, looking to Germany for inspiration on how to overcome the past. Tokyo Keizai University has even established a Center for Historical Reconciliation, thanks to support from German foundations such as the Friedrich-Ebert-Stiftung and the Goethe-Institut. The center invited Lily Gardner Feldman, a U.S. academic who has studied Germany's efforts to reconcile with other states, to speak about that country's experience. Among the recommendations she offered to her Japanese hosts was this: "The perpetrators must acknowledge the nature of the victims' grievances through some public act, for example a formal or informal apology, a legal act, a statement of willingness for a new relationship, symbolic visits to the location of atrocities, etc."[4]

This is the common refrain: Japan must learn to talk more like Germany, to apologize more profusely. Even better, it should do so in biblical terms: confessing and then atoning for its sins. Thus, Thomas Berger (2012) argues that Germany is a "model penitent" because, he argues, it has recognized its militarist past and openly sought forgiveness for its sins. Japan, by contrast, might be considered a "model impenitent" that has failed to atone or even confess.

My analysis is quite different, and confirms the old admonition that "actions speak louder than words." While I recognize the value of discourse and gestures, I believe that formalized cooperation invites reconciliation between states. This is how Germany managed to overcome the past, forging regional partnerships through NATO and even more actively through the European Union. It has shown its neighbors that it can be trusted, that it won't attempt to dominate or brutalize them again.

Japan has not taken, or been able to take, the same steps in Northeast Asia, where regionalism is woefully underdeveloped—thanks in large part to the United States. It has not seized, or been afforded, the opportunity to demonstrate its ability to cooperate through regional agreements. So it remains mistrusted. To achieve reconciliation with countries such as China and South Korea, Japan first "must become a trusted member of the community, a trusted resident in its local neighborhood—that is, Asia— and make everyone feel at home in its company," according to Wakamiya (1995: 280), a Japanese journalist.

Interestingly, Japan enjoys much better relations with nations in Southeast Asia, including Indonesia and Malaysia. This may reflect nothing more than the short duration of its occupation there (1942–45). But what about Taiwan, then, which Japan colonized for a half century—even longer than it colonized Korea? It, too, gets on relatively well with Japan today. Just as officials in Tokyo have worked hard to maintain formal ties of cooperation with their counterparts in Jakarta and Kuala Lumpur, agreeing (for example) to help build a supporting industry for automakers there, they have done the same with counterparts in Taipei, forging (for example) an agreement to share fishery resources.

Comparing Germany and Japan can be fruitful—but only if we do so carefully, evaluating the singular effect of different factors. The two countries have had very different experiences. Masuda, for example, notes that a Europe devastated by World War II benefited from the U.S.-funded Marshall Plan, which induced France to cooperate with West Germany. "There was no Marshall Plan in Asia," he reminded me.

This hints at a larger difference: As outlined in chapter 7, the U.S. pursued a multilateral approach in Europe after World War II, but hammered out a bilateral "hub-and-spokes" pattern in Asia. Regional institutions emerged in the former, embedding Germany in a set of cooperative agreements. Such institutions did not emerge in the latter, leaving Japan exposed to long-standing suspicion. Berger (2012: 238) seems to understand this important difference, but—like He (2009) and so many others— still emphasizes words and gestures, or "official narratives."

I have offered four case studies here. One of them shows that Germany was able to reconcile with France shortly after forging agreement on the European Coal and Steel Community and long before offering expressions of contrition or becoming economically intertwined. Another shows that Germany's concerted efforts to accommodate Poland's entry into NATO and the European Union won over its eastern neighbor, much more than expressions of contrition or economic exchange. We also saw that Japan has offered official apologies to China and South Korea, and has tried to compensate both countries for past misdeeds; in the 1980s and 1990s, it offered massive yen loans for Chinese infrastructure projects, and agreed in 1993 and 2015 to compensate Korean "comfort women" who were exploited by Japanese soldiers during World War II. But neither words nor gestures of contrition improved Japan's diplomatic ties with its Asian neighbors. Likewise, economic exchange with those countries appears to have had little impact. One constant in Japan's relations with South Korea and China is the near absence of formal-legal regionalism.

Although the three countries participate in the ASEAN Plus Three meetings that happen every year among the 13 countries of Northeast and Southeast Asia, they do not participate together in any significant regional organization. Granted, they all belong to Asia Pacific Economic Cooperation, which has a diverse membership, from Chile to Australia, on either side of the ocean; and they belong to East Asia Summit, which also has expanded geographically, to include India, Russia, and the United States. But neither group has much substance or clout. The United States, as noted earlier, has thwarted efforts by Asian states to participate in substantive, influential regional organizations that do not include the U.S.

Formal agreements between states demonstrate a credible commitment to cooperation, a willingness to forego the unilateral exercise of power that created a ghostly legacy of distrust in the first place. In addition to deterring the Soviet Union and later Russia, NATO has allowed Germany to show that it can collaborate with neighbors such as France and Poland to maintain the region's security. The pact represents a pledge to renounce the brutal militarism that had characterized Europe's major power in the past. Likewise, the project of regional integration (via the EEC, the EC, and then the EU) did more than promote trade among participating economies and boost the fortunes of Europe's farmers; it also allowed Germany to prove that it could work with its neighbors to improve the region's health and welfare.

To be sure, Germany's behavior in Europe has not always seemed collaborative or mutually uplifting. This was painfully evident especially in the financial crisis that engulfed Greece between 2010 and 2018. Critics complained that Germany sometimes behaved like a predator, running up a large trade surplus with neighbors and insisting that borrowers enact austerity measures in exchange for financial help from the European Central Bank.[5] Caporaso (2022), for example, suggests that Germany exploited its regional power to protect creditors, including itself, punish supposedly "profligate" debtors such as Greece, and momentarily jeopardize the entire Eurozone.

More often, though, Germany is viewed as a valuable, perhaps essential partner in the region. Neighbors today believe it is dedicated to a common cause; Germany has formally pledged to work with them to maintain regional security and enhance regional prosperity. In the wake of Moscow's invasion of Ukraine, Berlin immediately recommitted itself to NATO, and promised policies to shore up both its own economy, which is perilously dependent on Russian oil and gas, and to help stabilize the EU.

The conclusion offered in this book is not entirely revolutionary. Jennifer Lind (2009) already has taught us that heartfelt apologies from states not only fail to bring about reconciliation, they often trigger a nasty backlash from nationalist forces at home. Her analysis thus questions the conventional wisdom about official contrition, noting that the domestic convulsion following such statements can damage interstate relations even further. But while she shows us what doesn't work, she does not actually show us what does.

A few scholars outside the U.S. have begun to offer explanations that sound more like mine: Regionalism, not rhetoric, is the pathway to reconciliation; Germany's success in overcoming the legacies of its past is a function of formal cooperation, not grand gestures of contrition. Turek (2018: 47), a Pole, writes that Japan and its neighbors in Asia could "mirror European mechanisms and institutions. This role model—European integration—could serve as an inspiration. . . . The European Union is the institutional and political prolonging of reconciliation between Poland and Germany, but in a supranational dimension."

In the future, formal cooperation through regionalism may lose its power to heal interstate relations. Nationalism is on the rise throughout the world, even in Europatriotic Germany, fomenting right-wing skepticism about "entangling alliances" such as NATO or economic integration projects such as the EU. Nativists and antiglobalists, alarmed by the mobility of migrant labor and financial capital, and whipped up by political entrepreneurs, are calling for harder borders. Brexit is just one example of this global trend. Donald Trump's term (2017–21) as U.S. president is another.

Although his nationalist rhetoric rattled allies around the world, the former president may have—ironically and accidentally—revealed a path toward reconciliation in Northeast Asia, a path toward greater institutionalization of interstate ties there. If "America First" means that the United States does not, by definition, belong at the center of everything that happens in that region, perhaps Japan can step up and demonstrate the political will to forge significant agreements of its own with Asian neighbors such as South Korea and even China. We already have seen a positive if not permanent effect on Japan-Korea relations from a 2015 pact between the two countries to resolve the comfort women controversy and another, signed in 2016, to directly share military information (instead of relying on the U.S. as middleman). Likewise, Japan-China relations improved a bit, for a while, after 2018 deals on bilateral currency swaps, joint R&D projects, and collaborative infrastructure spending in Southeast Asia. Agreements like these demonstrate a commitment to cooperation, especially when they are extended and expanded. They allow Japan to reassure its neighbors that it is, at last, a trustworthy partner.

Even if not pursued under the isolationist banner of "America First," a less U.S.-centered security architecture in Asia also might contribute to interstate reconciliation. Multilateralism, rather than a Washington-dominated hub-and-spokes system, might push friendly Asian states to collaborate more. And a lighter U.S. military footprint in Japan, which now hosts more than 50,000 American troops, could enable Tokyo to exercise greater policy autonomy in the region. This would, in turn, cause Japan's neighbors to take it more seriously.

There are risks, of course, to a U.S. withdrawal from Asia, or even a major reduction in its presence there. President Biden, a more traditional foreign-policy maker, clearly understands that this could create a vacuum in the region—one that China might try to fill. But perhaps the Democratic administration in Washington will also recognize that Asian powers themselves—not only Japan, but South Korea, Indonesia, Malaysia, Thailand, Vietnam, and India—are capable of filling at least some of that void. For example, 11 states on both sides of the Pacific, including Japan, have moved ahead with a renamed trade deal after the Trump administration abandoned TPP in one of its first public declarations. (On the other hand, as if to highlight the risks of U.S. withdrawal, China has expressed an interest in joining the Comprehensive and Progressive Trans-Pacific Partnership.) This rare example of Asian regionalism without U.S. domination has shown, thus far, that Japan can afford to safely step outside the shadow of its patron state.

I will never forget a meeting I had several years ago with Tamamoto Masaru, one of Japan's sharpest social critics. He argued that Asian nations do not take Japan seriously because it remains a client, or perhaps even a child, of the United States. On policy matters, it behaves like a supplicant. And with respect to the past, it appears to remember almost nothing. Japan, he told me, "does not own its own history—it's an American-authored history. We have to reclaim our past if we want to become an agent of our own future."[6]

Notes

1. For 45 years after World War II, Europe's once-dominant continental power was divided into a capitalist, pro-U.S. West Germany and a communist, pro-Soviet East Germany. The latter dealt with Germany's bloody past in a rather simple way: It didn't. As an avowed antifascist state, East Germany declared itself clean; the stain of Nazism lingered only in Bonn. What about earlier misdeeds, such as the partition of Poland by Prussia and its co-conspirators? That too, was a different place, a disconnected time. So when I write here about "Germany," I am referring to the Federal Republic of Germany—which was West Germany from the end of World War II until 1990, and the unified state after that.

2. Evelin Lindner has launched the field of dignity/humiliation studies, which helps understand some (but certainly not all) types of events that create a dynamic or syndrome crying out for reconciliation. See especially Lindner (2006).

3. In his work on Northern Ireland, Love (1995) insists that reconciliation flows from contrition and forgiveness. Likewise, Feldman (2006) argues that, to achieve reconciliation, "perpetrators must acknowledge the nature of the victims' grievances through some public act, for example a formal or informal apology, a legal act, a statement of willingness for a new relationship, symbolic visits to the location of atrocities, etc."

4. The Rwandan Patriotic Front—a Tutsi-led force that ended the 1994 genocide and established an authoritarian government in Kigali—used a very localized version of the truth and reconciliation commission to foster healing throughout that country. *Gacaca* (meaning "on the grass under the elder's tree") allowed villagers to level complaints against Hutu villagers who participated in the killings, but did not organize them. The accused then had a chance to dispute the allegations, or recognize them and apologize to victims.

5. This taxonomy comes from George (2000).

6. Many scholars outside political science have adopted a similar approach. For example, Olick and Coughlin (2003), who are sociologists, suggest that international pressure forces insecure states to issue public apologies for earlier misdeeds.

7. See CBOS, "Stosunek do innych narodów" (Relations with Other Nations): https://www.cbos.pl/SPISKOM.POL/2022/K_021_22.PDF

8. See Genron NPO, "Public Opinion of Japan Drastically Falls among Chinese People in the Previous Year," October 28, 2021: https://www.genron-npo.net/en/opinion_polls/archives/5587.html

9. See, for example, https://www.theguardian.com/world/2015/mar/11/greece-sours-german-relations-further-demand-war-reparations

10. The Nazi genocide of European Jews may be sui generis. But more importantly, it represents an attack on an ethnic population that did not, until 1948, have its own nation-state. (And many of the European Jews targeted by Hitler were German.) If Israel had been a European country attacked by Germany during World War II, I certainly would have included it in this study.

11. Interview, August 5, 2009, Seoul.

12. Phone interview, April 22, 2006, Berlin.

13. This reflects a belief in Pax Mercatoria (the commercial peace). See Oneal and Russett (1999), Polachek (1980), and Rosecrance (1986).

14. Under Article 301 of its penal code, Turkey has—since 2005—banned speech that denigrates the nation. This law has been used against prominent citizens blaming Ottoman leaders for the 1915 genocide of Armenians.

15. Obama delivered other tepid statements acknowledging American mistakes in the past, upsetting conservatives. See, for example, Gardiner and Roach (2009).

16. Bundestag speech, May 27, 1994; *Bulletin, Presse-und Informationsamt der Bundesregierung*, May 30, 1994, 478 (quoted in Banchoff 1997).

17. Email, April 6, 2006.

18. Interviews with the author, Tokyo, July 12, 2011; and via email on September 20, 2021.

CHAPTER 2

1. One might also include the Allied firebombings of German cities (such as Dresden in February 1945) and the U.S. firebombings of Japanese cities (such as Tokyo in March 1945, when 100,000 civilians burned to death).

2. Interview, July 8, 2009, Paris.

3. Rosoux (2001: 193) does an especially good job of documenting how French elites, seeking to build a new and more-positive memory better suited for new and better times, have recast old hostilities between France and Germany as brotherly disputes. François Mitterand, she notes, referred to World War I and World War II as "civil wars in Europe." And Jacques Chirac recalled them, collectively, as "the long fratricidal war" that began in 1914.

4. Navigating my way through interwar history textbooks, I have relied heavily on Siegel (2002) and Shapiro (1997).

5. "Conférences pédagogiques du canton de Montpon: Registre des procès-verbaux, 1880–1925," Archives departmementales de la Dordogne (ADD) 4/T/107, quoted in Siegel (2002: 781).

6. My goal here is not to demonstrate the veracity of such claims; rather, I merely strive to show that they were widely believed and shared by French citizens. Hull (2005) makes perhaps the strongest argument on behalf of German exceptionalism (*sonderweg*) as a "military culture."

7. The quote is from Jules Isaac, a lycée professor and war veteran. See Malet and Grillet (1925: 1082).

8. Speech at Bar-le-Duc, July 28, 1946, quoted in Gildea (2002a: 66).

9. See Gildea (2002b: 14).

10. Napolean freed Warsaw from Prussian control in 1806.

11. See Ritter (1968: 180).

12. See Blackbourn (2000: 8).

13. See Davies (1982: 124).

14. The existence of this secret protocol to the Molotov-Ribbentrop "Non-Aggression" Pact was not revealed until 1945, well after the fall of Berlin. Until 1989, when an investigative team commissioned by President Mikhail Gorbachev released its findings, the Soviet Union continued to deny its own participation in the protocol.

15. This historical narrative draws heavily on Kulski (1976) and the Central Commission for the Investigation of German Crimes in Poland (1982).

16. In 1895, Russia, France, and Germany teamed up to pressure Japan to relinquish control of China's Liaodong Peninsula, a war spoil that it had acquired in the Treaty of Shimonoseki ending the first Sino-Japanese war.

17. Quoted in Okamoto (1970: 119).

18. I also interviewed Shoji Jun'ichiro on this and related topics, October 10, 2012, Tokyo.

19. I came across the sign in a 2006 visit to Seoul. On returning in 2018, after a renovation of the palace and its grounds, I could not find the sign again.

20. From Kim Sang-hyon, *Chae-il Hanguk-in* (Korean Residents in Japan) (Dankuk Research Institute Press, 1969): 38. Quoted in Lee (1990: 64).

21. Historians estimate that there were as many as 200,000 "comfort women" throughout Japanese-occupied Asia, and that about half of them were Korean.

22. Quoted in Keene (1971: 264).

23. The Nanjing Massacre Museum repeats this number so often, and in such dramatic ways, that it is seared into the visitor's consciousness. One exhibit occupies a dark chamber with a pool of water on the ground and small photographs of Chinese victims on the wall. A clock ticks in the background. Every twelve seconds, a different photograph is illuminated and a drop of water falls into the pool, triggering a loud *ping*. A sign delivers the equation: The Japanese military killed 300,000 Chinese over a six-week period, the equivalent of 1 every 12 seconds.

24. I visited the museum on July 16, 2011.

25. Fortunately, I am in good company. See, for example, Ragin 1987; Van Evera 1997.

26. Germany's per-capita GDP (in nominal terms) for the year 2021 was $50,788; France's was $45,028, and Poland's was $17,318 (more than one-third of Germany's level). Japan's per capita GDP in 2021 was $40,704; South Korea's was $35,196, and China's was only $11,891 (more than one-fourth of Japan's). These figures come from the IMF's World Economic Outlook database.

CHAPTER 3

1. Quoted in Herf (1997: 282).

2. European Union, "Declaration of May 9, 1950," europa.eu.int/abc/symbols /9-may/decl_en.htm

3. Interview with the author, Paris, July 6, 2009.

4. To promote his vision of reconciliation, Rovan created his own organization, the International Liaison and Documentation Office (Le Bureau International de Liaison et de Documentation) in 1945. The Paris-based group served as the model for another that emerged just three years later across the border in Ludwigsburg: the Franco-German Institute (Deutsch-Französisches Institut, or DFI).

5. Quoted in Maillard (1990: 89).

6. Quoted in Acheson (1969: 552).

7. Hitchcock (1998) disagrees with the prevailing view that France was forced by the U.S. to accommodate West Germany as part of its new Cold War strategy. He argues that European integration was, from the very beginning, a French plan.

8. Quoted in Campbell (1989: 61).

9. Cited by Marcussen et al. (1999: 622).

10. See https://www.annuaire-mairie.fr/jumelage-allemagne.html

11. See https://www.fgyo.org/resources-publications/fgyo-self-portrayal-short-version.html

12. I first interviewed Mr. Schäfer in Berlin, April 20, 2006. We had a follow-up conversation by email in October 2021. The quote comes from that conversation.

13. Mitterand was actually speaking here to Hans-Dietrich Genscher, the foreign minister of West Germany, not Kohl. The quote comes from Attali (1995: 364).

14. In an unusual case, German hooligans brutally attacked a French policeman at a 1998 World Cup soccer match in France. The victim later became Germany's guest of honor at its opening game in Euro 2016. See https://www.dailymail.co.uk/sport/sportsnews/article-3638192/Germany-welcomes-former-French-policeman-victim-1998-World-Cup-hooliganism-Euro-2016-opening-game.html

15. An interview in *Figaro*, January 20, 2003, quoted in Martens (2003: 41).

16. See Lizzy Davies, "Merkel Joins Sarkozy at Armistice Ceremony in Paris," *Guardian*, November 11, 2009.

17. See the *Guardian:* https://www.theguardian.com/world/2018/nov/13/merkel-joins-macron-in-calling-for-a-real-true-european-army

18. See *Financial Times:* https://www.ft.com/content/1dc45d1c-36bf-11e9-bb0c-42459962a812

Also note that the state-level negotiations were greased by collaboration between French and German economists, as reported by *Politico:* https://www.politico.eu/article/french-german-economists-launch-their-own-eurozone-plan/

19. See the *New York Times:* https://www.nytimes.com/2019/01/22/world/europe/france-germany-eu.html

20. See https://www.gmfus.org/news/transatlantic-relations

21. Lind actually goes further to argue that apologies can do more harm than good when they stimulate a domestic backlash, leading to denials by other public officials. The net effect, she suggests, referring specifically to Japan's relations with South Korea, may be negative.

22. See his speech as published in Deutscher Bundestag, *Stenographische Berichte, erste Wahlperiod*, September 27, 1951: 6697–98.

23. Lind (2008: 109) notes that only 11 percent of West Germans then supported the payment of compensation to Israel. Citizens were focused then on German, not Jewish, suffering.

24. This section draws heavily from Olick (1993).

25. Quoted in Herf (1997: 271).

26. Interview with the author, Berlin, July 22, 2009. Olick (1998: 551) supports this historiography; he says the late 1960s generated a new image of "Germany as a moral nation. Unlike the society of the 1950s, the new generation was willing to confront and draw more radical lessons from the past . . ."

27. Quoted in Herf (1997: 344–45).

28. Interview with the author, Berlin, July 22, 2009.

29. See the French Foreign Ministry site; available at https://www.diplomatie.go uv.fr/en/country-files/germany/france-and-germany/

30. In late 2018, Euractiv estimated that the number of German firms established in France was closer to 4,500; available at https://www.euractiv.fr/section/eco nomie/news/la-france-seduit-davantage-les-investisseurs-allemands/

For recent French investment in Germany, see https://amp2.handelsblatt.com/ german-connection-french-industry-has-a-preference-for-germany/23583306. html

31. See OECD statistics for "FDI flows by partner country" at OECD.Stat

32. Quoted in Moravcsik (1998: 104).

33. Telephone interview, April 22, 2006.

34. Kohl's May 27, 1994, speech is available in *Bulletin, Presse-und Informations-amt der Bundesregierung*, May 31, 1994, 478.

35. Quoted in Heuser (1998: 221).

36. Interview with the author, Paris, July 8, 2009.

37. Interview with the author, Dijon, July 10, 2009.

38. Phone interview, September 2, 2009.

39. Interview with the author, Paris, July 7, 2009.

CHAPTER 4

1. East Asia Institute and Genron NPO, "The 9th Japan-South Korea Joint Public Opinion Poll (2021)" available at http://www.eai.or.kr/main/english/program _view.asp?intSeq=20810&code

This number (39 percent) was actually lower than 2020, when 44 percent of South Koreans viewed Japan as a military threat, and way lower than 2015, when 58 percent did.

2. Asan Institute for Policy Studies, "South Koreans and Their Neighbors," April 2019: 8. See https://en.asaninst.org/contents/south-koreans-and-their-neighbors-2019/

3. A large minority of respondents (39%) did not choose sides. https:// www.japantimes.co.jp/news/2019/11/08/national/politics-diplomacy/nearly-half-south-koreans-back-north-vs-japan/

4. Interview, July 9, 2009, Brussels.

5. Interview, August 3, 2009, Seoul; and email exchange September 5, 2021.

6. *Chosun Ilbo*, June 8, 1949.

7. *Mainichi Shinbun*, December 21, 1955.

8. See Wakamiya (1998: 194).

9. See World Bank, "World Integrated Trade Solution" (WITS) data; also see Kimura (2013).

10. On August 4, 2009, I interviewed Yoon Mee-Hyang, the head of the Korean Council for the Women Drafted for Sexual Slavery by Japan, in Seoul. The interview was conducted in English, Japanese, and Korean (with translation). "Japan must recognize that this was a war crime, a crime against humanity," she told me. "So far it has just engaged in lip service." In 2020, after Yoon was elected to the National Assembly, she was accused by one of the surviving comfort women of exploiting them for personal and political gain. https://www.koreatimes.co.kr/www/nation/2020 /05/356_290099.html

11. The statement was issued on August 4, 1993, by Kono Yohei, chief cabinet secretary under Prime Minister Miyazawa, and continues to constitute the Japanese government's official position on the historical question of "comfort women." In addition to an apology, the Kono statement contains three significant findings: (1) The Japanese military did in fact play a direct and indirect role in establishing and operating the wartime "comfort stations"; (2) private and public officials often recruited women "against their will" to serve in these stations; and (3) the women "lived in misery at comfort stations under a coercive atmosphere." The statement can be found online at the website of the Ministry of Foreign Affairs: https://www .mofa.go.jp/a_o/rp/page25e_000343.html

12. *Yomiuri Shinbun*, December 23, 2013.

13. From *The Economist*, "Japan and South Korea: Remember the Noses," Feb. 17, 1996: 35.

14. BBC, "Attack on Japan Ministry Website," March 31, 2001.

15. "Cup cohosts' ties thaw, at least on individual level," *Japan Times*, June 29, 2002: 3.

16. See World Bank, *World Integrated Trade Solution* (WITS).

17. *Nikkei Weekly*, April 29, 2002.

18. See McLelland (2008).

19. Soh (2003: 164–71) tells this story well.

20. See, for example, *Asahi Shimbun*, "Panel Still Bickers over History Issues," March 25, 2010. For a more academic analysis, and one that compares the Japan– South Korea negotiations with the Germany-Poland negotiations, see Sakaki (2012).

21. The Seodaemun Prison is now a museum designed to educate Koreans, especially youth, about the Japanese occupation. Filled with bloody photographs and chilling exhibits, it encourages hostility toward Japan as it fosters pride in Korea.

22. See *Korea JoongAng Daily*, March 23, 2005.

23. Interview, July 7, 2006, Seoul. We exchanged emails more recently, and Lee told me he now blames Korean politicians as much as Japanese nationalists for the bilateral rift.

24. See figure 4.1.

25. See, for example, "Japan and Its history: The Ghosts of Wartime Past," *The Economist*, November 8, 2008.

26. See, for example, "Lee Presses Japan to Resolve 'Comfort Women' Issue," *Korea Times*, August 15, 2012.

27. Yonhap, August 22, 2018.

28. See Arrington and Yeo (2019).

29. See *Washington Post*, February 9, 2019, at https://www.washingtonpost.com/wo rld/asia_pacific/japan-south-korea-ties-worst-in-five-decades-as-us-leaves-alliance-un tended/2019/02/08/f17230be-2ad8-11e9-906e-9d55b6451eb4_story.html

30. See Daniel Sneider, "Cutting the Gordian Knot in South Korea-Japan Relations," *East Asia Forum*, April 4, 2022; available at https://www.eastasiaforum.org/20 22/04/04/cutting-the-gordian-knot-in-south-korea-japan-relations/

31. Ku (2008: 25) and Berger (2012: 200) combine survey results from the *JoongAng* newspaper with these *Dong-a* numbers to create a longer timeline.

32. *Japan Times*, May 15, 2013.

33. I relied here on Wakamiya (1998: 186–88).

34. See Wakamiya (1998: 199–201); and McCormack (1996: 233).

35. See *New York Times*, "Japanese Politician Reframes Comments on Sex Slavery," May 27, 2013.

36. *Japan Times*, "Seoul envoy: Mayor is odd man out," May 16, 2013.

37. *Korea Times*, January 25, 2021: https://www.koreatimes.co.kr/www/opinion/20 21/03/202_303012.html

38. Roh's speech was greeted with enthusiasm in Japan. Reading it, especially the new Korean president's pledge to help usher in a "Northeast Asia Era," "I felt my spirits lift," wrote Wada Haruki (2003), a historian at the University of Tokyo.

39. See Hatoyama's speech (November 15, 2009) at the conclusion of the APEC meeting in Singapore: https://japan.kantei.go.jp/hatoyama/statement/200911/15singa pore_e.html

40. In my August 4, 2009, interview at the Seoul office of the Korean Council for the Women Drafted for Military Sexual Slavery by Japan, Yoon Mee-hyang told me her group, perhaps the leading civil society organization representing Korean "comfort women," was not satisfied with the Kono statement. "It was insincere—nothing but lip service," she said. "We want the Japanese government to take responsibility for this terrible war crime."

41. Interview, August 3, 2009, Seoul.

CHAPTER 5

1. See figure 5.1.

2. Interview with the author, April 24, 2013, Warsaw.

3. In a November 2017 poll, CBOS found that 54 percent of Polish respondents agreed that Poland should demand reparations from Germany. But a plurality (45%) predicted that Poland would lose more than it gained by doing so; 31 percent predicted Poland would gain more than it would lose. See "Polish Public Opinion," at https://www.cbos.pl/PL/publikacje/public_opinion/2017/11_2017.pdf

4. The German-Polish Textbook Commission was founded in 1970 at a UNESCO gathering in Paris. Two years later, 11 historians from West Germany traveled to Warsaw for the first of many difficult but important dialogues about how to record the past.

5. Quoted in Feldman (2012: 236).

6. See, for example, Jacobsen and Mieczysław (1992: 498–501).

7. "Germany for the Germans," *Newsweek*, April 22, 1991.

8. "Biedrusko Journal; The Cold War Armies Meet, Just to Link Arms," *New York Times*, September 15, 1994.

9. Interview with the author, Berlin, April 24, 2006.

10. Interview with the author, Warsaw, April 10, 2006.

11. The issue first surfaced in 1998, when the Bundestag condemned the expulsion of Germans as "unlawful" (*unrecht*) and appeared to support the expellees' demands for "justice."

12. The entrenched identity of Poland as a "pure" victim-nation had already been challenged from within by the publication of a book (*Neighbors* by Jan Tomasz Gross) documenting Polish participation in the mass murder of Jews at Jedwabne in 1941.

13. Die Bundesregierung, "Speech by Chancellor Schröder on the 60th anniversary of the Warsaw Uprising," August 1, 2004. Available at: http://www.warsawupris ing.com/paper/schroeder.pdf

14. See, for example, *DerStandard*, "Sikorski: Ostsee-Pipeline gleicht 'Hitler-Stalin Pakt'" ("Sikorski: The Baltic Sea Pipeline Resembles the Hitler-Stalin Agreement"), May 8, 2006; at https://derstandard.at/2431077/Sikorski-Ostsee-Pipeline-gleicht-Hitler-Stalin-Pakt-

15. Interview with the author, Warsaw, April 12, 2006.

16. Interview with the author, Warsaw, April 11, 2006.

17. Interview with the author, Warsaw, April 22, 2013.

18. Jan Cienski, "Migrants carry 'parasites and protozoa,' warns Polish opposition leader," *Politico*, October 14, 2015; available at https://www.politico.eu/article/mi grants-asylum-poland-kaczynski-election/

19. This has been a long-standing meme for cartoonists and polemicists. Jon Henley, "Polish press invokes Nazi imagery as war of words with EU heats up," *Guardian* (UK), January 12, 2016; available at https://www.theguardian.com/world /2016/jan/12/polish-press-nazi-imagery-war-of-words-eu-angela-merkel

20. Jon Stone, "Support for EU membership reaches record high in Poland despite showdown with Brussels," *The Independent* (UK), January 9, 2018; available at https://www.independent.co.uk/news/world/europe/poland-eu-membership-suppo rt-for-membership-courts-rule-of-law-mateusz-morawiecki-juncker-a8149876.html

21. For more on this, see Marten-Finnis (1995: 256–57).

22. Sander (1995) argues that, despite official propaganda, Poles did not view East Germans as substantially different or better than West Germans. Textbooks generally treated them both as "Germans" who had viciously mistreated Poland over centuries.

23. The commission began by producing handbooks with shared glossaries for history teachers in each country. It later completed a joint history textbook.

24. Weizsacker was commemorating the 40th anniversary of the end of World War II. His speech resonated because it conveyed a feeling of collective guilt not only for crimes against Jews, but also against homosexuals, communists, Roma/ Sini, and Polish and well as Soviet citizens. In addition, it had an impact because the speaker was a member of the conservative CDU, which until then had viewed Germans as victims of the war. *Spiegel*, the German magazine, has published a transcript: http://www.spiegel.de/politik/deutschland/weizsaecker-rede-1985-8-mai-war-ein-tag-der-befreiung-a-354568.html

25. Davis (1999: 112–14) argues that West Germany was actually quite generous during this time, agreeing to reschedule Polish debt and promising new export-credit guarantees. But she also acknowledges that Bonn suspended its lending in 1986 due to concern over the slow pace of repayment.

26. Phillips (2001: 177) notes that Poles submitted 700,000 claims. By 1997, the foundation had spent all its money before it was able to compensate many of the alleged victims.

27. See Feldman (2012: 206–7).

28. See He (2009: 70–72).

29. See Newnham (2005: 473).

30. See Bandelj (2007: 46).

31. See OECD; available at https://data.oecd.org/fdi/inward-fdi-stocks-by-partner-country.htm

32. Interview with the author, Warsaw, April 14, 2006.

33. See, for example, Lebioda (2000: 165) and Lipski (1996: 262).

34. BBC Summary of World Broadcasts, "Speech by German Foreign Minister on Signing of Polish-German Treaty," November 14, 1990.

35. "Das transatlantische Netzwerk ausbauen und verstärken," a speech to the Chicago Council on Foreign Relations, Chicago, June 19, 1997, *Bulletin*, Presse-und Informationsamt der Bundesregierung, no. 63, July 30 1997: 751. Quoted in Feldman 1999: 337.

36. See University of Luxembourg, Centre Virtuel de las Connaissance sur l'Europe, "Community Funding Under the PHARE program (1990–1998)"; available at "Community Aid under the Phare programme (1990–1998)," https://www.cvce.eu/en/obj/community_aid_under_the_phare_programme_1990_1998-en-f3e52aeb-b34f-417a-92d8-06ddff880a5d.html

37. See Davis and Dombrowki (1997: 16), who use EC data from 1995. Other data and perspectives on this program can be found in Chessa (2004) and Fure (1997). At the end of 2003, on the eve of Polish accession, Onis (2004: 497) estimates that the EU had provided a total of nearly six billion euros in assistance to Poland through the INTERREG and PHARE programs.

38. Interview with the author, Berlin, July 20, 2009.

39. Helmut Kohl, "Rede von Bundeskanzler Helmut Kohl anlässlich der Eröffnung der Deutsch-Polnischen Industrie- und Handelskammer am 7. Juli 1995 in Warschau," in Presse- und Informationsamt der Bundesregierung (eds.) (1995): Bulletin Nr. 58, Bonn: 574.

40. See Rühe (1993). Some have questioned whether the defense minister spoke on behalf of Germany, or only for himself. Towpik (2011), however, persuasively argues that Chancellor Kohl eventually adopted this position.

41. For this discussion, I have relied heavily on Towpik (2011).

42. "Remembering Their War, Germans Embrace the First Victims," *New York Times*, September 2, 1999: A9.

43. See Feldman (2012: 246) and Newnham (2007: 212–213)

44. See Truszczynski (2011: 226) and Newnham (2007: 214)

45. See Newnham (2007: 212). Tewes (2002: 118) endorses this analysis: "For Germany, an enlargement without Poland was unimaginable and unacceptable. Since this was so, there was a tacit understanding in the EU that Poland would have to be in the first wave, even if it did not quite fulfill all the criteria as well as the other countries."

46. Interview with the author, Berlin, April 20, 2006. The diplomat asked me not to name him.

47. Interview with the author, Warsaw, April 23, 2013.

48. Freudenstein (1998: 49) believes Poland hungered to join European institutions not only for economic but also for political and cultural reasons. "EU membership is seen as a chance to catch up with European modernity, and thus to re-establish a contact which was lost not just at the beginning of the Second World War, but as far back as the beginning of the partition of Poland at the end of the eighteenth century."

49. See Buras (2013: 67–82).

50. See Buras (2013: 83–97).

51. Interview with the author, Warsaw, April 23, 2013.

CHAPTER 6

1. Interview with the author, Beijing, July 11, 2006.

2. I acknowledge that this is speculation; for all I know, the Chinese government may be correct in claiming that Jin Xide was in fact selling secrets to Japan and South Korea. Since the judicial system is not independent, we will never know for sure. Jin Xide was released from prison in late 2019, but remains incommunicado.

3. See Siyun Lin, "Nanjing Defense Campaign and Nanjing Massacre," in *China Weekly Report*, October 27, 2000: https://www.china-week.com/html/548.htm (cited in Xu and Spillman, 2010, footnote 26); also see Eykolt (2000: 25–26).

4. See He Yinan (2003: 13–14).

5. *People's Daily*, "The Situation of Japanese Peoples' Struggle" (editorial), July 7, 1950.

6. See Radtke (1990: 98).

7. He Yinan (2009: 135–36).

8. *People's Daily*, "Human Conscience Will Inevitably Win" (editorial), August 6, 1957.

9. See Hatch (2014: 372).

10. See Ma (2002).

11. Takahashi (1998: 149). *Ôshin* aired on NHK, Japan's public television station.

12. We now know the textbooks were not actually so "revisionist." Japanese leftists mischaracterized the content of the books, which led to overheated articles in Japanese media (especially *Asahi Shimbun*) and ultimately in Chinese media. See Rose (1998: 80–94).

13. *People's Daily*, June 30, 1982.

14. One of the first cases was filed in 1997 against the Japanese government and four construction companies that allegedly forced victims to dig tunnels and build hydroelectric plants in Nagano Prefecture during the war. That case was subsequently tossed out because it exceeded the statute of limitations (*Japan Times*, March 11, 2006). Japanese courts, including the Supreme Court, ultimately rejected about a dozen such slave labor cases. (See, for example, *Japan Times*, March 27, 2004; and *New York Times*, April 26, 2007.)

15. In 2006, while visiting a Nanjing bookstore, I came across the most purple example I ever found of this genre. Ma Yi's *Ugly Japanese* describes an amoral society guided by blind loyalty to the emperor and a faux religion (Shinto), resulting in "savagery within the depths of the soul" (3).

16. See Sato (2001: 12).

17. See Sawaji (2007: 7).

18. For example, see *Yomiuri's* Q&A from July 28, 2005, "Kiban kara wakaru nihon seifu reikishi ninshiki" (A basic understanding of the Japan government's reckoning of the past). *Yomiuri* later published a groundbreaking series of articles about World War II, and it editorialized in favor of a public and less controversial memorial to replace the Yasukuni Shrine.

19. The Japanese media marveled at Wen's speech. See, for example, *Yomiuri Shimbun*, "On kahō shushō enzetsu: Chūgoku no tai-nichi shisei ni henka ga mieta" (Wen Jiabao's speech: Change is seen in China's attitude toward Japan), April 13, 2007.

20. See Ministry of Foreign Affairs (2008).

21. I visited the museum in July 2011. The "reconciliation room," near the museum's exit, tries to thread the needle with this exhortation: "The Chinese government and people firmly insist that the two nations should live in friendship from generation to generation by taking history as a mirror to guide the growth of ties between the countries into the future."

22. Interview, Beijing, August 10, 2009.

23. Abe had always been skeptical of the claim that Japan's military coerced "comfort women" throughout Asia to serve as "sex slaves." He openly challenged this claim in March 2007, during his first term as prime minister, and appeared to do so again early in his second term (2014) when he commissioned a review of the Kono statement. He also questioned the conventional wisdom that Japan had invaded China in 1937, arguing that there is no commonly shared definition of "invasion." See Shoji (2015).

24. *New York Times*, November 10, 2014.

25. *Guardian*, June 1, 2016.

26. *Guardian*, January 18, 2017.

27. See Yoshida (1998: 138–40).

28. See Tian (1997: 103–4).

29. *New York Times*, October 24, 1992.

30. Mikyoung Kim (2008) provides data for subsequent years, including 1992, in "Myths, Milieu, and Facts: History Textbook Controversies," in Hasegawa and Togo, *East Asia's Haunted Present*. See figure 5.1 on p. 107. She cites "Shiyan Zhongguo Diaocha Wang" (China Japan Joint Poll), for years 1988–2002. I was unable to replicate her data set.

31. See Yamazaki (2006: 74–75, 148). She adds that right-wing groups (such as the Izokukai) and some LDP politicians criticized Hosokawa for his apology, which may have led him to refer to "acts of aggression" (rather than "war of aggression") in future statements. But she (p. 87) and Berger (2012: 181–82) also note that Japanese citizens overwhelmingly supported the prime minister.

32. The 1994 visit to Beijing is covered nicely by Austin and Harris (2001: 56).

33. See Wang Xiaodong and Wu Luping (1995).

34. See Amako (1998: 24). The December 1996 survey by *China Youth Daily* found that 14.5 percent had a good or very good impression of Japan; 41.5 percent had a poor or very poor impression. Others were just indifferent.

35. See Zhao (1993: 168).

36. See Hatch (2010: 80).

37. *New York Times*, August 14, 2015.

38. Statistics come from the World Bank's WITS data bank.

39. Seguchi (2021). Also see *The Economist* (November 19, 2019): https://www.economist.com/business/2019/11/09/japan-inc-has-thrived-in-china-of-late

40. See Japan External Trade Organization statistics at https://www.jetro.go.jp/en/reports/statistics.html

41. See China Statistical Yearbooks at http://www.stats.gov.cn

42. Armstrong (2010) offers some countervailing evidence.

43. Although CASS was responsible for both surveys, it may have used very different methodologies from one to the next. We know that its methodology was consistent between 2002 and 2010.

44. Media outlets generated many reports on this summit. See, for example, Yu Xiaodong, "China-Japan Relationship Back on Track," in *NewsChina*, January 2019: 12–15; and Shi Jiangtao, "China-Japan ties at 'historic turning point' after Shinzo Abe's visit, but can the goodwill hold?" in *South China Morning Post*, October 28, 2018, available at: www.scmp.com/news/china/diplomacy/article/2170469/china-japan-ties-historic-turning-point-after-shinzo-abes-visit

45. Although he maintained close personal relations with Prime Minister Abe, Trump falsely accused Japan of manipulating its currency, and continued to complain that it engages in unfair trade. In 2018, he called for steep tariffs on steel imports from Japan, but later granted several exemptions to the policy. Despite a similarly good personal relationship with President Xi, Trump also was fiercely critical of China, calling it a "strategic competitor" that uses "predatory" policies to achieve power. In 2018, he called for $50 billion in tariffs on a variety of Chinese products. China retaliated with its own tariffs on U.S. products. The trade war escalated with both sides proposing new or increased tariffs, but these were suspended in early 2020.

46. Komori (2006: 143) writes that "China and Japan have 'competed to cooperate' with ASEAN countries through the chain-reaction of their respective overtures to ASEAN."

47. Interview, Shanghai, July 13, 2006.

48. Interview, Tokyo, July 7, 2011, augmented by communication in July 2021. See also Tsugami (2003).

CHAPTER 7

A version of this chapter appeared in Min-hyung Kim and James A. Caporaso, eds., *Power Relations and Comparative Regionalism: Europe, East Asia, and Latin America* (New York: Routledge, 2022). Reproduced by permission of Taylor & Francis Group.

1. The IMF accords voting rights to states based on their financial contributions to the intergovernmental organization over time. The U.S. has about 17 percent of IMF voting rights—far more than any other state. (Germany and Japan each have about 6%.) Given that a "significant" decision by the Board of Governors requires an 85 percent supermajority, the U.S. is the only state with veto power in the IMF.

2. U.S. secretary of state John Foster Dulles coined the term "hub-and-spokes" to describe the pattern of American-led bilateral alliances with subordinate Asian allies.

3. If we include "Oceania" as part of Asia (and leaders in Oceania increasingly do), the 1951 ANZUS treaty set up the only multilateral security alliance in the region. It also happens to include the region's only majority-white countries: Australia and New Zealand.

4. "Humanities" or "Western Civilization" courses tend to start with the Greeks (Socrates and Sophocles), move through Italy (Dante), Germany (Goethe), France (Voltaire), and Great Britain (Chaucer and Shakespeare), and end up in the United States with Longfellow or perhaps Twain.

5. Robert Vitalis (2015) reminds us that *Foreign Affairs*, which published Buell's piece and remains the preeminent U.S. policy publication on international relations, was originally called the *Journal of Race Development*.

6. See Bernal (1994: 126).

7. See U.S. Senate (1949), "North Atlantic Treaty: Hearings Before the Committee on Foreign Relations," 81st Congress, 1st Session. Washington D.C., S. 206.

8. Of course, this "community" did not always exist. It was, like most things, socially constructed in the hothouse of interstate conflict. Before World War II, Henrikson (1975) notes, world maps drawn in the U.S. tended to show the cartographer's home country in the center, surrounded by two oceans. But in the early 1940s, as the U.S. first shipped supplies and then troops to besieged Europe, those maps began to take on a new form, with the Atlantic Ocean in the middle of a world apparently pivoting around the United States on "the west" and Europe on "the east."

9. U.S. Senate 1949, p. 380.

10. From his radio address to the nation, September 10, 1988 (*Public Papers of the Presidents of the United States*, p. 1152).

11. See Charles Yu (2020) for a fictional take on Hollywood's infantilization of Asian Americans.

12. Miller 1982: 134.

13. See Karnow (1989: 167–95).

14. See U.S. Senate, "Hearings before the Committee on Armed Services and the Committee on Foreign Relations," *Military Situation in the Far East*, May 1951, part 1, especially p. 312. To be fair, I should note that some Americans, including

John Foster Dulles, feared the strategic consequences of such racialized arrogance. At the same time, I will add that the Cold Warrior's view was an instrumentalist one that might not have reflected his actual feelings. He was concerned that Western attitudes might produce an antiwhite, procommunist backlash. See Koshiro (1999: 44).

15. MacArthur, of course, had also grossly underestimated Japanese military capabilities at the very start of World War II. Dower (1986: 105) notes that the general was stunned when, nine days after the attack on Pearl Harbor, Japanese warplanes wiped out his air force in the Philippines. He "refused to believe that the pilots could have been Japanese"; instead, he "insisted they must have been white mercenaries." But MacArthur was in good company. Dower (1986: 102–3) quotes other U.S. military analysts, including Fletcher Pratt, who—before Pearl Harbor—embraced rather complex racial theories about why the Japanese could not effectively wage war.

16. The friend who quoted Acheson was Walt Whitman Rostow, the development economist who worked closely with the U.S. State Department. See Isaacson and Thomas (1986: 698).

17. James Dao, "The World: Why Keep U.S. Troops?" *New York Times*, January 5, 2003.

18. Kevin Maher apparently made the remarks in a briefing to a group of American University students. Shortly after a report surfaced, Maher and the State Department complained that the remarks were made "off the record," but did not deny them. Much later, after he was dismissed, Maher gave an interview in which he called the report of his comments a "fabrication." But a professor who attended the briefing backed up his AU students. See David Vine, "Smearing Japan," at http://fpif.org/smearing_japan/

19. See, for example, Sloan 2005.

20. The exception came in early 2003, when the leaders of France and Germany came out firmly in opposition to President George W. Bush's planned invasion of Iraq. U.S. Defense Secretary Donald Rumsfeld said the two powers represented "Old Europe." Bush's successor, Barack Obama, worked hard to restore close relations with European allies; he was, on transatlantic policy, a proponent of old-fashioned multilateralism. Obama's successor, Donald Trump, campaigned as a unilateralist ("America First"), but after four years in office had only managed to weaken rather than irrevocably damage ties with Europe. Joe Biden, who defeated Trump in 2020, renewed transatlanticism.

21. See U.S. State Department (Acting Director of the Office of German and Austrian Affairs) 1949, p. 121.

22. Italy also joined NATO that year.

23. See transcript of Obama press conference with French president, April 3, 2009: https://www.govinfo.gov/content/pkg/PPP-2009-book1/pdf/PPP-2009-book1-doc-pg409.pdf

24. Whitelaw Reid, a member of the Peace Commission for the Philippines, may have been the first to describe the Pacific as an "American Lake"—in 1898. See McCormick (1967: 119). Within years, the term was de rigueur among expansionists (Beale 1962). MacArthur recast and racialized the concept in a 1949 speech (see Whiting 1968: 39).

25. The U.S. viewed Japan at this time as a fellow imperialist. In 1905, through the Taft-Katsura memorandum, it informally acknowledged Japanese control over the Korean Peninsula in exchange for Japan's recognition of U.S. control over the Philippines.

26. JCS Memorandum for Truman (September 9, 1947), FRUS 1947, Vol. 1, pp. 766–67, as quoted in Schaller (1985: 56–57).

27. In 1979, the U.S. normalized relations with mainland China and moved to end its treaty with Taiwan. At the same time, though, it adopted the Taiwan Relations Act, promising to supply defensive weaponry to the island.

28. Report of the Committee on Asian Regional Economic Development and Cooperation (chaired by Kenneth T. Young), U.S. Council on Foreign Economic Policy, Office of the Chairman, Special Studies Series, Box 3, Dwight D. Eisenhower Library, Abilene, KS, p. 1. Quoted in Hoshiro (2009: 402).

29. Quoted in *The Economist*, April 22, 2017: 6.

30. "A free and open Indo-Pacific region provides prosperity and security for all," according to the U.S. Defense Department (2018: 9), identifying China as a threat. "We will strengthen our alliances and partnerships in the Indo-Pacific to a networked security architecture capable of deterring aggression, maintaining stability, and ensuring free access to common domains."

31. See military.com, "Here's what it costs to keep U.S. troops in Japan and South Korea," March 23, 2021: https://www.military.com/daily-news/2021/03/23/heres-what-it-costs-keep-us-troops-japan-and-south-korea.html

32. I examine alternative explanations for this puzzle in Hatch (2022: 118–19).

CHAPTER 8

1. Interview with the author, Tokyo, June 29, 2006.

2. https://www.aicgs.org/events/2009/05/reconciliation-or-resentment/

3. https://aparc.fsi.stanford.edu/news/conference_compares_wartime_experiences_in_asia_and_europe_20110822

4. See Feldman (2006). Many other authors have also cited German "lessons" for Japan. For example, see Borggräfe (2011), who holds up the example of German compensation to victims of forced labor.

5. This has led to renewed calls from Greece for Germany to pay reparations for World War II, even though it settled claims long ago. See, for example, DW (Deutsche Welle), "Greece calls on Germany to negotiate over war reparations," April 6, 2019; available at https://www.dw.com/en/greece-calls-on-germany-to-negotiate-over-war-reparations/a-49059996

6. Interview with the author, Yokohama, July 3, 2006. For a fuller explication, see Tamamoto (2005/6).

References

Acheson, Dean. 1969. *Present at the Creation: My Years in the State Department*. New York: Norton.

Adenauer, Konrad. 1966. *Memoirs: 1945–1953*. Chicago: Regnery.

Alexander, J. C., and R. Gao. 2007. "Remembrance of Things Past: Cultural Trauma, the 'Nanking Massacre' and Chinese Identity." In *Tradition and Modernity: Comparative Perspectives*. Beijing: Peking University Press.

Amako, Satoshi. 1998. "Yuko ippento kara no tenkan" (Shifting from Reliance on Friendship). In *Nicchuu Kōryū no Shihanseki* (A Quarter Century of Sino-Japanese Exchange), edited by Amako Satoshi and Sonoda Shigeto. Tokyo: Tōyō Keizei Shinpōsha.

Armstrong, Shiro. 2010. "Interaction between Trade, Conflict and Cooperation: The Case of Japan and China." Canberra (ANU, Australia-Japan Research Centre): Asia-Pacific Economic Papers, No. 386.

Arrington, Celeste L., and Andrew Yeo. 2019. "Japan and South Korea Can't Get Along: Why America Needs to Help Its Allies Mend Fences." *Foreign Affairs* (July 31).

Asian Development Bank (ADB). 2022. "Asian Economic Integration Report 2022: Advancing Digital Services Trade in Asia and the Pacific." (February). https://www.adb.org/sites/default/files/publication/770436/asian-economic-integration-report-2022.pdf

Attali, Jacques. 1995. *Verbatim*. Vol. 3. Paris: Fayard.

Austin, Greg, and Stuart Harris. 2001. *Japan and Greater China: Political Economy and Military Power in the Asian Century*. Honolulu: University of Hawai'i Press.

Axelrod, Robert, and William D. Hamilton. 1981. "The Evolution of Cooperation." *Science* 211, no. 4489 (March): 1390–96.

Banchoff, Thomas. 1997. "German Policy towards the European Union: The Effects of Historical Memory." *German Politics* 6, no. 1 (March): 60–76.

Bandelj, Nina. 2007. "Supraterritoriality, Embeddedness, or Both? Foreign Direct

Investment in Central and Eastern Europe." In *Globalization: Perspectives from Central and Eastern Europe*, edited by Katalin Fábián. Oxford, UK: Elsevier.

Barbieri, Katherine. 2002. *The Liberal Illusion: Does Trade Promote Peace?* Ann Arbor: University of Michigan Press.

Baritz, Loren. 1985. *Backfire: A History of How American Culture Led Us into Vietnam and Made Us Fight the Way We Did*. New York: William Morrow.

Barkan, Elazar. 2000. *The Guilt of Nations: Restitution and Negotiating Historical Injustices*. New York: W. W. Norton.

Beale, Howard K. 1962. *Theodore Roosevelt and the Rise of America to World Power*. New York: Collier Books.

Beckmann, George M. 1962. *The Modernization of China and Japan*. New York: Harper & Row.

Beeson, Mark. 2005. "Rethinking Regionalism: Europe and East Asia in Comparative Historical Perspective." *Journal of European Public Policy* 12, no. 6: 969–85.

Benedict, Ruth. 1946. *The Chrysanthemum and the Sword: Patterns of Japanese Culture*. New York: Houghton Mifflin.

Berger, Thomas U. 2012. *War, Guilt, and World Politics after World War II*. New York: Cambridge University Press.

Bernal, Martin. 1994. "The Image of Ancient Greece as a Tool for Colonialism and European Hegemony." In *Social Construction of the Past: Representation as Power*, edited by George C. Bond and Angela Gilliam. London: Routledge.

Bi, Shihong. 2017. "China and Japan, in the Mekong Region: Competition and Cooperation." In *China-Japan Relations in the 21st Century: Antagonism Despite Interdependency*, edited by Lam Peng Er. Singapore: Palgrave Macmillan.

Blackbourn, David. 2000. "Conquests from Barbarism: Interpreting Land Reclamation in 18th Century Prussia." International Congress of Historical Sciences, Oslo.

Bledowski, Krzysztof. 2018. "How Poland and Germany Can Close Ranks." *The Globalist* (March 21). https://www.theglobalist.com/germany-poland-european-union-fiscal-policy-ecb-eurozone/

Borggräfe, Henning. 2011. "Compensation as a Mechanism of Reconciliation? Lessons from the German Payments for Nazi Forced and Slave Labor." *AICGS Transatlantic Perspectives* (October). https://www.aicgs.org/publication/compensati on-as-a-mechanism-of-reconciliation-lessons-from-the-german-payments-for-nazi-forced-and-slave-labor/

Boulding, Kenneth E. 1978. *Stable Peace*. Austin: University of Texas Press.

Brandt, Willy. 1992. *My Life in Politics*. New York: Viking.

Buell, Raymond Leslie. 1923. "Again the Yellow Peril." *Foreign Affairs* 2, no. 2 (December): 295–309.

Buras, Piotr. 2013. *Poland-Germany: Partnership for Europe? Interests, Opinions of Elites, Prospects*. Warsaw: Centre for International Relations.

Buras, Piotr, and Josef Janning. 2018. "Divided at the Centre: Germany, Poland, and the Troubles of the Trump Era." Policy brief for the European Council on Foreign Relations (December 19). https://www.ecfr.eu/publications/summary/div ided_at_the_centre_germany_poland_and_the_troubles_of_the_trump_era

Buruma, Ian. 2002. *The Wages of Guilt: Memories of War in Germany and Japan*. London: Phoenix, Orion Books.

Campbell, Edwina S. 1989. *Germany's Past and Europe's Future*. Washington, DC: Pergamon-Brassey's.

Caporaso, James A. 2022. "Germany and the Eurozone Crisis: Power, Dominance and Hegemony." In *Power Relations and Comparative Regionalism: Europe, East Asia and Latin America*, edited by Min-hyung Kim and James A. Caporaso, 18–43. New York: Routledge.

Carroll, Ross. 2008. *The Politics of Culpability: Apology and Forgiveness in International Society*. Ljubljana: University of Ljubljana.

Central Commission for the Investigation of German Crimes in Poland. 1982. *German Crimes in Poland*. New York: Howard Fertig.

Chessa, Cecilia. 2004. "State Subsidies, International Diffusion, and Transnational Civil Society: The Case of Frankfurt-Oder and Słubice." *East European Politics and Societies* 18, no. 1: 70–109.

Chōn, Yō-ok. 1993. *Ilbon-un ōpt'a* (The Japan that Does Not Exist). Seoul: Chisik kongjaksō.

Coffey, Luke. 2013. "EU Defense Integration: Undermining NATO, Transatlantic Relations, and Europe's Security." Background #2806 (June 6) for the Heritage Foundation. http://www.heritage.org/research/reports/2013/06/eu-defense-integration-undermining-nato-transatlantic-relations-and-europes-security

Conrad, Sebastian. 2003. "Entangled Memories: Versions of the Past in Germany and Japan, 1945–2001." *Journal of Contemporary History* 38, no. 1: 85–99.

Davies, Norman. 1982. *God's Playground: A History of Poland*. Vol. II: *1795 to the Present*. New York: Columbia University Press.

Davis, Patricia A. 1999. *The Art of Economic Persuasion: Positive Incentives and German Economic Diplomacy*. Ann Arbor: University of Michigan Press.

Davis, Patricia, and Peter Dombrowski. 1997. "Appetite of the Wolf: German Foreign Assistance for Central and Eastern Europe." *German Politics* 6, no. 1 (April): 1–22.

Dent, Christopher M. 2010. "Organizing the Wider East Asia Region." ADB Working Paper Series on Regional Economic Integration, No. 62 (November).

Deutsch, Karl W., Lewis J. Edinger, Roy C. Macridis, and Richard L. Merritt, 1967. *France, Germany and the Western Alliance: A Study of Elite Attitudes on European Integration and World Politics*. New York: Charles Scribner's Sons.

Dixon, Jennifer M. *Dark Pasts: Changing the State's Story in Turkey and Japan*. Ithaca: Cornell University Press, 2018.

Dower, John W. 1986. *War Without Mercy: Race and Power in the Pacific War*. New York: Pantheon Books.

Dreyer, June Teufel. 2014. "China and Japan: Hot Economics, Cold Politics." *Orbis* 58, no. 3: 326–41.

Drinnon, Richard. 1990. *Facing West: The Metaphysics of Indian-Hating and Empire Building*. New York: Schocken Books.

Dudden, Alexis. 2008. *Troubled Apologies: Among Japan, Korea, and the United States*. New York: Columbia University Press.

Duffield, John. 2001. "Why Is There No APTO? Why Is There No OSCAP? Asia-Pacific Security Institutions in Comparative Perspective." *Contemporary Security Policy* 22, no. 2: 69–95.

European Commission. 2013. "European Economy: Macroeconomic Imbalances:

France 2013." Occasional Papers #136 (April).http://ec.europa.eu/economy_fina nce/publications/occasional_paper/2013/pdf/ocp136_en.pdf

Eykolt, Mark. 2000. "Aggression, Victimization, and Chinese Historiography in the Nanjing Massacre." In *The Nanjing Massacre in History*, edited by Joshua Fogel. Berkeley: University of California Press.

Fairbank, John K. 1966. *United States Policy with Respect to Mainland China, Testimony before the U.S. Senate Committee on Foreign Relations* (March). Washington, DC: U.S. Government Printing Office.

Feldman, Lily Gardner. 1999. "The Principle and Practice of 'Reconciliation' in German Foreign Policy: Relations with France, Israel, Poland and the Czech Republic." *International Affairs* 75, no. 2: 333–56.

Feldman, Lily Gardner. 2006. "Germany's External Reconciliation as a Defining Feature of Foreign Policy: Lessons for Japan?" *AICGS Advisor* (April 28).

Feldman, Lily Gardner. 2012. *Germany's Foreign Policy of Reconciliation: From Enmity to Amity*. Lanham, MD: Rowman and Littlefield.

Feng, Zhaokui. 1992. "Riben fazhan he yinjin jishu de gishi" (Lessons from Japan's Development and Technology Transfer). *Riben Xuekan* (Japan Studies), 5.

Feng, Zhaokui. 2006. "Geopolitical Causes of Sino-Japanese Tension." *China Daily* (February 24): 4.

Fiske, John. 1885. *American Political Ideas: Viewed from the Standpoint of Universal History*. Boston: Houghton Mifflin.

Freudenstein, Roland. 1998. "Poland, Germany and the EU." *International Affairs* 74, no. 1: 41–54.

Friedberg, Aaron L. 1993/94. "Ripe for Rivalry: Prospects for Peace in a Multipolar Asia." *International Security* 18, no. 3 (Winter): 5–33.

Fure, Jorunn Sem. 1997. "The German-Polish Border Region: A Case of Regional Integration?" *ARENA Working Papers*. WP 97/19.

Gardiner, Nile, and Morgan Lorraine Roach. 2009. "Barack Obama's Top 10 Apologies: How the President Has Humiliated a Superpower." *Heritage Foundation Report* (June 2). https://www.heritage.org/europe/report/barack-obamas-top-10-apologies-how-the-president-has-humiliated-superpower

Gauthier and Deschamps. 1923. *Cours d'histoire de France* (History of France). Paris: Librairie Hachette.

Gebert, Konstanty, and Ulrike Guérot. 2012. "Why Poland Is the New France for Germany." *Open Democracy* (October 17). https://www.opendemocracy.net/en /why-poland-is-new-france-for-germany/

George, Alexander. 2000. "Foreword." In *Stable Peace Among Nations*, edited by Arie M. Kacowicz et al., xi–xvii. Lanham, MD: Rowman & Littlefield.

Gildea, Robert. 2002a. "Myth, Memory and Policy in France Since 1945." In *Memory and Power in Post-War Europe: Studies in the Presence of the Past*, edited by Jan-Werner Muller. Cambridge: Cambridge University Press.

Gildea, Robert. 2002b. *France Since 1945*. Oxford: Oxford University Press.

Gould, Erica R., and Stephen D. Krasner. 2003. "Germany and Japan: Binding versus Autonomy." In *The End of Diversity? Prospects for German and Japanese Capitalism*, edited by Kozo Yamamura and Wolfgang Streeck, 51–88. Ithaca: Cornell University Press.

Grimmer-Solem, Erik. 2012. "National Identity in the Vanquished State: German and Japanese Postwar Historiography from a Transnational Perspective." *History and Theory* 51, (May): 280–91.

Grosser, Alfred. 1967. *French Foreign Policy Under de Gaulle.* Translated by Lois Ames Pattison. Boston: Little, Brown.

Gustafsson, Karl. 2015. "Identity and Recognition: Remembering and Forgetting the Postwar in Sino-Japanese Relations." *Pacific Review* 28, no. 1: 117–38.

Haigneré, Claudie. 2004. "Coopération Franco-Allemande et Europe Élargie: Une Coopération Ouverte au Service de L'Union" (Franco-German Cooperation and European Enlargement: Open Cooperation for the Benefit of the EU). *Documents: Revue des Questions Allemandes* 59, no. 3: 69–91.

Hatch, Walter. 2010. *Asia's Flying Geese: How Regionalization Shapes Japan.* Ithaca: Cornell University Press.

Hatch, Walter. 2014. "Bloody Memories: Affect and Effect of War Museums in China and Japan." *Peace & Change* 39, no. 4: 366–94.

Hatch, Walter. 2022. "European Integration, Asian Subordination: U.S. Identity and Power in Two Regions." In *Power Relations and Comparative Regionalism: Europe, East Asia, and Latin America*, edited by Min-hyung Kim and James A. Caporaso, 103–26. New York: Routledge.

Hayner, Priscilla B. 2010. *Unspeakable Truths: Transitional Justice and the Challenge of Truth Commissions.* London: Routledge.

He, Yinan. 2003. "National Mythmaking and the Problems of History in Sino-Japanese Relations." Paper delivered at the Conference on Memory of War (January 24–25), MIT.

He, Yinan. 2009. *The Search for Reconciliation: Sino-Japanese and German-Polish Relations since World War II.* New York: Cambridge University Press.

Heginbotham, Eric, and Richard Samuels. 2018. "With Friends Like These: Japan-ROK Cooperation and U.S. Policy." Open Forum, *Asan Forum* (March 1). http://www.theasanforum.org/with-friends-like-these-japan-rok-cooperation-and-us-policy/

Hemmer, Christopher, and Peter J. Katzenstein. 2002. "Why Is There No NATO in Asia? Collective Identity, Regionalism and the Origins of Multilateralism." *International Organization* 56, no. 3 (Summer): 575–607.

Henrikson, Alan K. 1975. "The Map as an Idea: The Role of Cartographic Imagery During the Second World War." *American Cartographer* 2, no. 1: 19–53.

Heo, Seunghoon Emilia. 2012. *Reconciling Enemy States in Europe and Asia.* Hampshire, UK: Palgrave Macmillan.

Herf, Jeffrey. 1997. *Divided Memory: The Nazi Past in the Two Germanys.* Cambridge, MA: Harvard University Press.

Heuser, Beatrice. 1998. "Historical Lessons and Discourse on Defence in France and Germany, 1945–90." *Rethinking History* 2, no. 2: 199–237.

Hitchcock, William I. 1998. *France Restored: Cold War Diplomacy and the Quest for Leadership in Europe, 1944–1954.* Chapel Hill: University of North Carolina Press.

Hoshiro, Hiroyuki. 2009. "Co-Prosperity Sphere Again? United States Foreign Policy and Japan's 'First' Regionalism in the 1950s." *Pacific Affairs* 82, no. 3 (Fall): 385–405.

Hughes, Christopher. 2004. "The U.S.-Japan Alliance and the False Promises,

Premises, and Pretences of Multilateralism in East Asia." Unpublished paper for "International Conference on Creating an East Asian Community: Prospects and Challenges for Fresh Regional Cooperation." National University of Singapore (January).

Hull, Isabel V. 2005. *Absolute Destruction: Military Culture and the Practices of War in Imperial Germany*. Ithaca: Cornell University Press.

Hunt, Michael H. 1987. *Ideology and U.S. Foreign Policy*. New Haven: Yale University Press.

Huntington, Samuel P. 1996. *The Clash of Civilizations and the Remaking of World Order*. New York: Simon and Schuster.

Hyde-Price, Adrian. 2000. *Germany and European Order: Enlarging NATO and the EU*. Manchester: Manchester University Press.

Ikenberry, G. John. 2001. *After Victory: Institutions, Strategic Restraint, and the Rebuilding of Order After Major Wars*. Princeton: Princeton University Press.

Isaacson, Walter, and Evan Thomas. 1986. *The Wise Men: Six Friends and the World They Made*. New York: Touchstone.

Jackson, Patrick Thaddeus. 2006. *Civilizing the Enemy: German Reconstruction and the Invention of the West*. Ann Arbor: University of Michigan Press.

Jacobsen, Hans-Adolf, and Tomala Mieczysław. 1992. *Bonn-Warschau: 1945–1991. Die deutsch-polnischen Beziehungen, Analyse und Dokumentation* (Bonn-Warsaw, 1945–1991. The German-Polish Relationship: Analysis and Documentation). Cologne: Verlag Wissenschaft und Politik.

Jiang, Lifeng. 1989. "Zhongri lianhe jinxing de shehui yunlun diaocha shuoming le shenme" (Survey of Public Opinion on the Process of China-Japan Relations). *Riben Wenti* (Japan Studies) 2: 22–26.

Kansteiner, Wulf. 2006. "Losing the War, Winning the Memory Battle: The Legacy of Nazism, World War II, and the Holocaust in the Federal Republic of Germany." In *The Politics of Memory in Postwar Europe*, edited by Richard Ned Lebow, Wulf Kansteiner, and Claudio Fogu. Durham: Duke University Press.

Karatani, Kōjin. 1993. "The Discursive Space of Modern Japan." In *Japan in the World*, edited by Masao Miyoshi and Harry D. Harootunian, 288–316. Durham: Duke University Press.

Karnow, Stanley. 1989. *In Our Image: America's Empire in the Philippines*. New York: Random House.

Kawashima Shin. 2018. "Kankei 'Seijōka' no—koda to shite Abe hōchū" (Abe's Visit to China: An Effort to Normalize Relations). *Asahi Shinbun (WebRonza)* (October 30). https://webronza.asahi.com/politics/articles/2018102900003.html

Keene, Donald. 1971. *Landscapes and Portraits: Appreciations of Japanese Culture*. Tokyo: Kodansha International.

Kennan, George F. 1967. *Memoirs: 1925–1950*. Boston: Little, Brown.

Keohane, Robert. 1984. *After Hegemony: Cooperation and Discord in the World Political Economy*. Princeton: Princeton University Press.

Kim, Jin-myung. 1993. *Mugunghwa kkochi pieot seumnida* (The Rose of Sharon Blooms Again). Seoul: Saeum.

Kim, Jiyoon, Karl Friedhoff, and Chungku Kang. 2012. "The Asan Monthly Opinion Survey, July 2012." Seoul: Asan Institute for Policy Studies.

Kim, Mikyoung. 2008. "Myths, Milieu, and Facts: History Textbook Controversies in Northeast Asia." In *East Asia's Haunted Present: Historical Memories and the Resurgence of Nationalism*, edited by Tsuyoshi Hasegawa and Kazuhiko Togo, 94–118. Westport, CT: Praeger.

Kimura, Kan. 2013. "Nikkan kankei shūfuku ga muzukashii hontō no riyū" (The Real Reason Why It Is So Difficult to Repair Japan-Korea Relations). Nippon. com (December 20). https://www.nippon.com/ja/in-depth/a02701/

Kimura, Kan. 2019. *The Burden of the Past: Problems of Historical Perception in Japan-Korea Relations*. Translated by Marie Speed. Ann Arbor: University of Michigan Press.

Komori, Yasumasa. 2006. "The New Dynamics of East Asian Regional Economy: Japanese and Chinese Strategies in Asia." *Pacific Focus* 21, no. 2 (Fall): 107–49.

Komori, Yoshihisa. 2018. "Taichū ODA: sengo saidaikyū shippai" (Foreign Aid to China: Japan's Biggest Postwar Failure). *Sankei Shinbun* (October 26). https://www.sankei.com/world/news/181026/wor1810260002-n1.html

Koo, Min Gyo. 2005. "Economic Interdependence and the Dokdo/Takeshima Dispute between South Korea and Japan." *Harvard Asia Quarterly* 9, no. 4: 24–35.

Koshiro, Yukiko. 1999. *Trans-Pacific Racisms and the U.S. Occupation of Japan*. New York: Columbia University Press.

Ku, Yangmo. 2008. "International Reconciliation in the Postwar Era, 1945–2005: A Comparative Study of Japan-ROK and Franco-German Relations." *Asian Perspective* 32, no. 3: 5–37.

Kulski, W.W. 1976. *Germany and Poland: From War to Peaceful Relations*. Syracuse, NY: Syracuse University Press.

Kuwahara, Yasue. 2014. "Hanryu: Korean Popular Culture in Japan." In *The Korean Wave: Korean Popular Culture in Global Context*, edited by Yasue Kuwahara, 213–21. New York: Palgrave Macmillan.

Lam, Peng Er. 2006. *Japan's Relations with China: Facing a Rising Power*. Sheffield, UK: Routledge.

Lavisse, Ernest. 1921. *Nouveau cours d'histoire. Histoire de France: cours moyen* (A New History of France: For Primary Students). Paris: Librairie Armand Colin.

Lebioda, Tadeusz. 2000. "Poland, *die Vertriebenen*, and the Road to Integration with the European Union." In *Poland and the European Union*, edited by Karl Cordell. London: Routledge.

Lee, Chong-sik. 1985. *Japan and Korea: The Political Dimension*. Stanford: Stanford University Press.

Lee, Jung-bok. 1992. "The Japan Problem and Korea-Japan Relations." Unpublished paper prepared for the Korea-Japan Intellectual Exchange Conference, Seoul, June 11–14.

Lee, Jung-hoon. 1990. "Korean-Japanese Relations: The Past, Present and Future." *Korea Observer* 21, no. 2 (Summer): 159–78.

Lieberson, Stanley. 1991. "Small Ns and Big Conclusions: An Examination of the Reasoning in Comparative Studies Based on a Small Number of Cases." *Social Forces* 70, no. 2: 307–20.

Lind, Jennifer. 2008. *Sorry States: Apologies in International Politics*. Ithaca: Cornell University Press.

Lind, Jennifer. 2009. "The Perils of Apology: What Japan Shouldn't Learn from Germany." *Foreign Affairs* 88, no. 3 (May–June): 132–46.

Lind, Jennifer. 2013. "Sorry, I'm Not Sorry: The Perils of Apology in International Relations." *Foreign Affairs* (November 21). https://www.foreignaffairs.com/articl es/united-states/2013-11-21/sorry-im-not-sorry

Lindner, Evelin. 2006. *Making Enemies: Humiliation and International Conflict*. Westport, CT: Praeger Security International.

Lippmann, Walter. 1947. *The Cold War: A Study in U.S. Foreign Policy*. New York: Harper & Brothers.

Lipski, Jan Józef. 1996. "Polen, Deutsche und Europa" (Poland, Germany and Europe). In *Wir Müssen uns Alles Sagen: Essays zur Deutsch-Polnischen Nachbarschaft* (We Have to Tell Each Other: Essays on the German-Polish Neighborhood), edited by J. J. Lipski, 253–64. Warsaw: Deutsch-Polnischer Verlag.

Lipson, Charles. 1984. "International Cooperation in Economic and Security Affairs." *World Politics* 37, no. 1 (October): 1–23.

Lochner, Louise Paul. 1942. *What About Germany?* New York: Dodd, Mead and Co.

Love, Mervyn T. 1995. *Peace Building Through Reconciliation in Northern Ireland*. Aldershot, UK: Avebury.

Lu, Huiru. 1998. "An Analysis of Japan's ODA Loans to China." In *Riben wenti yanjiu* (Studies in Japanese Affairs), no. 1. Quoted in Austin and Harris (2001: 175).

Lundestad, Geir. 2003. *The United States and Western Europe Since 1945*. Oxford: Oxford University Press.

Ma, Licheng. 2002. "Dui-Ri guanxi xin siwei" (New Thinking on Sino-Japanese Relations). *Zhanlüe yu Guanli* (Strategy and Management), no. 6 (December): 41–56.

Ma, Yi. 2006. *Chou lou de Riben ren* (The Ugly Japanese). Jinan: Shandong Publishing House.

Maillard, Pierre. 1990. *De Gaulle et l'Allemagne: Le rêve inacheve*. Paris: Plon.

Malet, A., and P. Grillet. 1925. *XIXe Siècle: Histoire Contemporaine (1815–1920)*. Paris: Librairie Hachette.

Marcussen, Martin, Thomas Risse, Daniela Engelmann-Martin, Hans-Joakim Knopf, and Klaus Roscher. 1999. "Constructing Europe? The Evolution of French, British and German Nation-State Identities." *Journal of European Public Policy* 6, no. 4: 614–33.

Markovits, Andrei S., and Simon Reich. 1997. *The German Predicament: Memory and Power in the New Europe*. Ithaca: Cornell University Press.

Marten-Finnis, Susanne. 1995. "Collective Memory and National Identities: German and Polish Memory Cultures: The Forms of Collective Memory." *Communist and Post-Communist Studies* 28, no. 2: 255–61.

Martens, Stephan. 2002-3. "Pour un nouveau prisme d'analyse de l'entente franco-allemande" (Toward a New Analytical Framework for Understanding the Franco-German Alliance). *La revue internationale et strategique* 48 (Winter): 13–21.

Martens, Stephan. 2003. "Les relations franco-allemandes depuis 1963." *Notes et Etudes Documentaires* no. 5174-75: 39–63.

McCormack, Gavan. 1996. *The Emptiness of Japanese Affluence*. Armonk, NY: M. E. Sharpe.

McCormick, Thomas. 1967. *China Market*. Chicago: Quadrangle.

McLauchlan, Alastair. 2001. "Korea/Japan or Japan/Korea? The Saga of Co-hosting the 2002 Soccer World Cup." *Journal of Historical Sociology* 14, no. 4 (December): 481–507.

McLelland, Mark J. 2008. "'Race' on the Japanese Internet: Discussing Korea and Koreans on '2-Channeru.'" *New Media Society* 10, no. 6: 811–29.

McNamara, Dennis L. 1990. *The Colonial Origins of Korean Enterprise: 1910–1945*. New York: Cambridge University Press.

Merritt, Richard L., and Donald J. Puchala. 1968. *Western European Perspectives on International Affairs: Public Opinion Studies and Evaluations*. New York: Praeger.

Miller, Gary J. 1992. *Managerial Dilemmas: The Political Economy of Hierarchy*. New York: Cambridge University Press.

Miller, Stuart Creighton. 1982. *Benevolent Assimilation: The American Conquest of the Philippines, 1899–1903*. New Haven: Yale University Press.

Ministry of Foreign Affairs (Japan). 2008. "Joint Statement between the Government of Japan and the Government of the People's Republic of China on the Comprehensive Promotion of a 'Mutually Beneficial Relationship Based on Common Strategic Interests.'" (May 7). http://www.mofa.go.jp/region/asia-paci/china/joint0805.html

Moravcsik, Andrew. 1998. *The Choice for Europe: Social Purpose and State Power from Messina to Maastricht*. Ithaca: Cornell University Press.

Nagy, Stephen R. 2018. "Is Trump Pushing China and Japan Together? Not Quite." *National Interest* (October 25). https://nationalinterest.org/feature/trump-pushing-china-and-japan-together-not-quite-34302

Newnham, Randall E. 2005. "Germany and Poland in the EU Enlargement Process." *Canadian American Slavic Studies* 39, no. 4 (Winter): 469–88.

Newnham, Randall E. 2007. "Globalization and National Interest in EU Enlargement: The Case of Germany and Poland." In *Globalization: Perspectives from Central and Eastern Europe*, edited by Katalin Fábián. Oxford, UK: Elsevier.

Nye, Joseph S., Jr. 2010. "An Alliance Larger than One Issue." *New York Times*, 7 January.

Ogburn, Charlton. 1953. "Memorandum by the Regional Planning Adviser in the Bureau of Far Eastern Affairs to the Assistant Secretary of State for Far Eastern Affairs." *Foreign Relations of the United States, 1952–4*. Vol. XII, Part 1 (document 85); available at http://history.state.gov/historicaldocuments/frus1952-54v12p1/d85

Okamoto, Shumpei. 1970. *The Japanese Oligarchy and the Russo-Japanese War*. New York: Columbia University Press.

Olick, Jeffrey K. 1993. "The Sins of the Fathers: The Third Reich and West German Legitimation, 1949–1989." PhD diss., Yale University.

Olick, Jeffrey K. 1998. "What Does It Mean to Normalize the Past?" *Social Science History* 22, no. 4 (Winter): 547–71.

Olick, Jeffrey, and Brenda Coughlin. 2003. "The Politics of Regret: Analytical Frames." In *Politics and the Past: On Repairing Historical Injustices*, edited by John Torpey, 37–62. Lanham, MD: Rowman and Littlefield.

Oneal, John R., and Bruce Russett. 1999. "Assessing the Liberal Peace with Alternative Specifications: Trade Still Reduces Conflict." *Journal of Peace Research* 36, no. 4: 423–42.

Öniş, Ziya. 2004. "Diverse but Converging Paths to European Union Membership: Poland and Turkey in Comparative Perspective." *East European Politics and Societies* 18, no. 3: 481–512.

Pękala, Urszula. 2016. "At a Crossroads? German-Polish Reconciliation in Light of the Recent Changes in the Polish Government." *AICGS publications* (May 20).https://www.aicgs.org/publication/at-a-crossroads-german-polish-reconciliation-in-light-of-the-recent-changes-in-the-polish-government/

Pew Center for Global Research. 2016. "Hostile Neighbors: China vs. Japan." http://www.pewglobal.org/2016/09/13/hostile-neighbors-china-vs-japan/

Pflüger, Friedbert. 1996. "Polen: Unser Frankreich im Osten" (Poland: Our France in the East). In *Aussenpolitik im 21 Jahrhundert. Die Thessen der Jungen Aussen-politiker*, edited by W. Schäuble und R. Seiters, 183–92. Bonn: Bouvier Verlag.

Phillips, Ann L. 2000. *Power and Influence after the Cold War: Germany in East-Central Europe*. Lanham, MD: Rowman & Littlefield.

Phillips, Ann L. 2001. "The Politics of Reconciliation Revisited: Germany and East-Central Europe." *World Affairs* 163, no. 4 (Spring): 171–91.

Polachek, Solomon W. 1980. "Conflict and Trade." *Journal of Conflict Resolution* 24, no. 1 (March): 57–78.

Poulos, James. 2015. "France Is at War . . . With Germany." *Foreign Policy* (November 17). https://foreignpolicy.com/2015/11/17/france-is-at-war-with-germany-isis-europe/

Prokop, Jan. 1993. *Universum polskie: literatura, wyobraźnia zbiorowa, mity polityc-zne* (The Polish Universe: Literature, Collective Imagination, and Political Mythology). Krakow: Universitas.

Radtke, Kurt W. 1990. *China's Relations with Japan, 1945–83: The Role of Liao Cheng-zhi*. Manchester: Manchester University Press.

Ragin, Charles C. 1987. *The Comparative Method: Moving Beyond Qualitative and Quantitative Strategies*. Berkeley: University of California Press.

Ritter, Gerhard. 1968. *Frederick the Great: A Historical Profile*. Berkeley: University of California Press.

Rose, Caroline. 1998. *Interpreting History in Sino-Japanese Relations*. London: Routledge Curzon.

Rosecrance, Richard. 1986. *The Rise of the Trading State: Commerce and Conquest in the Modern World*. New York: Basic Books.

Rosoux, Valérie-Barbara. 2001. "National Identity in France and Germany: From Mutual Exclusion to Negotiation." *International Negotiation* 6: 175–98.

Ross, Robert S. 2013. "Managing a Changing Relationship: China's Japan Policy in the 1990s." Strategic Studies Institute, U.S. Army War College.

Rovan, Joseph. 1945. "L'Allemagne de nos Mérites" (The Germany We Deserve). *Esprit* 11, no. 115 (October): 529–40.

Rozman, Gilbert. 2002. "China's Changing Images of Japan, 1989–2001: The Struggle to Balance Partnership and Rivalry." *International Relations of the Asia-Pacific* 2: 95–129.

Rühe, Volker. 1993. "Shaping Euro—Atlantic Policies: A Grand Strategy for a New Era." *Survival* 35: 2.

Rusk, Dean, and Khomen Thanat. 1962. Joint Statement, Washington, DC (March 6). Department of State Bulletin 46 (1187).

Sakaki, Alexandra. 2012. "Japanese-South Korean Textbook Talks: The Necessity of Political Leadership." *Pacific Affairs* 85, no. 2 (June): 263–85.

Sander, Richard P. 1995. "The Contribution of Post–World War II Schools in Poland in Forging a Negative Image of the Germans." *East European Quarterly* 29, no. 2 (Summer): 169–87.

Sato Kazuo. 2001. "The Japan-Chin Summit and Joint Declaration of 1998: A Watershed for Japan-China Relations in the 21st Century?" Brookings Institution working paper. https://www.brookings.edu/research/the-japan-china-summit-and-joint-declaration-of-1998-a-watershed-for-japan-china-relations-in-the-21st-century/

Sato, Takeo, and Norbert Frei. 2011. *Sugisaranu kako to no torikumi: Nihon to Doitsu* (Confronting the Past that Does Not Pass: Japan and Germany). Tokyo: Iwanami Shoten.

Sawaji Osamu. 2007. "Good Neighbors: Japan and China Grassroots Exchange." *Japan Journal* 3, no. 11 (March): 6–10.

Schaller, Michael. 1985. *The American Occupation of Japan: Origins of the Cold War.* New York: Oxford University Press.

Seguchi, Kiyoyuki. 2021. "Why Japanese Firms Are Not Withdrawing from China Despite the Spread of COVID-19." Canon Institute for Global Studies (January 21). Available at https://cigs.canon/en/article/20210121_5587.html

Shapiro, Ann-Louise. 1997. "Fixing History: Narratives of World War I in France." *History and Theory* 36, no. 4: 111–30.

Shoji, Jun'ichiro. 2011a. "Nicchū to Doitsu-Porando ni okeru Rekishi to Wakai: Sono Kyōtsūten to Soūiten o Chūshin to Shite" (History and Reconciliation between Japan and China versus Germany and Poland: Commonalities and Differences). In *Rekishi to Wakai* (History and Reconciliation), edited by Kurosawa Fumitaka and Ian Nish. Tokyo: University of Tokyo Press.

Shoji, Jun'ichiro. 2011b. "What Should the 'Pacific War' Be Named? A Study of the Debate in Japan." *NIDS Journal of Defense and Security* no. 12 (December): 45–81. National Institute for Defense Studies, Tokyo.

Shoji, Jun'ichiro. 2015. "Sengo nana-jūnen, taishou subeki 'kako' to wa?" (Seventy Years after World War II, What Is the "Past" We Should Be Focused On?). *NIDS Komentarii* no. 45 (May 13). http://www.nids.mod.go.jp/publication/commentary/pdf/commentary045.pdf

Siegel, Mona. 2002. "'History Is the Opposite of Forgetting': The Limits of Memory and the Lessons of History in Interwar France." *Journal of Modern History* 74 (December): 770–800.

Sil, Rudra, and Peter J. Katzenstein. 2010. *Beyond Paradigms: Analytical Eclecticism in the Study of World Politics.* New York: Palgrave Macmillan.

Skubiszewski, Krzysztof. 1992. "Polen und Deutschland in Europa an der Schwelle des 21. Jahrhunderts" (Poland and Germany in Europe on the Threshold of the Twenty-First Century). In *Bonn-Warschau 1945–1991. Die Deutsch-Polnischen Beziehungen. Analyse und Dokumentation*, edited by Hans Adolf Jacobsen and Mieczysław Tomala, 518–23. Köln: Verlag Wissenschaft und Politik.

Sloan, Stanley R. 2005. *NATO, the European Union, and the Atlantic Community: The Transatlantic Bargain Challenged.* Lanham, MD: Rowman & Littlefield.

Soh, Chunghee Sarah. 2003. "Politics of the Victim/Victor Complex: Interpreting South Korea's National Furor over Japanese History Textbooks." *American Asian Review* 21, no. 4 (Winter): 145–78.

Song Qiang, Zhang Zangzang, Qiao Bian, et al. 1996. *Zhongguo Keyi Shuo Bu* (The China That Can Say No). Beijing: Chinese Joint Press of Industry and Commerce.

Spiro, David. 1999. *The Hidden Hand of American Hegemony: Petrodollar Recycling and International Markets*. Ithaca: Cornell University Press.

Stokes, Bruce. 2013. "France and Germany: A Tale of Two Countries Drifting Apart." *Pew Research Center: Global Attitudes and Trends* (May 13). https://www .pewglobal.org/2013/05/13/france-and-germany-a-tale-of-two-countries-drifting-apart/

Stoneman, Mark R. 2008. "Die deutschen Greueltaten im Krieg 1870/71 am Beispiel der Bayern." In *Kriegsgreuel: Die Entgrenzung der Gewalt in kriegerischen Konflikten vom Mittelalter bis ins 20. Jahrhundert*, edited by Sönke Neitzel and Daniel Hohrath, 223–39. Paderborn: Ferdinand Schöningh.

Takahashi Kazuo. 1998. "The Impacts of Japanese Television Programs: Worldwide Oshin Phenomena." *Journal of Regional Development Studies* no. 1: 143–56.

Takahashi Kosuke. 2014. "Shinzo Abe's Nationalist Strategy." *The Diplomat* (February 13).

Tamamoto, Masaru. 2005/06. "How Japan Imagines China and Sees Itself." *World Policy Journal* (Winter).

Tewes, Henning. 2002. *Germany, Civilian Power, and the New Europe: Enlarging NATO and the European Union*. New York: Palgrave.

Thomson, James C. 1967. "Dragon Under Glass: Time for a New China Policy." *Atlantic Monthly* (October): 55–61.

Thomson, James Claude, Peter W. Stanley, and John Curtis Perry. 1981. *Sentimental Imperialists: The American Experience in East Asia*. New York: Harper & Row.

Tian, Huan. 1997. *Zhanhou Zhongri Guanxi Wenxianji* (Documents on Postwar Sino-Japanese Relations). Vol. 2: 1971–1995. Beijing: Zhongguo Shehui Kexue Chubanshe.

Timmerman, Martina. 2014. "Tri-Regional Partnering on Reconciliation in East Asia: Pivotal to Shaping the Order of the Twenty-first Century?" *AICGS Policy Report 59*. American Institution for Contemporary German Studies, Johns Hopkins University.

Towpik, Andrzej. 2011. "Republika Federalna Niemiec wobec polskiej akcesji do NATO. Dorobek i perspektywa wspólnego udziału w kształtowaniu bezpieczeństwa europejskiego" (The Federal Republic of Germany and Poland's Accession to NATO: Achievements and Prospects in Shaping European Security). In *Przełom I wyzwanie. XX lat polsko-niemieckiego traktatu o dobrym sąsiedztwie I przyjaznej współpracy 1991–2011* (Breakthrough and Challenges: 20 Years of the Polish-German Treaty on Good Neighborliness and Friendly Relations), edited by Witold M. Góralski, 225–45. Warsaw: Elipsa.

Trouillot, Michel-Rolph. 1995. *Silencing the Past: Power and the Production of History*. Boston: Beacon Press.

Truszczyński, Jan. 2011. "Polska-Niemcy-Europa. Droga do akcesji w Unii Europejskiej" (Poland-Germany-Europe: The Road to Accession in the European Union). In *Przełom i wyzwanie. XX lat polsko-niemieckiego traktatu o dobrym sąsiedztwie i przyjaznej współpracy 1991–2011* (Breakthrough and Challenges:

20 Years of the Polish-German Treaty on Good Neighborliness and Friendly Relations), edited by Witold M. Góralski, 246–75. Warsaw: Elipsa.

Tsugami Toshiya. 2003. *Chūgoku Taitō: Nihon wa nani o nasubeki ka* (The Rise of China: What Should Japan Do?). Tokyo: Nihon Keizai Shimbunsha.

Turek, Justyna. 2018. "Europeanisation of Reconciliation: Polish-German Lesson for Asian States?" In *Postwar Reconciliation in Central Europe and East Asia: The Case of Polish-German and Korean-Japanese Relations*, edited by Olga Barbasiewicz, 19–52. Berlin: Peter Lang.

U.S. Defense Department. 2018. *National Defense Strategy of the United States of America: Sharpening the American Military's Competitive Edge*. https://dod.defense.gov/Portals/1/Documents/pubs/2018-National-Defense-Strategy-Summary.pdf

U.S. Senate. 1949. "North Atlantic Treaty: Hearings Before the Committee on Foreign Relations, 81st Congress, 1st Session." Washington, DC: U.S. Government Printing Office.

U.S. State Department (Acting Director of the Office of German and Austrian Affairs). 1949. "U.S. Policy Respecting Germany." Document 52 of *Foreign Relations of the United States, 1949*, Vol. III. http://history.state.gov/historicaldocuments/frus1949v03/d52

U.S. State Department (Assistant Secretary of State for European Affairs). 1954. "Memorandum to the Secretary of State on Southeast Asia Pact." Document 304 of *Foreign Relations of the United States, 1952–54*, Vol. XII, Part 1, *East Asia and the Pacific*. https://history.state.gov/historicaldocuments/frus1952-54v12p1/d304

Van Evera, Stephen. 1997. *Guide to Methods for Students of Political Science*. Ithaca, NY: Cornell University Press.

Vitalis, Robert. 2015. *White World Order, Black Power Politics: The Birth of American International Relations*. Ithaca: Cornell University Press.

Wada, Haruki. 2003. "The Era of Northeast Asia." *Asia-Pacific Journal: Japan Focus* 1, no. 3 (March 14).

Wakamiya, Yoshibumi. 1995. *Sengo hoshu no Ajia Kan* (The Postwar Conservative View of Asia). Tokyo: Asahi Shimbun Publishing.

Wakamiya, Yoshibumi. 1998. *The Postwar Conservative View of Asia: How the Political Right Has Delayed Japan's Coming to Terms with Its History of Aggression in Asia*. Tokyo: LTCB International Library Foundation.

Wang, Xiaodong, and Wu Luping. 1995. "Young Urban Chinese Evaluate the Year 1994." *Zhongguo qingnian bao* (China Youth Daily), edited by Ma Mingjie (January 21), FBIS-CHI-95-050; cited in Austin and Harris 2001: 69.

Weingartner, James. *A Peculiar Crusade: Willis M. Everett and the Malmedy Massacre Trial*. New York: New York University Press.

Whiting, Allen S. 1968. *China Crosses the Yalu: The Decision to Enter the Korean War*. Stanford: Stanford University Press.

WTO. 2018. World Trade Statistical Review. https://www.wto.org/english/res_e/statis_e/wts2018_e/wts18_toc_e.htm

Wu, Zhigang. 2008. "Research on Japan's ODA to China and Its Contribution to China's Development." Unpublished paper presented at the ninth workshop on the Chinese economy, Kyoto Sangyo University, Japan (March 21).

Xiao Jiwen. 1998. *Riben: Yige Bukeng Fuzui de Guojia* (Japan: A Country that Refuses to Admit Its Crimes). Nanjing: Jiangsu Renmin Chubanshe.

Xiao, Yong. 1992. "Riben de jinyan yu zhongguo de gaige" (Japan's Experience and China's Reform). In *Riben Xuekan* (Japan Studies), 5.

Xu, Bin, and Gary Alan Fine. 2010. "Memory Movement and State-Society Relationships in Chinese World War II Victims' Reparations Movement Against Japan." In *Northeast Asia's Difficult Past*, edited by Mikyoung Kim and Barry Schwartz, 169–89. Houndmills, Basingstoke, Hampshire (UK): Palgrave Macmillan.

Xu, Xiaohong, and Lyn Spillman. 2010. "Political Centres, Progressive Narratives and Cultural Trauma: Coming to Terms with the Nanjing Massacre in China, 1937–1979." In *Northeast Asia's Difficult Past*, edited by Mikyoung Kim and Barry Schwartz, 101–28. Houndmills, Basingstoke, Hampshire (UK): Palgrave Macmillan.

Yamazaki, Jane W. 2006. *Japanese Apologies for World War II: A Rhetorical Study*. London: Routledge.

Yoder, Jennifer A. 2008. "No Longer on the Periphery: German-Polish Cross-Border Relations in a New Institutional Context." *German Politics and Society* 26, no. 3 (Autumn): 1–24.

Yoshida, Yutaka. 1998. *Nihonjin no Sensō-kan* (Japanese Views of War). Tokyo: Iwanami.

Young, Kenneth. 1965. "Asia's Disequilibrium and American Strategies." In *The United States and Communist China*, edited by W. W. Lockwood. Princeton, NJ: Haskins Press.

Yu, Charles. 2020. *Interior Chinatown: A Novel*. New York: Vintage Books.

Zhao Quansheng. 1993. "Japan's Aid Diplomacy with China." In *Japan's Foreign Aid: Power and Policy in a New Era*, edited by Bruce M. Koppel and Robert M. Orr. Boulder: Westview Press.

Index

Note: Page numbers in *italics* indicate figures.

Abe Shinzo: denialism by, 99, 151n23; and Japan-South Korean relations, 57, 58, 63, 67; and Murayama statement, 99, 102, 106; and nationalism, 97, 99; relations with Trump, 152n45; relations with Xi, 1, 97, 99, 100, 111; and Sino-Japanese cooperation, 97–98, 100, 111; and Yasukuni visits, 97, 99, 105
Acheson, Dean, 123
Action Reconciliation Service, 32, 39
Adenauer, Konrad, 29, 31, 33, 38, 39
agriculture, 24, 34, 85, 128, 138
Airbus, 33, 128
Akihito (Emperor), 50, 57, 59, 60, 101
Alexander, J. C., 91–92
American (or Anglo-Saxon) Lake, 130, 154n24
analytical eclecticism, 12, 117
anti-Muslim views, 77, 121
apologies and contrition: anthropomorphizing states, 11; conventional approach to, 11; domestic backlashes to, 11, 62–63, 138; as element of reconciliation, 3–4, 135–36; as explanatory factor, 27, 135–36, 137; and Franco-German relations, 29, 37–41;

and German-Polish relations, 78–81; and Japan-South Korean relations, 48, 49, 50, 52, 55, 57, 59–63; Murayama statement, 52, 57, 60, 95, 99, 102; and national culture, 7; in official discourse, 2, 10; and Sino-Japanese relations, 89, 93, 95, 96, 100–106, 113
Armenian genocide, 11, 17, 142n14
Asahi Shinbun (newspaper, Japan), 150n12
Asan Institute for Policy Studies, 61
ASEAN (Association of Southeast Asian Nations), 66, 112, 115, 134, 152n46
ASEAN Plus Three (APT), 66, 112, 134, 137, 147n39
ASEAN Regional Forum (ARF), 112
Asia. *See* U.S.-East Asian relations; *specific countries*
Asian Development Bank (ADB), 111
Asian Infrastructure Investment Bank, 111
Asian Monetary Fund, 112, 116, 129, 134
Asian Women's Fund, 52, 62
Asia Pacific Economic Cooperation (APEC), 99, 112, 137
Auriol, Vincent, 31

Austin, Greg, 96
Australia, 125, 132, 153n3
authoritarian states, 27–28
Axelrod, Robert, 13

Bao Ge, 96
Baritz, Loren, 124
Barkan, Elazar, 2–3
Beckmann, George M., 124
Beeson, Mark, 117, 129
Belt and Road Initiative, 111
Benedict, Ruth, 7
Berger, Thomas, 2, 5, 10, 38, 136, 137,
  147n31, 152n31
Bi, Shihong, 111
Biden, Joe, 129, 132, 139–40, 154n20
bilateralism: U.S. promotion of "hub-
  and-spokes" model in Asia, 12,
  115–16, 129–34, 137. *See also* Franco-
  German relations; German-Polish
  relations; Japan-South Korean rela-
  tions; multilateralism; Sino-Japanese
  relations
bilateral trade. *See* economic
  interdependence
Bismarck, Otto von, 18, 22
Bledowski, Krzysztof, 86
Bosnia, 17
Boulding, Kenneth E., 4
Brandt, Willy, 33, 39, 71–72, 79
Bretton Woods system, 125
Brexit (2016), 15, 37, 129, 139
Buell, Raymond Leslie, 118
Buras, Piotr, 88
Buruma, Ian, 8

Cambodia, 110, 111
Caporaso, James A., 138
Carroll, Ross, 4, 10
Center Against Expulsions (Germany),
  75–76
Chang Ki-young, 50
Chiang Kai-shek, 26, 91, 122, 130–31
Chiang Mai Initiative, 112
China: anti-Japanese feeling in, 5, 8,
  103, 104, 108; economy of, 9, 28,
  64–65, 66, 106–10, 143n26, 152n45;
  and multilateralism in Asia, 139–40;
  regime type, 27–28; U.S. relations

with, 122–23, 130, 131–32, 134. *See
  also* Sino-Japanese relations
China Daily (newspaper, China), 90, 102–
  3, *104, 109*, 110
China-Japan Innovation Cooperation
  Mechanism, 111
China Youth Daily (newspaper, China),
  102, 152n34
Chinese Communist Party (CCP), 26,
  91–94, 95, 96, 105, 123
Chirac, Jacques, 34, 35, 85, 142n3
Chŏn Yŏ-ok, 53
Chosun Ilbo (newspaper, S. Korea), 7, 49
Christian Democratic Union (CDU),
  Germany, 32, 37, 38, 70
Christianity, 7
Chun Doo-hwan, 50, 59
civil society: and Franco-German relations, 32, 33, 45; and German-Polish
  relations, 74, 79; and Sino-Japanese
  relations, 94, 97–98
Clark, Wesley, 128
Clayton, Will, 120
Clinton, Bill, 85
Coffey, Luke, 128–29
Cold War (1947–91): effect on bilateral
  relations, 27; and German-Polish relations, 71–73; and Japan-South Korean
  relations, 50; and Sino-Japanese relations, 91–95; and U.S. involvement
  in European multilateralism, 126–28,
  133; and U.S. paternalism in Asia,
  124, 133; and U.S. West-East divide,
  119–20
collective memory: in China, 26, 91–
  92, 94; and Franco-German relations, 19–21, 35, 39–40, 142n3; and
  German-Polish relations, 75–76, 84;
  in Germany, 38–39; and historical
  revisionism, 55, 57, 90, 99–100, 105,
  113; importance in global affairs, 1–3;
  and interstate reconciliation, 12; and
  Japan-South Korean relations, 53
"comfort women": apologies for, 60;
  compensation to, 48, 52, 58, 62, 67,
  137; Japanese denials of, 57, 63, 99,
  151n23; and Japan-South Korean
  relations, 25, 48, 51, 52, 57, 58, 62,
  63, 67; Kono statement on, 52, 57,

146n11, 147n40; media on, 51; number of, 25, 143n21; Yoon on, 146n10, 147n40

commercial peace, 64–65, 106, 109, 110, 142n13

Common Agricultural Policy (CAP) of EU, 85, 128

Common Security and Defense Policy of EU, 87, 128

communism: and Franco-German relations, 31; and German-Polish relations, 73, 79; and U.S. West-East divide, 118–19, 133. *See also* Chinese Communist Party

compensation for damages. *See* reparations

Constitutional Treaty (2004, abandoned), 35

Constructivism (IR), 9–10, 12, 116–17, 133–34

contrition. *See* apologies and contrition

cooperation: as explanatory factor, 12–14, 27, 136–39; and Franco-German relations, 42–45, 137; and German-Polish relations, 83–86, 87, 137; and Japan-South Korean relations, 65–68, 137, 139; and Sino-Japanese relations, 100, 110–13, 137, 139; U.S. encouragement of in Europe, 129

Cot, Pierre, 21

credible commitment, 2, 12–16, 43, 48, 127, 137

cultural identity: and U.S. involvement in Asia, 116, 133–34; U.S. "Western" identification with Europe, 12, 117–21

culture: and Franco-German cooperation, 34; Japanese, 53, 54–55; Korean, 24, 53, 54–55; national norms of, 7–8, 9, 10

Czech Republic, 77, 85

defense. *See* security

de Gaulle, Charles, 20, 31, 33

Demesmay, Claire, 46

Democratic Party of Japan (DPJ), 98, 106, 132

democratic states, 9, 27–28, 51

Deng Xiaoping, 93–94

denials: and Japan-South Korean rela-

tions, 57, 62–63, 99, 151n23; and Sino-Japanese relations, 95, 99, 105, 151n23

development level, as explanatory factor, 27, 28

Diaoyu/Senkaku islands, and Sino-Japanese relations, 8, 97, 98, 99, 105–6, 110, 113

Dixon, Jennifer M., 2

Dokdo/Takeshima islands, and Japan-South Korean relations, 8, 48, 53, 56, 57, 58

domestic politics: and apologies, 11, 62–63, 138; as explanatory factor, 9, 10

Dong-a Ilbo (newspaper, S. Korea), 57, 60

Dreyer, June Teufel, 109

Dudden, Alexis, 49, 56, 62

East Asia. *See* U.S.-East Asian relations; *specific countries*

East Asia Economic Group (EAEG), 115–16, 129, 134

East Asian Community, 66, 132

East Asia Summit, 66, 112, 137

East Germany (German Democratic Republic, or GDR), 141n1; and German-Polish relations, 71, 73, 148n22; and unification of Germany, 6, 34, 73–74

Eastland, James, 120

economic interdependence: as explanatory factor, 9, 27, 137; and Franco-German relations, 41–42, *43, 44*; and German-Polish relations, 72, 73, 75, 81–83, 87; and Japan-South Korean relations, 48, 50, 58, 64–*65, 66*; and Sino-Japanese relations, 93–94, 106–10; U.S. involvement in European multilateralism, 125–26

Eisenhower, Dwight D., 119

Elysée Treaty (1963), 33, 35

employer-employee relationships, 14

Eurocorps, 34, 37, 128

Europe: "European project" of alliance-building, 29–30, 31–37, 41–45; U.S.-Western European relations, 115, 117–21, 125–29

European Atomic Energy Community (Euratom), 32, 43

European Banking Union, 86
European Central Bank, 5, 35–36, 138
European Coal and Steel Community (ECSC), 29–30, 31, 32, 43, 115, 119, 127, 137
European Commission, 31, 36
European Communities (EC), 30, 73, 75, 83–84, 138
European Court of Justice, 77
European Defense Agency, 128
European Economic Community (EEC), 30, 32, 43, 127, 138
European Union (EU): and Brexit, 15, 129, 139; Common Agricultural Policy, 85, 128; Common Security and Defense Policy, 87, 128; establishment of, 30–31, 127; and Eurozone crisis, 35–36, 138; expansion of, 34; and Franco-German relations, 30, 31, 33, 34–36, 37, 44; and German-Polish relations, 71, 77–78, 83, 84, 85–86, 87–88, 137, 139; and Germany, 136; military force of, 37; and U.S., 129
European University Viadrina, 84
Eurozone crisis (2010–17), 5–6, 35–36, 77, 88, 138
Expellees' Association (Germany), 75–76

Fairbank, John, 124
Faure, Maurice, 43
Federal Republic of Germany. *See* West Germany
Feldman, Lily Gardner, 135–36, 141n3
Feng, Zhaokui, 101, 112
Fine, Gary Alan, 96
Fischer, Joschka, 85
Fiske, John, 118
forced labor. *See* slave labor
foreign aid. *See* Official Development Assistance
foreign direct investment (FDI), 81–82, 107
Forster, Johann Georg, 21
Foundation for Polish-German Reconciliation, 79–80
France: economy of, 28, 41–42, 143n26; and Eurozone crisis, 35–36; and expansion of EU, 34; and Haiti, 11. *See also* Franco-German relations

Franco-German relations, 29–46; 1945–1951, 30–31; 1952–1963, 32–33; 1964–2010, 33–35; 2011–, 35–37; and collective memory, 19–21; contrition and discourse in, 37–41; economic interdependence in, 41–*42, 43, 44*; formal cooperation in, 15, 42–45, 137; in post–World War II period, 29–30, 127; and public opinion, 39, *40*, 41, *43, 44*; and war crimes, 6
Franco-German Youth Office, 33
François, Étienne, 41, 45
Franco-Prussian War (1870–71), 6, 18, 20
Frederick II (Frederick the Great), 21
Freudenstein, Roland, 86, 150n48
Friedberg, Aaron L., 8
Fujio Masayuki, 63
Fukuda Yasuo, 98

game theory, 12–13
Gao, R., 91–92
Gates, Robert, 132
Gebert, Konstanty, 87
General Agreement on Tariffs and Trade (GATT), 125–26
General Security of Military Information Agreement (GSOMIA, 2016), 57, 58, 68, 139
Genscher, Hans-Dietrich, 83
geography, 7, 10
geopolitics, as explanatory factor, 27
German Democratic Republic. *See* East Germany
German-Polish relations, 70–88; 1945–1990, 71–74; 1991–2003, 74–75; 2004–2014, 75–77; 2015–, 77–78; contrition and discourse in, 78–81, 87; and cultural narratives, 9; economic interdependence in, 72, 73, 75, 81–83, 87; formal agreements, 72, 74; formal cooperation in, 15, 83–86, 87, 137; and partitions of Poland, 21–22; and public opinion, 5, 70, 78, *80*, 81, *82*, 85, 88; and war crimes, 6, 18, 21–22
German-Polish Textbook Commission, 79, 148n4
Germany: compared with Japan, 6–8, 135–36; culture of, 7–8; economy of,

9, 28, 41–*42*, 143n26; and Eurozone crisis, 5–6, 35–37, 138; geography of, 7; historical memory in, 38–39; influence of history on, 1–2; official apologies by, 2, 10, 78–81; postwar government of, 32; and regionalism, 9, 15; success in relations with neighbors, 5–6, 12; unification of, 6, 34, 73–74, 127; war crimes of, 6, 20. *See also* East Germany; Franco-German relations; German-Polish relations; Prussia; West Germany

Goulard, Sylvie, 30, 45
Greece, 5–6, 35, 138, 155n5
Grosser, Alfred, 15–16, 29
GSOMIA (General Security of Military Information Agreement, 2016), 57, 58, 68, 139
Guérot, Ulrike, 87
Guomindang (GMD, KMT, Nationalist Party), China and Taiwan, 91, 92
Gustafsson, Karl, 98
Gyeongbokgung (Seoul, South Korea), 23–24, 68

Haigneré, Claudie, 34
Haiti, 11
Hamilton, William D., 13
Harriman, W. Averell, 119
Harris, Harry, 131
Harris, Stuart, 96
Hashimoto Ryutaro, 102, 105
Hashimoto Toru, 63
Hatoyama Yukio, 66, 98, 132
Hayner, Priscilla, 4
He, Yinan, 5, 9, 137
Hemmer, Christopher, 112, 117, 131
Heritage Foundation, 128–29
Herzog, Roman, 80
Hirohito (Emperor Shōwa), 50, 59, 60, 93, 100
historical memory. *See* collective memory
historical revisionism, 55, 57, 90, 99–100, 105, 113
historiography. *See* collective memory
history textbooks. *See* textbooks
Hitchcock, William I., 127, 144n7
Hitler, Adolf, 6, 22, 142n10

Hollande, François, 36
Holocaust, 6, 17, 78, 142n10
Hosokawa Morihiro, 52, 60, 101, 152n31
Hughes, Christopher, 132–33
Hu Jintao, 98
Hungary, 77, 83, 85
Huntington, Samuel, 121
Hyde-Price, Adrian, 83

identity. *See* cultural identity
Ikenberry, G. John, 126
Ilbon-un ôpt'a (The Japan That Does Not Exist) (Chôn), 53
imperialism: Japanese, 23, 24–26, 48; Prussian/German, 18, 21–22; U.S., 118, 121–22, 129–30
India, 17, 137, 140
Indonesia, 23, 136, 140
institutions, 2, 135–40. *See also* cooperation; European Union (EU)
Intermediate-Range Nuclear Forces Treaty, 88
International Monetary Fund (IMF), 73, 116, 153n1
international relations (IR): answers about Japan/Germany disparity by, 8–10; concept of reconciliation in, 4–5; and prisoner's dilemma scenario, 13–14
INTERREG, 84, 149n37
interstate conflicts: examples of, 17–18. *See also* reconciliation
Iraq, U.S. invasion of (2003), 17, 35, 86, 154n20
Ireland, 35, 117
"Iron Curtain," 72, 119
Ishihara Shintaro, 106
Islam, 77, 121
Israel, 29, 38, 78, 142n10, 145n23
Izokukai (Bereaved Families Association), 96–97, 105, 152n31

Jabko, Nicolas, 45
Jackson, Patrick Thaddeus, 119, 120
Janning, Josef, 88
Japan: compared with Germany, 6–8, 135–36; culture of, 7–8, 10; economic relations with U.S., 152n45; economy of, 9, 28, *109*, 143n26; geography of,

Japan (*continued*)
7, 10; influence of history on, 1–2; Meiji period, and emulating imperialism of the West, 23; nationalism in, 94–95; official apologies by, 2, 10, 52, 57, 60, 95, 99, 100–102; and regionalism in Asia, 9, 15, 115–16; relations with neighbors, 8–9; and U.S. bilateralism, 115–16, 130, 131, 132, 134, 139–40; U.S. military bases in, 124–25, 132; U.S. occupation of, 130. *See also* Japan-South Korean relations; Sino-Japanese relations
Japan-China Policy Dialogue on the Mekong Region, 110–11
Japan New Party, 52
Japan Socialist Party, 52
Japan-South Korea formal agreements: General Security of Military Information Agreement (GSOMIA, 2016), 57, 58, 68, 139; normalization treaty (1965), 25, 49, 58, 59, 62; pact on comfort women controversy (2015), 62, 67, 139
Japan-South Korean relations, 47–69; 1948–1992, 48–51; 1992–2001, 51–54; 2001–2015, 54–58; 2015–present, 58–59; contrition and discourse in, 48, 59–63; and Dokdo/Takeshima claim, 8, 48; economic interdependence in, 9, 54, 64–65, 66; formal cooperation in, 65–68, 137, 139; and Japanese imperialism, 23–25; and popular culture, 54–55; and public opinion, 47, 56–57, 60–62, 64–65, 67; and war crimes, 18
Japan Times, 54
Jiang Zemin, 96, 102
Jin Xide, 90–91, 150n2

Kaczynski, Jaroslaw, 77
Kaczynski, Lech, 76, 77
Kaifu Toshiki, 50, 59–60
Kansteiner, Wulf, 38
Kanzo, Uchimura, 25
Karnow, Stanley, 130
Katzenstein, Peter J., 12, 112, 117, 131
Kawashima Shin, 111
Kim Chang-gi, 7
Kim Dae-jung, 49, 52–53, 60, 96

Kim Hak-soon, 51
Kim Jin-myung, 53
Kimura Kan, 64
Kim Young-sam, 51–52, 53, 60
Kniefall (December 1970), 72, 79
Knirsch, Hubert, 75
Kohl, Helmut, 15; and Franco-German relations, 33–34, 39–40, 44–45; and German-Polish relations, 72–73, 79, 83, 84–85
Koizumi Jun'ichiro, 55–56, 90, 96–97, 102, 105
Komori, Yasumasa, 152n46
Komori, Yoshihisa, 105
Kono statement (1993), 52, 57, 63, 146n11, 147n40, 151n23
Koo Min Gyo, 64
Korea. *See* Japan-South Korean relations; North Korea; South Korea
Korean Council for the Women Drafted for Military Sexual Slavery by Japan, 51, 62, 146n10, 147n40
Kubota Kenichiro, 63
Kuomintang. *See* Guomindang

Lam, Peng Er, 110
Laos, 111
Lavisse, Ernest, 20
Law and Justice Party (PiS), Poland, 71, 76, 77, 88
Lee Jung-bok, 51, 56–57, 146n23
Lee Myung-bak, 57
Liaodong Peninsula, 23, 143n16
Liberal Democratic Party (LDP), Japan, 52, 55, 95, 132, 152n31
Liberalism (IR), 9
Lieberson, Stanley, 27
Li Keqiang, 98
Lind, Jennifer, 5, 10, 11, 37–38, 63, 138, 144n21, 145n23
Lippmann, Walter, 119
Luce, Henry, 122
Lundestad, Geir, 126
Lutz, Thomas, 39
Luxembourg Agreement (1952), 38

MacArthur, Douglas, 123, 130, 154n15, 154n24
Macron, Emmanuel, 1, 37

Malaysia, 115, 129, 136, 140
management, corporate, 14
Manchuria, 23, 25, 26, 89
manga, 54, 55
Mann, Thomas, 32
manufacturing: and cooperation, 14; and
   Franco-German relations, 29–30, 31,
   33; and German-Polish relations, 75,
   82; and imperial Germany, 18; and
   Japan-South Korean relations, 50, 58;
   and Sino-Japanese relations, 94, 99,
   104, 107
Mao Zedong, 26, 91–92, 113
Markovits, Andrei S., 31
Marshall, George, 120
Marshall Plan, 31, 115, 120, 126, 136–37
Martens, Stephan, 44
Masuda Masayuki, 135, 136–37
Mazowiecki, Tadeusz, 73
McLauchlan, Alastair, 54
McNamara, Dennis L., 24
media: Franco-German cooperation on,
   34; and Japan-South Korean rela-
   tions, 53, 54–55; and Sino-Japanese
   relations, 94, 96, 99–100. *See also*
   textbooks
medical experiments, 6, 26, 89
memory. *See* collective memory
Merkel, Angela, 1, 5–6, 35, 36–37, 76, 81
Meyer, Till, 45
military. *See* security
Miller, Gary J., 14
Mill's method of difference, 27
Ministry of Education (Japan), 50, 55,
   95, 105
Mitterand, Francois, 33–34, 39–40,
   142n3
Miyazawa Ki'ichi, 51, 60
modernization theory, 123–24
Molotov-Ribbentrop Pact (1939), 76,
   143n14
monetary system, European, 34, 86, 125,
   127. *See also* economic interdependence; Eurozone crisis (2010–17)
monetary systems, East Asian, 111, 112,
   115–16
Monnet, Jean, 31
Monnet Plan, 31
monuments and museums: and German-

Polish relations, 72, 75, 79; and Japan-
   South Korean relations, 24, 67, 68,
   146n21; and Sino-Japanese relations,
   94, 98, 101, 102
Moon Jae-in, 58, 67, 68
Motoya Toshio, 99
Movement for Correcting Japanese
   Textbooks, 55
Mugunghwa kkochi pieot seumnida (The
   Rose of Sharon Blooms Again) (Kim),
   53
multilateralism, 12; in Asia, 129–33,
   139–40; in Europe, 12, 29–30, 31–33,
   115–16, 119–20, 125–29, 133, 137,
   154n20. *See also* European Union;
   North Atlantic Treaty Organization;
   regionalism
Murayama statement (1995), 52, 57, 60,
   95, 99, 102
Murayama Tomiichi, 52, 60, 95, 102
Museum of Chinese People's Resistance
   Against Japanese Aggression (Beijing,
   China), 94
museums. *See* monuments and museums
music, 54
Muslims: anti-Muslim views, 77, 121

Nagano Shigeto, 105
Nagy, Stephen, 111
Nakasone Yasuhiro, 50, 59, 95, 101
Nanjing Massacre (1937), 25–26, 91–92,
   99–100, 105
Nanjing Massacre Museum, 26, 98,
   143n23
nationalism: and German-Polish relations, 75–76, 77–78; and Japan-South
   Korean relations, 55–57; as obstacle to
   cooperation through regionalism, 139;
   and Sino-Japanese relations, 90, 99
nativism, 119, 139
NATO. *See* North Atlantic Treaty
   Organization
natural gas pipelines, 76, 88
neoliberal institutionalism (IR), 9, 12,
   13, 64
neoliberalism (economic ideology),
   55
New York Times (newspaper, U.S.),
   99

North Atlantic Treaty Organization (NATO), 2, 154n22; Asian multilateralism compared with, 112, 131; and Franco-German relations, 32–33, 37, 43, 127; German involvement in, 15, 127, 136, 138–39; and German-Polish relations, 71, 73, 75, 83, 84–85, 86, 87, 137; and U.S., 15, 115, 119–20, 126, 128–29

Northeast Asian History Foundation, 68

North Korea, 47, 58, 112, 125

nuclear bombings (Hiroshima and Nagasaki), 11, 18, 25, 93, 125

nuclear weapons, 18, 32, 47, 53, 58, 88, 112

Nye, Joseph, 132

Obama, Barack, 11, 129, 132, 154n20

Obuchi Keizo, 52–53, 60, 96, 102

Occidentalism, 117–19

Oder-Neisse Line, 72, 74

Official Development Assistance (ODA), and Sino-Japanese relations, 93–94, 98, 100, 103 5

Ogburn, Charlton, 123

Oh Koo Sak, 54

Okazaki Katsuo, 63

Okinawa, 18, 124–25, 132

Organization for European Economic Cooperation, 126

Ôshin (TV show), 94

Ostpolitik, 71–72, 79, 81

Pacific islands, U.S. imperialism in, 129–30

Pacific War (1941–45), 23, 25, 99. *See also* World War II (1939–45)

Pakistan, 17

Park Chung-hee, 49

Park Geun-hye, 58

Park Joon-woo, 48

paternalism, U.S., 121–24

Pax Mercatoria. *See* commercial peace

peace, stable, 4

Pękala, Urszula, 87

People's Daily (Renmin Ribao) (newspaper, China), 92, 93, 95

People's Republic of China (PRC). *See* China

Perry, John Curtis, 122

Pflüger, Friedbert, 70

PHARE (Poland and Hungary Assistance for the Restructuring of their Economies), 83–84, 149n37

Philippines, the, 116, 118, 121–22, 129–30, 131, 154n15, 155n25

Phillips, Ann, 5, 149n26

Poland: anti-German feeling in, 5, *80, 82*; economy of, 28, *82*, 143n26; in EU policy caucus (Weimar Triangle), 34; Germany's militarism against, 6; Germany's reconciliation with, 15; partition of, 21, 22; and U.S. under Trump regime, 88. *See also* German-Polish relations

Pompidou, Georges, 33

popular culture, 54–55, 94, 96

Portsmouth Treaty (1905), 23

Potsdam Conference (1945), 72

Poulos, James, 36

power: regional structures of, as explanatory factor, 8–9, 12; unilateralism, 15, 131, 137, 154n20; and U.S. involvement in Asia, 116, 133–34. *See also* imperialism; multilateralism

prisoner's dilemma scenario, 13–14

protests, and Sino-Japanese relations, 95, 97, 98

Prussia, 6, 18, 20, 21–22

Prussian Trust, 76

public opinion: of EU, 36; and Franco-German relations, 39–41, *43, 44*; and German-Polish relations, 70, 76, 78, *80,* 81, *82,* 85, 88; on Germany, among neighbors, 5–6; on Japan, among neighbors, 5; and Japan-South Korean relations, 47, 56–57, 60–62, 64–65, *67*; and Sino-Japanese relations, 102–*3, 104, 108,* 109, 110, 113

qualitative analysis, 27

racism: and German-Polish relations, 21; and U.S.-Asia relations, 12, 23, 116, 121–25, 133–34; and U.S.-European relations, 117–21

Reagan, Ronald, 50, 73, 79, 120

Realism (IR), 8–9, 10, 12–13, 116–17, 118, 133–34
reciprocity, 13
reconciliation, 1–3; as completed (Franco-German), 45–46; defining, 3–5, 141n3; and geographical explanations, 7; and moral/cultural explanations, 7–8, 9–10. *See also* apologies/ contrition; cooperation; economic interdependence
refugees, Poland's refusal to accept, 77, 86
regime type, as explanatory factor, 27–28
Regional Comprehensive Economic Partnership, 112
regionalism: and Franco-German relations, 42–45; and German-Polish relations, 83–86; and Germany-Japan comparison, 12, 15–16, 48, 91, 137–39; and Japan-South Korean relations, 65–68; and Sino-Japanese relations, 110–13; U.S. undermining of in Asia, 12, 115–16, 129–33. *See also* cooperation; European Union (EU)
Reich, Simon, 31
Reischauer, Edwin, 49
Rémond, Bruno, 19
Renmin Ribao (People's Daily) (newspaper, China), 92, 93, 95
reparations: to "comfort women," 48, 52, 58, 62, 67, 137; foreign aid instead of, 48, 49, 62, 89, 98, 103–5, 106; and German-Greek relations, 142n9, 155n5; and German-Polish relations, 71, 72, 76, 78, 79, 80, 81, 87, 88, 147n3, 149n26; from Germany and/or German industry, 38, 78, 81, 87, 145n23, 155n4; from Japan and/ or Japanese industry, 95, 99, 137; and Japan-South Korean relations, 48, 49, 52, 58, 62, 63, 137; and Sino-Japanese relations, 89, 93, 96, 101, 103–5, 137
Republic of China. *See* Taiwan
Republic of Korea (ROK). *See* South Korea
revanchism, 2, 22, 49, 73
revisionism. *See* historical revisionism
Rhee, Syngman, 49, 130
Roh Moo-hyun, 56, 65–66, 147n38

Roh Tae-woo, 50, 59
Roosevelt, Franklin Delano, 119, 122
Roosevelt, Theodore, 23
Rosati, Dariusz, 86, 88
Rosoux, Valérie-Barbara, 39–40, 142n3
Ross, Robert S., 101
Rovan, Joseph, 30, 144n4
Rozman, Gilbert, 101
Rühe, Volker, 74–75, 84
Rumsfeld, Donald, 86, 154n20
Rusk-Thanat statement (1962), 131
Russia: in East Asia Summit, 137; and German-Polish relations, 18, 21, 76, 84, 88; and war with Japan, 23–24. *See also* Soviet Union
Russian invasion of Ukraine (February 2022–), 2, 78, 129, 138
Rwandan genocide (1994), 17, 141n4

Sakhalin Island, 23, 51
Sakurai Shin, 105
Sarkozy, Nicolas, 35
Schäfer, Roland, 33
Schäuble, Wolfgang, 45
Schmidt, Helmut, 39, 72, 79
Schröder, Gerhard, 35, 76, 80–81, 85
Schuman, Robert, 29–30
Schuman Plan, 31
Schwall-Düren, Angelica, 75
Schwan, Gesine, 84
security: Common Security and Defense Policy of EU, 87, 128; Franco-German cooperation on, 32, 34, 37; German-Polish cooperation on, 74–75, 87; Japan-South Korean cooperation on, 57, 58, 68; and Polish-U.S. cooperation, 88; and Sino-Japanese relations, 99, 111–12; United Nations Security Council, 14, 97, 105; U.S. involvement in European multilateralism, 125–26, 128–29; U.S. military bases in Asia/Pacific, 124–25, 131–32, 139–40. *See also* North Atlantic Treaty Organization
Senkaku/Diaoyu islands, and Sino-Japanese relations, 8, 97, 98, 99, 105–6, 110, 113
Seodaemun Prison (Seoul, South Korea), 24, 68, 146n21

Seoul, South Korea, 23–24
Serbia, bombing of, 128
sex slaves. *See* "comfort women"
shame vs guilt, 7–8
Shiina Etsusaburo, 49
Shin Gil-sou, 68
Shin Yong-ha, 48
Shoji, Jun'ichiro, 5, 23, 143n18
Sikorski, Radoslaw, 77
Sil, Rudra, 12
Single European Act (1987), 127
Sino-Japanese relations, 89–114;
    1949–1981, 91–94; 1982–2005, 94–
    97; 2006–, 97–100; contrition and
    discourse in, 89, 93, 96, 100–106, 137;
    and Diaoyu/Senkaku islands, 8, 97, 98,
    99, 105–6, 110, 113; economic inter-
    dependence in, 9, 93–94, 106–10, 137;
    formal agreements, 93, 99, 100; formal
    cooperation in, 100, 110–13, 137, 139;
    and Japanese imperialism, 23, 25–26;
    and land claims, 8, 97, 98, 105–6; and
    public opinion, 5, 90, 96, 97–98, 101,
    102–3, 104, 108, 110; and war crimes,
    18, 25–26, 89, 93, 94, 95, 96
Sino-Japanese war, first (1894–95), 25,
    89, 143n16
Sino-Japanese war, second (1937–45),
    25–26, 89
"sister city" or "sister region" organiza-
    tions, 32, 45
six party talks, 112, 133
Skubiszewski, Krzysztof, 83
slave labor: and German-Polish rela-
    tions, 22, 81; and Japan-South Korean
    relations, 51; and Sino-Japanese rela-
    tions, 95, 99, 151n14; and U.S. history,
    117. *See also* "comfort women" (sex
    slaves)
social Darwinism, 23, 118
Social Democratic Party (SPD), Ger-
    many, 39, 72, 79, 80–81, 85
socialists, 36, 52
social media, 55, 97
South Africa, 4
Southeast Asia Treaty Organization
    (SEATO), 131
South Korea (Republic of Korea, or
    ROK): anti-Japanese feeling in, 8, 9,

47–48, 67; economy of, 28, 64–65, 66,
    143n26; Japan's invasion/annexation/
    occupation of, 24; regime type of, 28;
    and U.S. bilateralism, 116, 131; U.S.
    military bases in, 124; U.S. occupation
    of, 130. *See also* Japan-South Korean
    relations
Soviet Union: collapse of, 87, 120, 128;
    and German-Polish relations, 22,
    71, 72, 73; and Molotov-Ribbentrop
    Pact, 76, 143n14; and Sino-Japanese
    relations, 92–93, 110; support for N.
    Korea, 130; support for N. Vietnam,
    17; and U.S. involvement in European
    multilateralism, 126–28, 133; and U.S.
    West-East divide, 119–20
Spencer, Herbert, 23
Spillman, Lyn, 91
sports, 53–54, 144n14
stable peace, 4
Stanley, Peter W., 122
Steinbach, Erika, 75–76
Stokes, Bruce, 36

Taft, William Howard, 122
Taft-Katsura memorandum (1905),
    155n25
Taiwan: and Chinese civil war, 26, 91;
    Japanese relations with, 23, 136; U.S.
    relations with, 116, 121, 123, 131,
    155n27
Takeshima/Dokdo islands, and Japan-
    South Korean relations, 8, 48, 53, 56,
    57, 58
Tamamoto Masaru, 140
Tamogami Toshio, 57, 105
Tanaka Kakuei, 93, 100
television, 34, 54, 94
territorial disputes. *See* Senkaku/Diaoyu
    islands, and Sino-Japanese relations;
    Takeshima/Dokdo islands, and Japan-
    South Korean relations
textbooks: and Franco-German rela-
    tions, 19–20, 38, 142n4; and German-
    Polish relations, 72, 77, 79, 148n22;
    and Japan-South Korean relations,
    50, 55; and Sino-Japanese relations,
    26, 90, 91, 92, 95, 96, 97–98, 105, 113,
    150n12

Thadden, Rudolf von, 7, 44
Thailand, 100, 111, 131
Thomson, James C., 122, 123
Time magazine, 122
Togo Kazuhiko, 99
tourism, 42, 54, 81, 107
trade. *See* economic interdependence
trade intensity: and Franco-German
    relations, 41, *43*, *44*; and German-
    Polish relations, 81–*82*; and Japan-
    South Korean relations, 64; and
    Sino-Japanese relations, 107–*8*
Trans-Pacific Partnership, 112, 132, 134,
    140
Treaties of Rome (1957), 32, 127
Treaty of Lisbon, 35, 119, 128
Treaty of Maastricht (1992), 15, 34, 128
Treaty of Nice (2001), 15
Treaty of Paris (1951), 15, 31, 127
Treaty of Peace and Friendship (1978),
    93
Treaty of Versailles (1919), 22
Treaty of Warsaw (1970), 72
Treaty on Good Neighborly Relations
    and Friendly Cooperation (1991), 74
Trouillot, Michel-Rolph, 2
Trump, Donald: and German-Polish
    relations, 88; and NATO, 15, 129;
    and Sino-Japanese relations, 111; and
    U.S.-Asian relations, 15, 111, 125,
    132, 139, 152n45; and U.S.-European
    relations, 129, 154n20
trust, and cooperation, 13–14
Truszczyński, Jan, 83
truth and reconciliation commissions, 4,
    141n4
Tsugami Toshiya, 113
Tsunekawa, Keiichi, 15–16
Turek, Justyna, 138–39
Turkey, 11, 142n14
21 Demands (1915), 25, 89, 122
twinning. *See* "sister city" or "sister
    region" organizations

Ukraine, invasion of (2022), 2, 78, 129,
    138
unilateralism, 15, 131, 137, 154n20
Unit 731 and Museum (Harbin, China),
    26, 89, 94, 96

United Kingdom: Brexit (2016), 15, 37,
    129, 139
United Nations, 14
United Nations Security Council, 14,
    97, 105
United States, 115–34; apologies
    by, 11, 142n15; and bilateralism
    in Asia, 12, 115–16, 129–34, 137;
    and creation of UN, 14; cultural
    relationship to Asia, 121–25, 133;
    cultural relationship to Europe,
    117–21, 133; and Franco-German
    relations, 31, 127; French trust for,
    37; and German-Polish relations,
    73, 88; imperialism in Asia, 129–34;
    influence on outcomes in Europe
    and Asia, 2, 8, 12, 133–34, 136–37;
    invasion of Iraq (2003), 17, 35, 86;
    and Japan-South Korean rela-
    tions, 49, 68; military bases in Asia,
    124–25, 132; and multilateralism in
    Europe, 115, 119–20, 125–29, 133,
    137; and postwar global hegemony,
    125–29; relations with Vietnam, 10,
    17; and Sino-Japanese relations, 91,
    92, 111–13, 114, 122
U.S.-East Asian relations, 10, 115–16,
    121–25, 129–33
U.S.-Japan Security Treaty (1951), 131,
    132
U.S. State Department: and anti-Asian
    racism, 123, 124–25; on European
    project, 128; on SEA pact, 131
U.S.-Western European relations, 115,
    117–21, 125–29

Vietnam, 10, 110, 124, 140
Vietnam War (1955–75), 10, 17, 123,
    124
Vogel, Wolfram, 46

Wakamiya, Yoshibumi, 59, 136
Walt, Stephen, 118
Warsaw Pact, 71, 126
Weimar Triangle, 34, 74
Weizsacker, Richard von, 79, 149n24
Wen Jiabao, 98
Western civilization, cultural identity of,
    117–21

West Germany (the Federal Republic
of Germany, or FRG) (1949–1990),
141n1; contrition by, 29, 37–38; entry
into NATO, 15, 32, 127; Europeanization of, 43; and Franco-German relations, 30–34, 37–*40*, 41, 43–44; and
German-Polish relations, 71, 78–79,
83–84; and unification of Germany, 6,
34, 127. *See also* Franco-German relations; Germany
whiteness, 117–18. *See also* racism
Wilson, Woodrow, 118
women. *See* "comfort women"
World Cup soccer matches, 53–54,
144n14
World War I (1914–18): and Franco-
German relations, 6, 19–20, 35, 39;
and German-Polish relations, 22; U.S.
involvement in, 118
World War II (1939–45): and Franco-
German relations, 6, 20–21, 29–30,
38–39; and German-Polish relations, 6, 22; and Japan-South Korean
relations, 23, 25, 57; and postwar US
global hegemony, 125–27; and postwar US imperialism in Asia, 130–31;
and Sino-Japanese relations, 23, 93;
U.S. involvement in, 119

Wu, Zhigang, 103–4
Wu Yi, 97

Xiao, Yong, 101
Xi Jinping, 1, 99, 111, 152n45
Xu, Bin, 96
Xu, Xiaohong, 91

Yamazaki, Jane W., 59, 152n31
Yasukuni Shrine, Japanese official visits
to, 57, 98, 151n18; by Abe, 99, 105,
110; by Hashimoto, 105; by Koizumi,
56, 90, 97, 105, 113; by Nakasone,
50, 95
Yoder, Jennifer A., 84
Yomiuri Shinbun (newspaper, Japan), 98,
151n18
Yoon Mee-hyang, 146n10, 147n40
Yoon Suk-yeol, 59
Yoshimi Yoshiaki, 51
Young, Kenneth, 123–24

Zha Daojiong, 98
Zhou Enlai, 93, 100
Zhu Rongji, 96
Ziemer, Klaus, 77